CONSERVATORIES AND GARDEN ROOMS

CONSERVATORIES AND GARDEN ROOMS

SUSAN CONDER AND DONALD JOHNSON

WINDWARD

Editors: Susanne Mitchell, Pat Sinclair

Art editor: Edward Pitcher

Designers: Trevor Vertigan, Gordon Robertson

Picture research: Moira McIlroy

Production: Richard Churchill

Published by Windward,
an imprint owned by W.H.Smith & Son Limited
Registered No. 237811 England
Trading as WHS Distributors,
St. John's House, East Street, Leicester LE1 6NE

ISBN 0 7112 0432 2

Printed and bound in Italy by L.E.G.O. S.p.A.

Contents

Introduction

The origin of the conservatory dates back some 250 years when oranges were cultivated in this country rather more as a status symbol than for their fruit. They were grown in 'orangeries', which were glazed and heated additions to the aristocratic home. Later on, in pre-Victorian times, the popularity of the orangery was eclipsed by that of the palm house, and many large glass houses were erected to provide an atmosphere of far-off lands.

It was during the Victorian era, a time when scientific development and research began to move on at a pace, that it was discovered that reflection of the sun's light and heat was reduced to a minimum if the angle at which the light struck the glass could be maintained as near as possible to a right angle. As a result, the Victorian conservatories tended to use curved glass, which both looked attractive and also transmitted the maximum amount of sunlight.

The acquisition of conservatories began to spread to the Victorian middle classes with the abolition of that quite extraordinary tax, the window tax, and, by the turn of the century, smaller conservatories were being added to existing houses.

For some strange reason the interest in domestic conservatories waned after the turn of the century and did not pick up again until the 1970s when a slow, but rapidly increasing come-back commenced.

Conservatory building was labour intensive and this, in itself, restricted sales. However, a post-war trend was the development of modular units. These were first used for simple wooden home extensions, but were later extended to traditional conservatories, and now it is possible to build a 'Victorian-style' conservatory from units at a realistic cost and with all the modern comforts of double glazing, electric heating, single length panes and suchlike.

During the past thirty years there has been a parallel development in a conservatory, or 'lean-to' – call it what you will – that is used more for plant growing than for display and relaxation. A third and contemporary development has been the 'home extension' or garden room, which is built to a higher building specification to enable it to be used as an additional living room.

Making the Choice

It is all too easy to go along to a display centre, fall for a particular make of conservatory, and order it there and then; but buy in haste and live to regret it. There is much to be considered when buying a conservatory, and the would-be purchaser should settle down comfortably with pencil and paper and work out exactly for what purpose the conservatory is required.

The decision as to why you want a conservatory and for what you are going to use it *must* be decided in advance because it will influence not only the kind of structure, but the type of glazing, roofing, ventilation, doors, and even the actual siting on the house. It may even alter the legal planning and building requirements.

The fundamental questions to be asked are, 'Is the prime use (1) for growing plants, (2) for displaying plants, (3) for entertaining and 'tea and cucumber sandwiches' in the summer, or (4) to make an extra permanent living area for meals, for sleeping in or somewhere for the children to play in?' The answers to these questions must be thought out carefully with an eye to the future. It really is not a good idea to have nice furniture and a carpeted floor in a cheap greenhouse type of structure with overlapping panes of glass that may let in water during a storm.

For Growing Plants

The best structure for this purpose is little different from a lean-to greenhouse but possibly with curved eaves to soften the effect. Since growing is the prime consideration, there will be staging and watering equipment, potting soil and so on, and there must be room to walk around and attend to the plants; ventilation and shading will be chosen to suit the plants rather than for the comfort of human occupants.

The Display Conservatory

This, in many ways, is the most satisfying. The plants are grown in containers and can be moved to give the best artistic effect when relaxing in the room. Water spillage will be minimal so the floor can be covered, but ventilation and shading will have to be a compromise to suit all the likely occupants.

For Entertaining

The ideal for this purpose is the luxury conservatory with large panes of glass and a structure built for its appearance.

For convenience the plant growing and sun lounge areas of a wide conservatory can be separated so that watering does not disrupt relaxation.

Home Extension

For this purpose a solid insulated roof has to be used as well as double glazing and all the other conveniences of a room in the house, the aim being to make the conservatory as much a part of the house as possible.

Dual Purpose

The real difficulty arises when the choice works out somewhere between two divisions. The answer then, if the pocket will allow it, is to go up one stage. The problem is that the cost spread of conservatories is wider even than that of cars. At the time of writing you can pay as little as £500 for a very basic structure and up to £10,000 for a luxury made-to-measure design. For a comfortable well-equipped leisure room £2,000 to £4,000, according to size, would be a useful figure to work on; a 'growing room' would cost less. Obviously with such a wide variation in costs, it is vitally important to get it right the first time because if you make the wrong decision you cannot, as with a car, go along to the dealer and part exchange it for another one.

Perhaps the most difficult requirement to accommodate is a dual-purpose building that is to be used as a garden room for leisure activities but also for growing – not displaying – plants. The light and moisture requirements for the plants and the staging requirements necessitate that the 'growing' area must be separate – say up one side – because you can't really mix sun beds with watering cans, so the shape of the structure needs to be wide rather than deep. The dual-purpose conservatory will also present contradictions when it comes to shading, watering, heating and ventilation, all of which will have to be something of a compromise. These matters are discussed elsewhere in this book.

Buying the Structure

When the moment of truth arrives and you are ready to place the order, do try to see your short-listed choice already erected: you can then tell better how well it is finished and particularly see the details of the glazing, which are seldom shown in the leaflets. In view of

the high expenditure involved it is worthwhile travelling quite a journey to see one 'in the flesh' as it were.

Whether you can accept a standard unit (which works out cheapest), a modular system planned to suit your needs, or a custom built structure, will depend on how complicated your site is: usually the maker's erector will look at the situation and advise you on this. Cost may persuade you to buy at the bottom end of the price range, but bear in mind that a really good conservatory that can function as an extra day-time room can enhance the value of the house when the time comes to move.

Siting the Conservatory

Having decided to invest in a conservatory, the next decision is where to site it. Most people put their extensions outside their patio or french doors, so there is then no further scope for variation. If, however, the extension is to be entered from the garden, there may be, especially in the case of the older houses in large gardens, an opportunity to choose the best position. Again, the answer is 'it all depends'. Life is full of 'ifs and buts'. If you want the conservatory as a sun room, there is one answer, but if you want it as a growing room the answer is different.

Blending with the architectural style of the house, this timber framed conservatory has side doors, and entrance is from the garden. Customers can easily satisfy their needs nowadays from a wide range of structures.

Sun rooms tend to be used in spring, autumn and winter: in the summer you can generally relax out of doors, at other times you can do with as much sun as possible. The ideal, then, is to face south, or better still south-west, to catch the evening sun.

The morning sun will come in from the side, but few people are in their sun rooms at 6 a.m.

For a growing room the situation is different. A south aspect can cause astronomically high temperatures in the summer, with the heat reflected off the house wall, and it is going to be very difficult indeed to keep the plants happy by providing adequate shade and ventilation. Few plants enjoy temperatures of over 27°C (80°F).

For a growing room a westerly aspect is ideal because it is also pleasant to work in during the evening. An easterly aspect will give enough light for growing but it is not very pleasant for pottering in when you come home from work and it is certainly not much good for sunbathing.

If you only have a northerly aspect available, then it is doubtful if it is worth the cost of a conservatory unless you need the extra room for the children to play in. If circumstances leave you with no alternative but a northerly aspect, then take the extension out as far as possible, even if you have to sacrifice length to do so. This will let in the maximum amount of morning and evening sun from the east and the west.

Structure and Materials

You may think a conservatory is just a conservatory, but this just is not so. That is why it is absolutely essential to collect the catalogues of all the makes in your price range and then take the time and trouble to get around and see those on your short list already erected. It is really surprising how small details can affect the 'feel' of a conservatory when you are inside it. For example, even relatively unimportant things, like uncovered nuts and bolts, can be quite irritating as you lay back in your chair relaxing. Glazing methods, which are dealt with later (page 18), can make all the difference between a conservatory feeling like a greenhouse or more like an extension to the house: indeed, glazing, particularly of the roof, can change the whole atmosphere in the conservatory. So, indeed, can the spacing of the glazing bars (the uprights that hold the glass). Wide spacing makes for a pleasant feeling of spaciousness inside the conservatory.

SHAPE

Broadly speaking modern conservatories are available in three basic styles, namely the traditional Victorian style, the modern rectangular shape, and more recently, an import from the United States, a structure with curved eaves. Most are constructed of aluminium, but wood is still used and the latest development is a framework of uPVC, a polyvinyl chloride plastic treated against ultra-violet light.

Unfortunately all these options are not open to the buyer whose means are very limited, because the cheapest conservatories, at little more than greenhouse prices, are also built like greenhouses with the same kind of slotted aluminium extrusions and, except in positions where Building Regulations forbid it, small overlapping panes of glass held by clips. Whilst such a structure offers somewhere to sit and to grow plants, you cannot get away from the greenhouse feeling. In fact, it seems that some manufacturers are using the title conservatory for a structure which is really a lean-to greenhouse. On the other hand, a few makers have taken their basic lean-to, and for a relatively small extra cost have smartened up the appearance generally, eliminated overlapping panes of glass, at least in the roof, provided double glazing and generally made the whole thing presentable.

The more expensive structures offer greater variation in design. At the top of the price range you can have your conservatory custom built, but the firms that used to specialise in this type of service are these days offering a compromise by stocking a large number of prefabricated modules which allow a very attractive traditional 'Victorian' structure to be built up quite quickly. Sometimes a 'post and panel' system of construction is used, which conforms very well to house construction, and almost always 'traditional' conservatories are mounted on a low wall about 45cm (18in) high. This is best built of bricks and, if necessary, rendered to match the original building, although full depth glass panes can always be supplied as an alternative. Decoration can be added in the form of timber or cast aluminium friezes along the horizontal roof lines and finials on the gables or tops of octagonal models.

The better quality conservatories have a roof structure designed to bear the weight of ladders and the weight of a person carrying out maintenance either of the conservatory or of the house. The cheaper conservatories, on the other hand, must be treated like

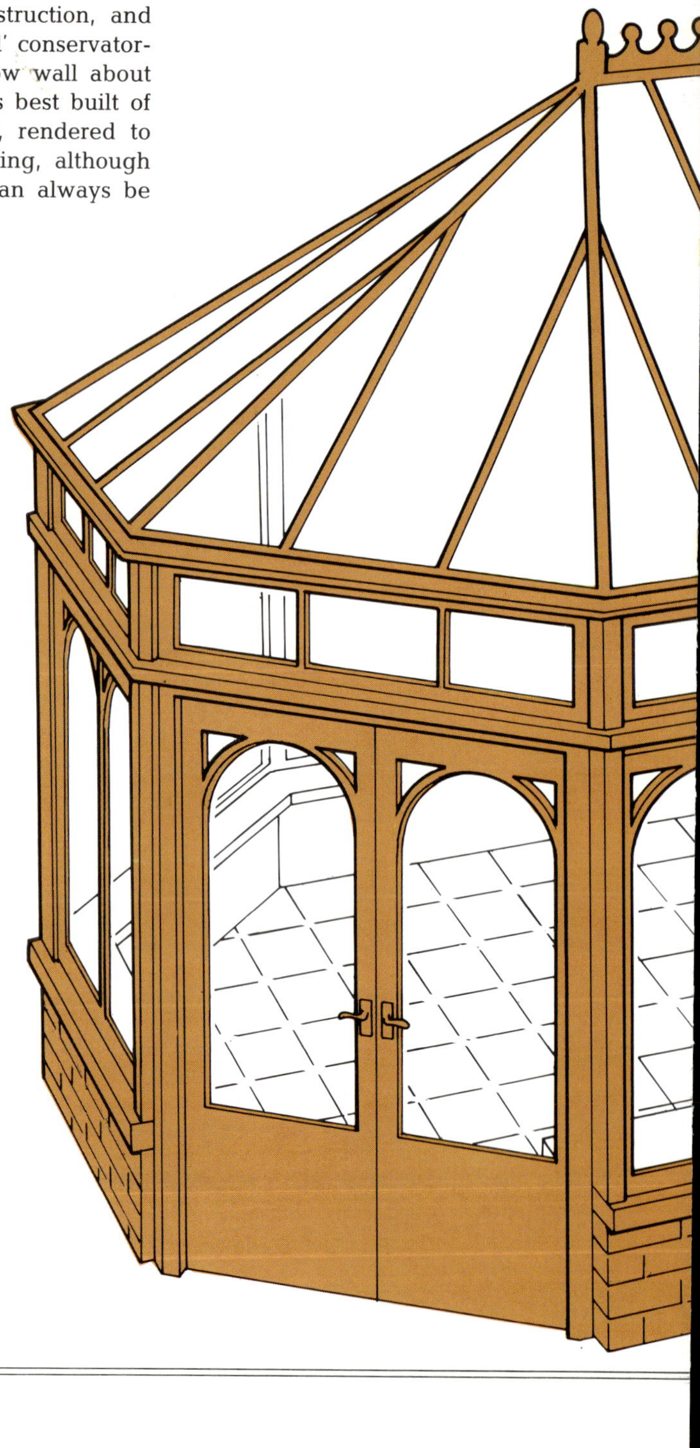

With ridge cresting and decorative moulding, a Victorian style conservatory makes an elegant addition to the house. Modular units allow flexibility in choosing size and design.

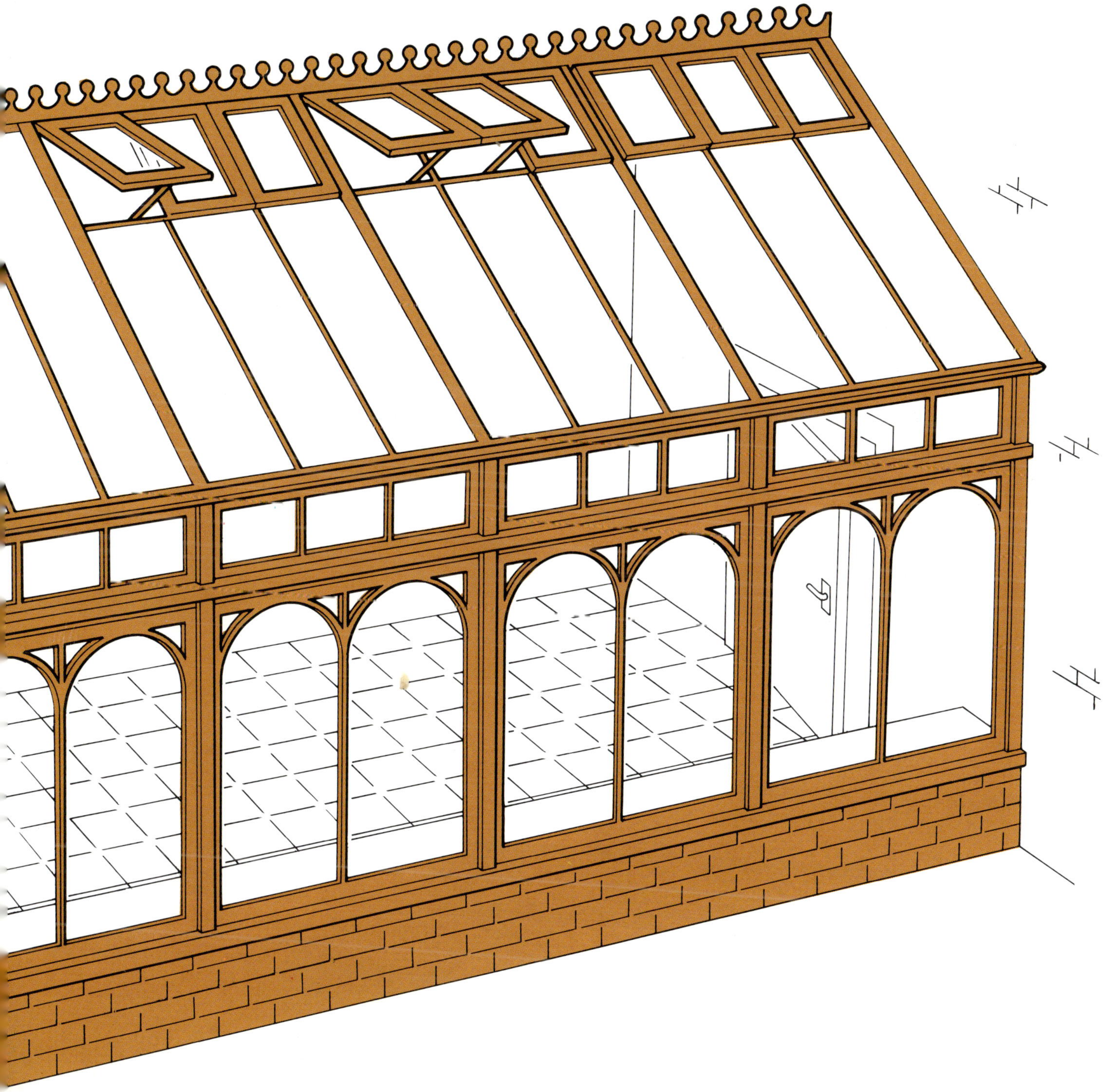

greenhouses from this point of view and the weight taken by suitable boards and ladders. Admittedly, modern methods of construction are so good that little maintenance should be required on any except the wooden-framed ones.

In between the cheap greenhouse conservatory and the expensive 'Victorian' classic designs, lies a vast choice of modern designs. They fall into two areas – one a traditional, square-edged rectangular shape and the other the modern, sleek, curved-eave conservatory. Both are available within the same price structure and choice is a matter of personal taste, although it may well be

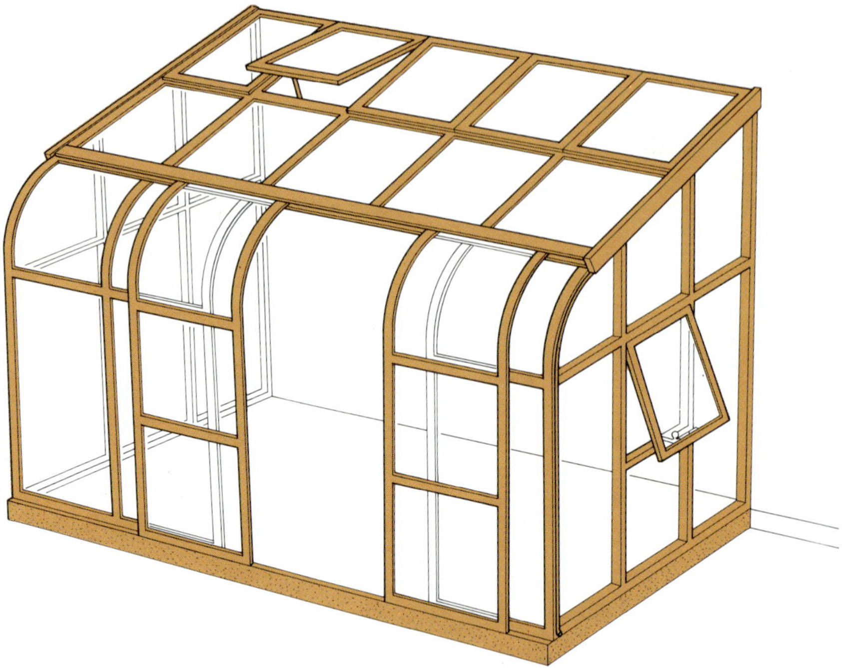

Right and below, the modern lines of curved aluminium eaves. Painted bronze or dark brown to harmonize with brickwork, they can be glazed either in plastic or toughened safety glass.

that the traditional rectangular design is less likely to go out of fashion. Both types are available with glass to the ground or with solid lower 'kick' panels, which may be advisable where there are children. Such panels also give a snug, room-like feeling to the conservatory and also can easily be insulated to reduce heat loss, whether they are of wood, aluminium, concrete or brick.

The rectangular conservatory lends itself particularly well to being fitted to a bungalow because it is possible to design a structure with adequate eave height and yet with a ridge low enough to go under the bungalow eaves. One maker overcomes this problem by having a ridge which is adjustable for height over as much as 43cm (17in).

In general, a high roof increases the volume of air inside the conservatory and this makes it easier to achieve a stable climatic condition inside. That is why the old Victorian buildings always had high roofs, very often dome shaped. On the other hand, a disadvantage of the high roof is the heat loss in winter, which can materially increase the fuel bills, something to be thought about in these days. Hot air rises, so you have to heat the top air space before the heat reaches ground or staging level. Some form of blind could be fitted to the back wall inside the conservatory and brought into use during the winter to provide a false ceiling and reduce air circulation upwards, but this would keep out light. (See shading, page 29.)

The rectangular conservatory resembles the traditional lean-to greenhouse, suitable for fitting snugly under low eaves, but, with access from the interior, it also provides extra living space.

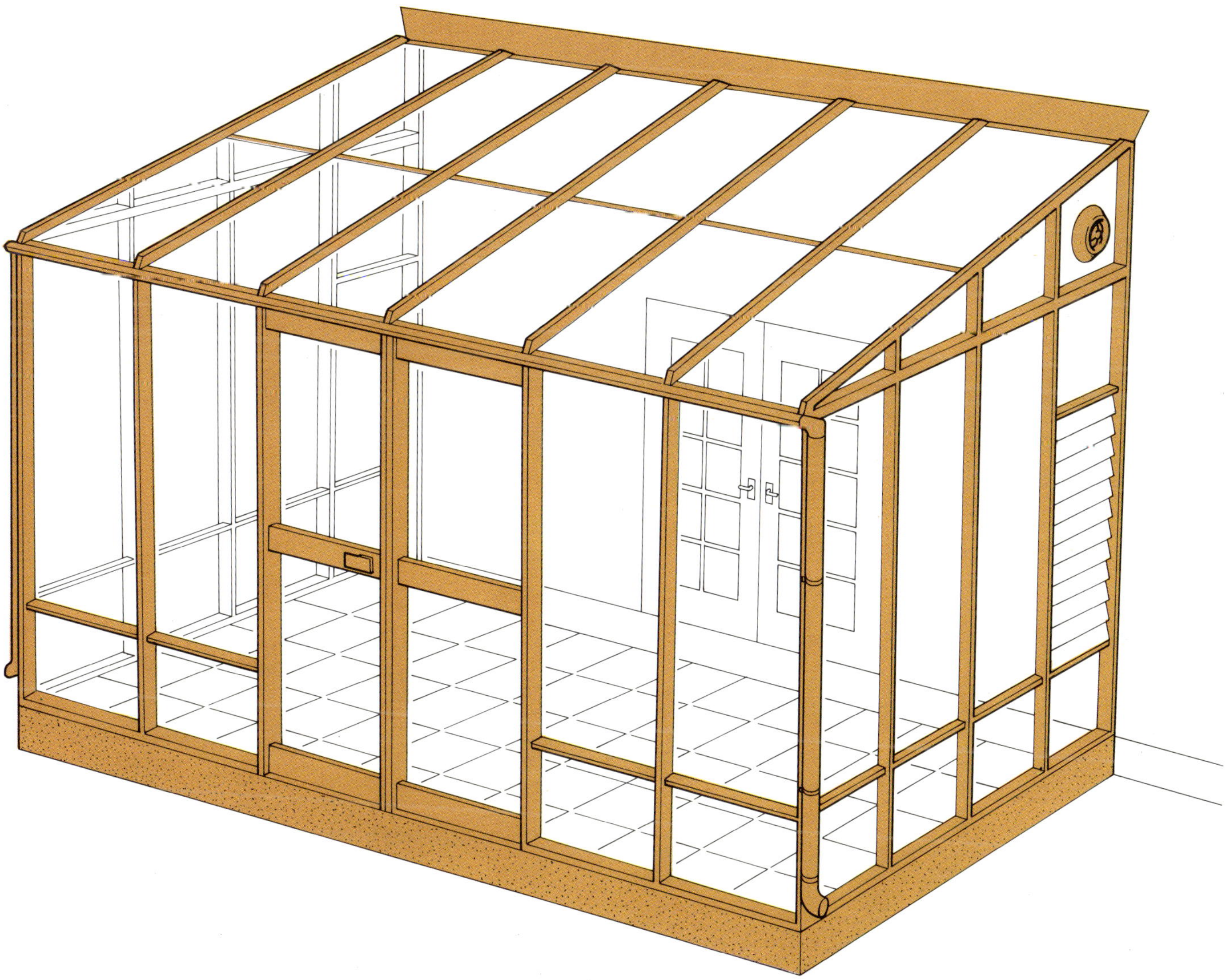

HOME EXTENSIONS

These are really conservatories with solid roofs and designed to be lived in all the year round. The main difference, apart from the roof, is not in the basic structure but in the detail needed to meet the more stringent Building Regulations, particularly in the matter of heat losses. The roof of a home extension is usually made of softwood boarding on timber rafters and covered with several layers of roofing felt. It can also be insulated with a glassfibre quilt and lined with plasterboard. Changes in Building Regulations are currently under discussion and reference should be made to the Local Authority for the latest developments.

FRAMEWORK

The traditional rectangular conservatory can be obtained with aluminium or timber framing. Aluminium, even if unpainted, needs no maintenance, whereas even cedar wood needs treatment from time to time, but timber framing is warmer. In fact, experiments have shown that heat losses in a timber conservatory can be reduced by as much as 20 per cent compared with aluminium framing, unless this has a 'thermal break', as is sometimes the case when double glazing is used. This is a method of construction whereby the inner part of the aluminium frame is insulated from the outer part, usually by plastic. This prevents transfer of heat to the outer part which is subject to prevailing weather conditions, especially to chilling by winds.

Timber framing will also prevent condensation, which is inevitable on metal frame structures because of the warm moist conditions in the conservatory.

The framework, whether of wood or aluminium, is substantial in the quality conservatories because it is usually supporting large panes of thick (up to

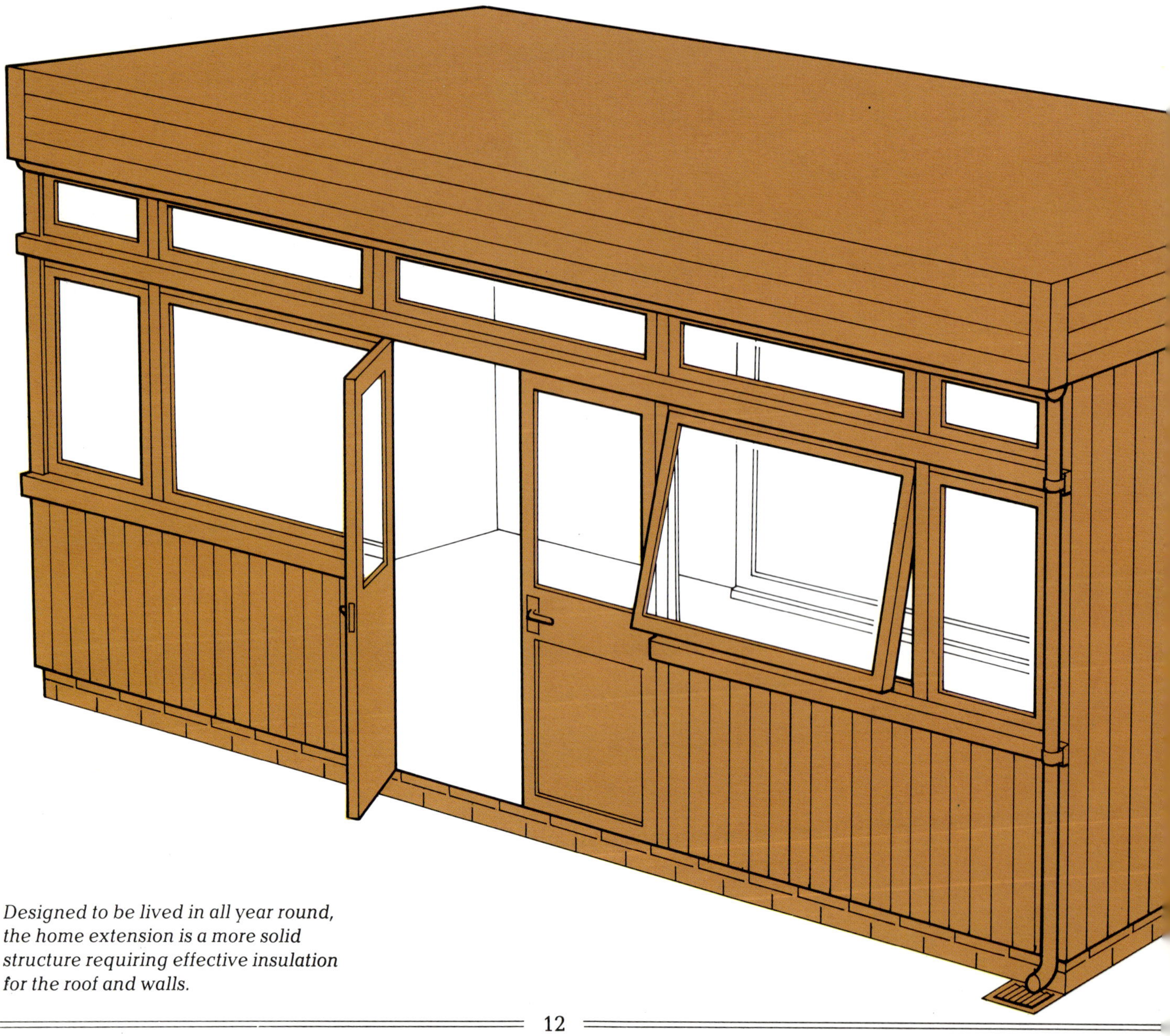

Designed to be lived in all year round, the home extension is a more solid structure requiring effective insulation for the roof and walls.

6mm), sometimes double-glazed glass – as much as twice the thickness of greenhouse glass. These large panes look attractive and provide more light.

Aluminium

Many of the aluminium-framed conservatories, even those that are painted, have slots in the structure members like greenhouse glazing bars. The makers argue that this makes it easy to put up shelves and other greenhouse accessories. This is undeniable, but it does not look all that attractive and after a time collects dirt and is very difficult to clean. There is much to be said for the smooth surface of box or square section supports, even if they do have to be drilled to take equipment. (One manufacturer will supply a white plastic beading to cover the unused slots, and this is a good compromise.)

Heat losses in aluminium, double-glazed conservatories can be reduced with an insulating strip separating the inner and outer parts of the framework.

If you favour a conservatory with curved eaves, you will have to accept an aluminium framework, but take a note of the size of the framework sections and check whether the glazing of the curved sections is in plastic or glass; in the long term the latter will be preferable. (See glazing on page 20.) Incidentally, conservatories with curved eaves are generally only available in 2.4m (8ft) widths, but there are a couple of makes which are 3m (10ft) wide. Because the sliding front doors on a curved-eave conservatory actually include the curved-eave portion, there is an exceptional feeling of spaciousness and, of course, fresh air, compared with opening the doors of a conventional rectangular conservatory. This is quite an important point to be borne in mind.

Wood

Conservatories constructed of wood, unless in the luxury class, are invariably of traditional rectangular construction. Although it is possible to obtain them glazed right to the base, it is more usual for them to be half-boarded or made to fit on a low brick wall. It is, of course, easy to screw fittings and accessories into the wood and the half-boarded area can be lined and even wallpapered.

Timber conservatories normally have hinged doors, single at the side and double at the front, but it is possible to obtain a wooden structure with aluminium sliding patio doors. It may not look in keeping but it is very practical.

Cedar is the preferred wood as it requires only minimal maintenance by treating with a special preservative. Cedar is sometimes offered primed to take a paint finish, but because of the nature of the wood this is not recommended, except for the special microporous paints that resist peeling and flaking.

Deal or other whitewoods are satisfactory provided a suitable wood preservative has been applied, but the surface will have to be painted regularly, sometimes as much as annually, and painting glazing bars with the glass in position is no fun. Alternatively, you can use a cedar preservative on a white wood structure and this is much easier to apply.

Although wood roof glazing is conventional there is much to be said for the aluminium bar fitted to some timber structures. Compression plastic sealing, in which the glass lies on a flexible plastic strip, is generally used, but one up-market manufacturer uses conventional type of lead strip sealing. Another maker uses cedarwood beading to retain the glass, instead of the putty and sprigs used in the cheaper structures.

There is a marked difference between makes amongst the cheaper timber-framed conservatories so that it is advisable, when comparing prices, to check the thickness of the main supports and the frames that hold the glass. Remember that cedar is much more expensive than ordinary white wood, and check if the protective finish is included in the price or is an extra. One manufacturer of

wooden conservatories uses PVC treated against sunlight for the window frames, which reduces maintenance. The same firm offers an unusual sloping fascia in cedar shingles (tiles) or bituminous felt tiles.

uPVC

Finally, one manufacturer is offering the whole basic structure in uPVC, an ultraviolet light-inhibited polyvinyl chloride. It is white in colour, does not need painting, only washing, and has an extremely good heat loss value. (U-factor 2.5.) It can also be worked like wood and would seem to be the material of the future.

FINISHES

Although natural finish aluminium cannot rust, it does deteriorate in appearance, particularly in coastal and industrial districts where salt spray and acid fumes respectively will attack it. As a result a white deposit collects, but this should not be removed because, unlike rust, it acts as protection to the metal underneath.

A white or bronze paint finish is available from most firms today. Often the paint is applied by an electrostatic process in which the paint spray is attracted on to the metal electrically, as in an electroplating process. The result is a very even coating, but even more important, the paint reaches those areas, like glazing bar slots, which would be almost impossible to reach by brush. Electrophoretic paint used by some firms is a dipping method. Acrylic finish is a paint that has resin added followed by a baking process that produces a particularly attractive and durable finish.

Finishes for wood have already been discussed, but it is worth mentioning the cedar finishes based on linseed oil. These give the wood a delightful gold tone which really is most attractive, but over the years this finish picks up the dirt, which is very difficult to remove, and the whole structure eventually goes very dark. Left to its own devices, cedar does not rot but turns a grey colour. Polyurethane varnish is sometimes recommended for wood other than cedar, but cracking and subsequent lifting of the surface can be a major problem on the type of wood used for conservatories.

GUTTERING

Neat guttering is important, particularly above a structure with curved eaves where unsightly guttering could so easily spoil the appearance. Interestingly, one firm takes the downpipe quite tidily down the inside corner of the conservatory.

The most expensive extensions which, even if of modular construction, are intended to look part of the house, usually have guttering of a similar pattern to that of the house. Plastic has replaced iron, even on houses, and the guttering supplied is usually in 10-cm (4-in) wide plastic in white, black, grey or brown. Conventional plastic guttering of smaller size is usually supplied with timber-framed conservatories.

The guttering on the rectangular conservatory is normally a conventional run along the eaves, sometimes in square section to conform to the general 'square-edged' appearance.

Various forms of guttering are used on conservatories with curved eaves. Those models that have doors at the ends instead of double-doors at the front, often have no guttering at all, the rainwater running down the front glass, but where sliding patio doors are incorporated, guttering becomes essential. This is usually a box or square section above the doors taking the water to the end where a downpipe may follow the curved contours of the glass. Alternatively, it may, more obtrusively, use a rather obvious square section downpipe at the side. If it can be positioned where it is not intrusive, a rainwater butt is useful as many plants, especially the azalea family, do not respond well to the alkalinity of most mains water.

DOORS

Most firms will offer a wide variation in door positions, although there are some that still only offer end doors like a greenhouse, optionally sliding or hinged. Sliding patio doors at the front are the best for a sun room, although here again one firm believes that double hinged doors, like french doors, are better. If the doors are hinged make sure the hinges, and indeed the door locks too, are of non-rusting material. Brass is used in quality timber conservatories. Door heights can vary but should be over 1.8m (6ft), a point worth bearing in mind for there is nothing worse than having to duck your head every time you go through the door. Some doors are as much as 2m (6½ft) high.

A gutter is a necessity over sliding patio doors. The inset shows how square section guttering need not spoil the lines of a curved framework.

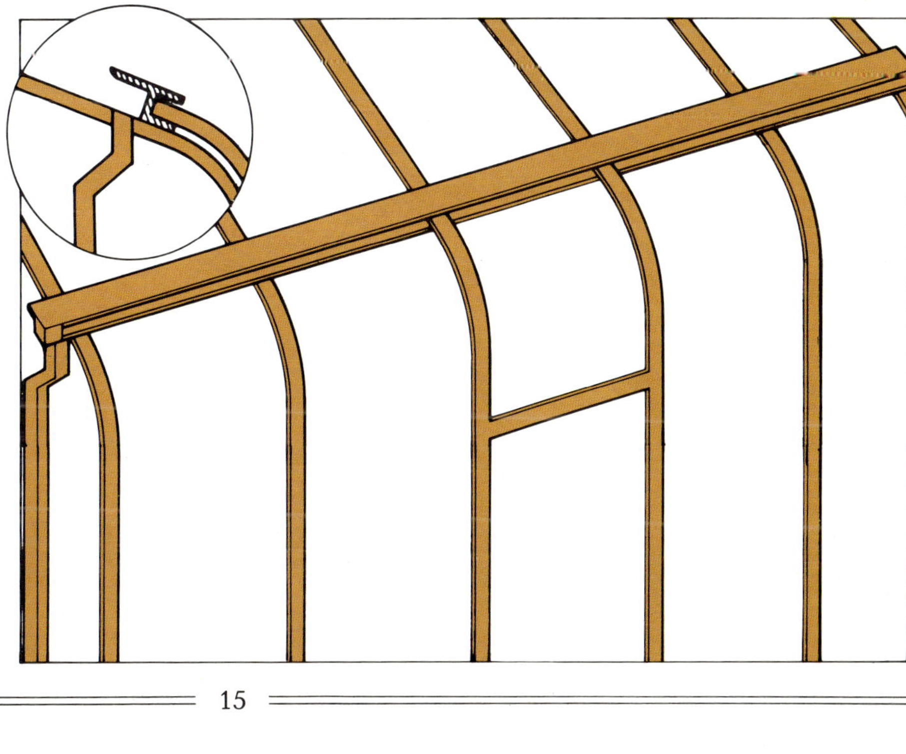

The atmosphere of a Victorian conservatory has been captured here by this wonderful array of mature plants.

Constructing the Conservatory

PLANNING PERMISSION

Planning permission for the addition of a conservatory will most likely not be required unless the area is one where the law allowing 'permitted development' has been withdrawn, such as often applies along the coastal belt. Planning permission will also be required if your house has already been extended and the addition of a conservatory brings the total extension to over 70cu m (2472cu ft). It is worth noting that even non-enclosed areas, such as a carport, are included in this total.

The local authority building inspector will, however, require a set of plans to check that the conservatory conforms to the Building Regulations, particularly in respect of matters like drains, manholes and foundations. The manufacturer will almost always provide you with the necessary guide lines and will very often provide the plans for you to submit to your local authority.

The local authority will also lay down the requirements for the foundations. Generally the structure frame can rest on an overall concrete slab about 10cm (4in) deep laid over 10cm (4in) of hardcore. The concrete at the edges will need to be thickened to 30cm (12in) or more. There may be variations where the building is situated in areas of unstable clay. As requirements vary according to the Authority's interpretation of the regulations the first thing to do is to have a word with your local inspector.

Where the conservatory does not cover a house door, regulations are not likely to be so stringent, particularly if it is a lean-to greenhouse type of structure for which the manufacturers will frequently offer a metal base made to fit. This is designed to be laid in the soil and is a suitable method if only part of the conservatory floor is to be paved or concreted, while part is left as a soil border in which to grow plants. Ordinary horticultural glass is permitted (but not recommended) under these circumstances.

Where the building rests on a dwarf wall, which will necessarily abut against the house, a damp course will be needed, and a damp-proof membrane lapped to the damp course will have to be applied to the concrete floor slab and topped with the usual cement and sand screed that will form the final floor.

Below, a pool gives another dimension to conservatory gardening. Right, climbing plants add a distinctive touch to a profusion of foliage.

Building Regulations can affect the siting of the conservatory. If the structure is of wood, you may have to site it 2m (6½ft) from the boundary fence to comply with fire regulations. If it has be nearer than this, then a fire resistant end will be required, and most manufacturers can supply this. Again the manufacturers will advise you as to whether the material they have used conforms to the Fire Regulations (British Standard 476).

MAINS SERVICES

The question of providing mains services in the conservatory should be considered before erection. The actual method used and the routing must depend upon where they run in the house itself, but a water supply is of prime importance if you are intending to grow many plants. If there is an outside garden water tap it should be fairly easy to run a plastic pipe from here to the conservatory, with a second tap inside the conservatory. This will allow the supply to be turned off at the main tap during frosty weather. If you do not make provision at this stage, every drop of water for the plants will have to carried by hand in watering cans, and if

you have a side staging area for young plants or propagation this will be no mean feat.

Electricity is essential. A double 13 amp socket outlet should be the minimum, as two-way adaptors are not to be recommended. Each piece of equipment must be correctly fused at its own plug. This socket will have to be taken as a spur – usually from a ring main – in the house, as will the central lighting. If you plan to use the conservatory as a plant house involving a heater, propagator, indoor plant watering, or automatic misting and so on, at least four outlets should be installed at the outset on the side where they are going to be needed. It is sometimes possible to use the slots in the glazing bars as a conduit. Such work must be installed by a professional electrical engineer or, if not, inspected and passed by the Electricity Board. If you intend to do it yourself, consult the current edition of Regulations for Electrical Equipment in Buildings, Section K. A growing room must be humid, so for safety's sake it is worth looking into the provision of an earth leakage trip which will cut off the mains instantly should there be an earth leakage (a shock) through you personally or through any piece of equipment.

A gas main will be needed if you intend to use this form of heating, be it a free-standing heater or balanced flue and, again, if you want to tap off the house central system, consider this in relation to the position of the structure.

ERECTING THE STRUCTURE

A buyer with the necessary 'diy' expertise can erect most types of conservatories, thus saving a good deal of money, sometimes as much as a third of the cost of the conservatory, but all suppliers will either do the erection for the purchaser or sub-contract it out to a local agent, if necessary.

Most conservatories are fixed to the house wall with screws through a wall bar supplied and the ridge of the conservatory. A smooth flat wall surface is required for this, but minor irregularities can be covered with the flashing strip that is supplied with the conservatory. Usually this strip is of some form of plastic but some luxury conservatories use conventional lead flashing. A very uneven wall may have to be made good and a timber sub-frame constructed by the erectors.

GLAZING

Glazing is quite a high proportion of the cost of a conservatory, but it is nevertheless an extremely important aspect and must be considered carefully. A conservatory that does not cover a house entrance door may be glazed to greenhouse standards, although this is not recommended. It means that small panes of glass are used, each overlapping the other by about 6mm (¼in), laid on the glazing bars on a strip of mastic or flexible pvc tubing to form a reasonably watertight joint. However, after a year or so, dirt collects in the overlap and the moisture in the overlap causes green algae to grow, and the whole thing begins to look rather messy unless a laborious cleaning process is undertaken every year. If the glazing is not done well there can be draughts and horizontally driven rain can leak through the roof overlaps. The glass is usually 3-mm thick horticultural glass, single glazed, and condensation can cause drip problems. All this leads to a conclusion that such a structure is really only suited to a plant room with perhaps the odd 'occasional chair' for relaxing in on cold but sunny days. The greenhouse effect is further heightened by the fact that most makes – not all – have the glass panes secured externally by a whole lot of rather ugly spring clips of one type or another.

However, such a structure is reflected in the price, which is comparable with a greenhouse. One or two manufacturers try to improve the external appearance by using capping, in one case black plastic strips which cover the joint between the glass and the glazing bar, whilst in another make the actual glass pane is secured by aluminium capping in place of clips.

When a conservatory covers a house door, British Standard Specification 6262 should be adhered to. This means using toughened glass to eave level and for the doors to prevent cuts if anyone falls through a window.

Another matter of glazing generally, is the size of the panes and, particularly in the roof, of the cross bars which often exist for support even when the glazing is in one long piece. The advantage of a large unobstructed area of glass is that it gives a feeling of spaciousness, almost

Glazing the conservatory with reeded glass is a practical way of gaining privacy or hiding an unsightly view.

as if you are sitting in the garden, but some people may prefer the 'cosiness' of a conservatory on a dwarf wall. Nevertheless, too many glazing bars make a conservatory feel small.

Roof Glazing

The regulations on roof glass depend upon how far out the conservatory projects. If this is up to 2m (6ft), then horticultural glass is occasionally used. However, it is not be recommended since heavy snow or a tile from the roof could shatter it with devastating effect. It is advisable to use toughened glass, either 3mm thick or, better and more widely used, 4mm thick. The advantage of toughened or safety glass, which is widely used for car windscreens, is that should it shatter, it disintegrates into a mass of small pieces with comparatively blunt edges compared with the lethal slivers of glass produced by ordinary glass.

Give consideration to support and glass strength for the roof in areas that have heavy snow or where the conservatory roof could receive snowfall

Planting boxes, shelving and hanging baskets are used to display a variety of foliage and flowering plants.

from the roof of the house. Snow guards at house roof level are a sensible precaution.

There is a fair choice of materials for roof glazing. In addition to toughed glass there is glass fibre, which is strong and safe and has the effect of diffusing sunlight without making it dark.

Polycarbonate is expensive but it is light and immensely strong. In the double and triple glazed forms available, in clear or brown tinted, it offers up to 40 per cent reduction in loss of heat radiated through the roof, with a corresponding reduction in condensation. It is one of the best materials for roofing and has a not unpleasant reeded appearance.

In the old days obscured Georgian wired glass was used in roofs for safety and this is still obtainable in traditional 'Victorian' conservatories, though it is a matter of opinion as to whether you like it, since the wire is clearly visible.

Some manufacturers offer 2½-mm laminated glass which does not even break up like toughened glass.

The cheaper timber-framed conservatories almost always have the roof glazed in corrugated PVC. The roof glazing is usually set in the same way as the wall glass, but a couple of up-market manufacturers use aluminium glazing bars with a wooden structure to simplify maintenance. In one case lead wings are dressed on to the glass to provide a permanent weather-tight seal.

Side Glazing

So far as the vertical walls are concerned, the larger and wider the panes of glass, the more pleasant the 'atmosphere' in the conservatory. It is particularly important for a sun room used for relaxation, but large panes necessitate thick glass for safety's sake, particularly in the doors. Toughened glass, too, is really an essential, apart from the B.S.S. recommendations already referred to. Some cheaper conservatories have a 3-mm thick toughened glass, but it is advisable not to go below 4-mm. Some manufacturers use a 6-mm glass.

Double Glazing
If you are heating the conservatory either for the plants or yourself, double glazing will pay for itself, materially reduce external noise and almost eliminate condensation. Factory-sealed double glazed units are frequently employed and are easily fitted in the now common plastic strip seals which surround the glass and provide a virtually watertight seal. However, apart from the glazing clips used on the cheap conservatories, the old sprigs and putty system is still to be found on many wooden structures, with its corresponding maintenance problems as the putty hardens over the years.

There is some difference in the air gaps on the double glazed units. Very small gaps are not so efficient as the larger gaps (up to optimum) and it is interesting to see that one manufacturer has now achieved a 12-mm air gap, no doubt made possible by the fact that his structure framework is of uPVC instead of aluminium. If you live in an area where noise is a problem, such as under an aircraft flight path, then wide air gap double glazing can make an appreciable difference.

Curved Eaves
Many of the conservatories that have curved eaves use a plastic pane in the curved area. Even though this may be ultra-violet stabilized, it is almost sure to discolour with age. However, glass curved panels are now available and these can even be obtained in toughened glass. This may be a more important advantage than is immediately apparent, because the curved plastic, which eventually deteriorates, might not be obtainable when replacements are needed.

All these general considerations can apply equally to a timber-framed building or one built of aluminium, and they should also be checked out even when it is decided to employ a local builder to design and build an extension, as opposed to buying a proprietary make. Some builders, used to conventional houses, may not always be aware of the properties of modern materials, like polycarbonate, for instance.

An extractor fan is one of the most effective ways of removing hot air and keeping the atmosphere buoyant during warmer weather.

MAINTENANCE
Routine maintenance on the majority of conservatories will be negligible. Mill-finished aluminium, that is the natural silver-coloured aluminium, needs only an occasional wash. In areas of high industrial pollution it will acquire a white powder and tend to pock-mark, but this is of no consequence. In fact, the white deposit is best left on as, unlike iron oxide or rust, it serves as a protection against further deterioration. Aluminium used for conservatories should be to the appropriate British Standard Specification.

Anodised aluminium requires only washing but take care not to scratch the coloured anodized surface with anything sharp. The widely used paint finished aluminium is also maintenance-free requiring only a wash, but the life of the paint depends upon the quality of the finish. A baked finish, similar to that used on cars or caravans, gives several years service before any powdering – caused by the sun – becomes noticeable. White uPVC plastic also requires no maintenance other than washing.

Wooden finishes are a different proposition altogether. White wood or deal, even if treated with a preservative, will need periodic rubbing down, priming and repainting at regular intervals, the actual interval depending upon the district in which the conservatory lies. It will need to be done at least every time the house is repainted. Cedar on the other hand, will not rot, but will need a colour treatment every three years or so to prevent it going grey. Linseed oil-based preservatives look good when first applied but tend to become sticky and collect the dirt, which is then almost impossible to remove. Cedar is sometimes painted, but it is important to use one of the special porous paints that allow the wood to breathe.

Glass is generally bedded in plastic seals and these will give trouble-free service for a very long time. The glass in timber frames can be retained in slots and so require no maintenance, but where the old-fashioned sprigs and putty is used, you can expect to have to renovate this from time to time if water leakage is to be avoided.

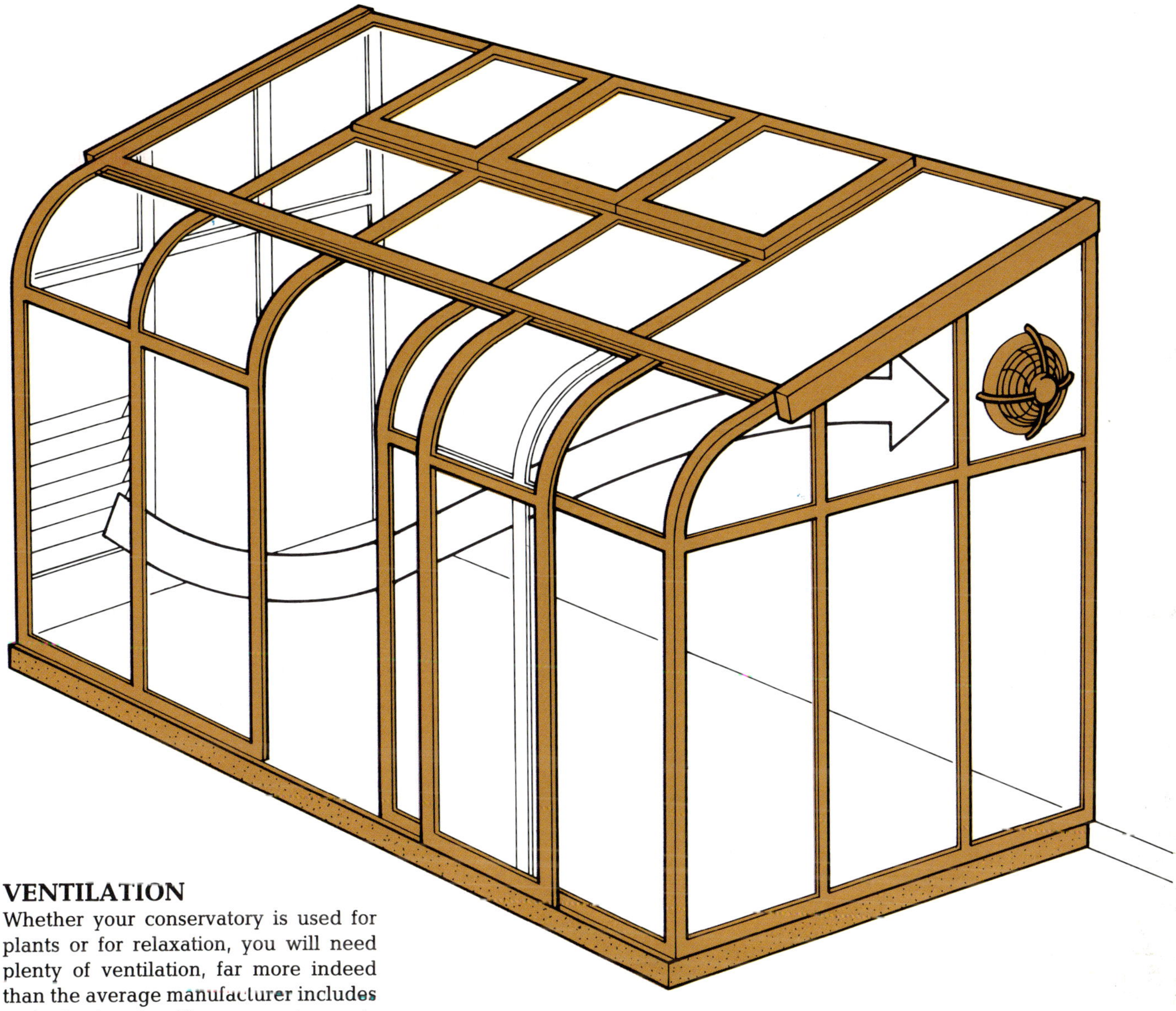

VENTILATION

Whether your conservatory is used for plants or for relaxation, you will need plenty of ventilation, far more indeed than the average manufacturer includes in the basic price. However, extra vents can always be supplied. Even in spring and autumn the midday sunshine can be unbearably hot behind glass but both plants and human beings need to cool off without draughts, so the positioning of vents is all important.

Hot air rises, so the principle is to let the hot air out as high as possible and introduce cool air low down. Therefore, some form of roof ventilation would seem to be ideal, and so it is, provided the vents will not leak in storm conditions. Because of this, if you live by the sea or on an exposed hill where force 10 winter gales are the norm, it may be a good thing to avoid ventilators actually fitted in the roof itself. As a compromise some manufacturers provide the option of full length ventilation at the ridge, a position that does tend to get some protection from the house or bungalow roof overhang. Even so, in exceptionally windy areas, it may still be wise to forgo roof ventilation altogether and use an electric extractor fan of the Vent Axia type mounted as high as possible in the side of the conservatory. Such fans can, incidentally, be thermostatically controlled so that they come on automatically when the air becomes too hot.

One way to counter overheating in the conservatory and encourage air flow is to place the extractor fan high and diagonally opposite a low louvre vent.

For those who are in a sufficiently sheltered position to use roof ventilation without leakage, there is a variety of forms to choose from, and ideally the ventilators should run the full length of the conservatory.

There are simple greenhouse vents and stays, but these, because of the height of the roof, may well be difficult to operate. Much better than these (which are really just bars with holes in them) is the two-position catch which is operated by a long pole supplied with the conservatory. Alternatively, the ventilators which take the form of top hung panes of glass can be controlled by an automatic non-electric arm. The temperature at which the arm operates can be pre-set and the ventilation will then look after itself when you are away from home.

Also available to operate roof ventilators is a remote window-operating gear.

All you have to do is turn a handle which operates a chain opener through a steel conduit – both neat and effective. Some up-market models have the handle operated by an electric motor which can, if required, be temperature controlled.

Exceptional summer heat can best be expelled by opening doors, and this is where front patio or double hinged doors come into their own compared with the single side doors fitted to many models. But it is unwise to rely only on the doors for ventilation, since you will not want to leave them wide open when you go out for the day.

Types of Ventilation

The ventilators or windows themselves come in a variety of types, but they are almost always bedded on a flexible material, like compressible PVC, to make a good seal against rain. At the lower end of the price bracket, ventilation is almost always effected by greenhouse windows with greenhouse type stays that can project rather disagreeably into the conservatory area and give you a jab in the ribs if you are in the wrong place at the wrong time. However, a popular window in the middle price bracket conservatories has a neat two-position stay which pushes the base of a top hung window out about 23cm (9in) or so and yet will lock it firmly closed, at the same time the fitting lying almost flush with the wall. Unfortunately there are no intermediate positions with this type of fastener, unlike one range of conservatories that has top hung windows fitted with friction stays to allow an intermediate position to be selected. The stay is in two parts. A friction disc joining the two parts can be tightened to lock the window in any position.

Technically, for the plant room, there is much to be said for a louvre window mounted fairly low down. It allows the entry of cool air and can be set in any intermediate position so that the cool air can be directed upwards out of the way of plants and people. This is undoubtedly the best system but it does not look very decorative in a sun room, either from the inside or the outside. However, it has the advantage of being very easily

Left, the house lime, Sparmannia africana, makes an effective, and easily grown, floor-standing specimen plant.

controlled automatically, even without the use of electricity, to open anywhere between about 16-21°C (60-70°F). In the case of louvre windows, the sharp edge of the exposed glass is usually removed, but, even so, it is not the ideal type of window for a room that children play in, although the windows can be fitted out of the way at the top of the side of the conservatory.

One of the most intriguing types of window is the 'tilt and turn', a remarkably clever combination that allows a side hung window to open outwards like a house window yet is also capable of tilting inwards on a bottom hinge. Since hot air rises, it is obviously more efficient to have the window opening at the top than at the bottom. The window frame incidentally, like the whole conservatory structure, is made of ultraviolet stabilized, white PVC. A point to bear in mind is that top and bottom hung windows, with their relatively small projection of opening, are much safer for people moving around outside the conservatory than conventional side hung casement windows.

Fans

Even when the outside air is cold, the conservatory can get quite stuffy, and to counter this a small, air circulating fan of the greenhouse type is beneficial. One model, in particular, can actually divert the hot air downwards. A recent development is a small fan which is let into a pane of glass and is operated by a solar battery – that is an electric fan which is driven by energy from the sun's rays.

Ventilation is probably far more important than you imagine. You will need it for personal comfort for six months of the year and the plants need a buoyant atmosphere all the year round. More

Two position stay which will firmly lock a top hung window and not intrude into the conservatory space.

plants are lost through a combination of stagnant atmosphere and overwatering than anything else. Remember it is better to have too many ventilators than too few.

HEATING

Heating the conservatory depends on many factors and is not so straightforward as dealing with a greenhouse because it has also to be considered as a living room.

Paraffin heaters are not really in the running; they need almost daily maintenance, they can be knocked over, they discharge a considerable amount of water vapour and there is always a certain amount of smell. Greenhouse-type gas heaters are very cheap to run, but also produce water and the gas has to be plumbed in. They are worth considering when the conservatory is used mainly for plants as they can be thermostatically controlled, but there is some evidence that the fumes can be harmful to some plants, such as orchids. Certainly any quite small leakage of unburnt gas is harmful.

An extension of the house central heating, where this is possible without too high capital expenditure, is ideal with supplementary electric heating. Best of all, because of its cleanliness and accurate temperature control, is some form of electric heating. Electricity is the most expensive to use (except on Economy 7 night heating) but the high cost per unit of heat is partially offset because, unlike gas and paraffin heaters, no permanent ventilation is required and temperature control can be

A manually operated roof vent with simple bar stay that can be adjusted with the help of a pole.

set quite accurately. Electricity compares favourably with other fuels at the lower temperature settings especially up to say, 7°C (45°F).

Domestic Central Heating

Apart from the initial cost of installation, the cheapest running cost will be obtained by using a room-type hot water radiator connected into the domestic central heating installation. The ease or difficulty of doing this will depend upon a multitude of factors which will vary from house to house. Such factors are whether the radiators run off a ring main or if the supply to each radiator is taken back to a main distribution panel in the hot water cupboard; whether the pipes are full size, small bore or microbore; whether the pipes are laid in a concrete floor or whether they are in suspended floors (which will make the extension easier); whether it is a house or a bungalow (when the extension can be taken through the roof space).

In any event the radiators in the conservatory will need to have their own thermostats fitted so that the temperature can be controlled regardless of the house radiators. They will probably have to be installed against the wall of the house, but better distribution of heat will be possible if they can be placed at the sides or front of the conservatory. This may be possible when the bottom part of the conservatory walls is solid and not glazed.

Supplementary electric heating will be essential because many people switch off their central heating at night by a time controller; it can also be switched off by the master thermostat in the living room or hall, and the glass-walled conservatory will cool down much more rapidly than the interior of the house. The electric heater should have a thermostat incorporated so that it comes on automatically if the temperature in the conservatory falls below, say, 7°C (45°F). To attempt to run an independently controlled heating system from the domestic installation without electric boost heating would require elaborate control gear and would prove very expensive.

Gas Heating

If there is a gas main accessible to the conservatory, gas heating will almost certainly prove to be the cheapest method of providing heat. This can be done by using a free-standing unit of the type supplied for greenhouses or, where the conservatory has a suitable outside wall for mounting, a small balanced flue gas heater can be employed.

The free-standing heater has slightly greater efficiency but many disadvantages. For one thing, air has to be provided for combustion and this means that a ventilator must be left open permanently with the attendant loss of heat, yet failure to do this will result in incomplete combustion and the production of dangerous fumes. Even at best, a minute amount of ethylene is produced and this is harmful to many plants, but, on the other hand, gas heaters produce a useful amount of carbon dioxide which is beneficial to plant growth. The higher the temperature to which the conservatory is heated, the greater the

Right, very much a living room extension, this conservatory holds an interesting mix of furniture and plants.

possible damage from ethylene gases.

There are, in fact, two types of free-standing greenhouse heaters on the market. One has a pilot light and the other a 'modulating' main jet. The pilot type is usually more expensive to buy but cheaper to run, since, when the thermostat turns the heat 'off', there remains only a low gas consumption for the pilot light. This can be around the equivalent of 100 watts. The modulating type only turns down the main flame, which saves complication, but in some cases the 'off' position still results in a gas flame the equivalent of nearly 1 kw. Only a few natural gas heaters can be set to operate at below 4°C (40°F) and for frost protection only but electric heating can be set lower and more accurately and for that reason the running cost of electric heating will not be much higher.

The free-standing gas heaters can be fitted with a different jet to allow them to be operated on bottled gas. This will certainly save the gas installation cost, but the actual running cost will be more than double that of natural gas. If bottled gas is used, then it should be propane, not butane which ceases to vaporise well above the level of freezing point, which is when you need it most.

If the conservatory has an outside wall the alternative method of heating by natural gas is to use a small thermostatically controlled balanced flue heater of the kind used in bedrooms. In this type

Automatic window opening devices, like the type shown here, are set when the conservatory is at the desired temperature. They react continuously to similar heat levels, pushing open the windows by hydraulic action.

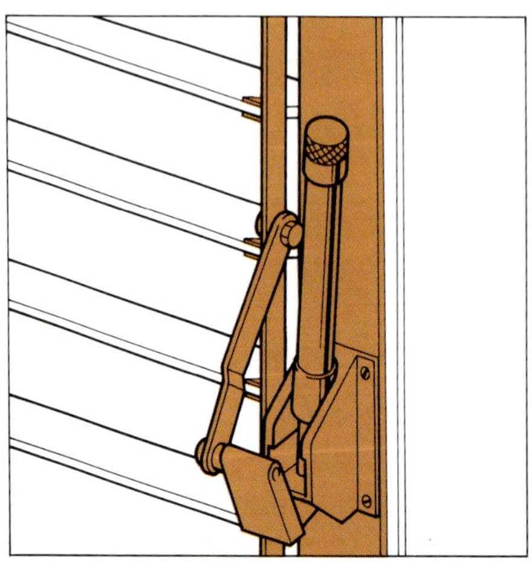

All these foliage plants benefit from some heat in winter. Shown here are ferns, Ficus benjamina and codiaeum.

fresh air is ducted into the heater from outside, and the burnt gas is also led out to the atmosphere after passing through a heat exchanger. The room air passes over the hot 'radiator' of the heat exchanger, just as in a car heater, and is circulated by convection. This has the advantage that no by-products of combustion of any kind are led into the conservatory itself, and the running costs are low.

Most gas heaters are fitted with a flame failure device to ensure that the gas supply is switched off automatically if the flame blows out. Ignition may be by hand with a match or with piezo crystal and push button to produce the spark.

Electric Heating

Electric heating is clean, automatic, needs very little attention and negligible maintenance. You just switch on and forget it. Although electricity per unit of heat produced is by far the most expensive fuel – at least three times that of gas – the fact that permanent ventilation is not required and very accurate temperature control can be maintained, makes it competitive, particularly when the minimum temperature setting is not above 7°C (45°F).

There are two basic types of equipment: tubular heaters and fan heaters. Tubular heaters give the best distribution of heat and do not create a draught when you are sitting in your sun lounge.

Fan heaters do not require any installation work – you just plug them into the nearest socket – and they do prevent stagnant conditions that lead to fungus troubles on plants.

Tubular Heaters

The tubular heaters used in conservatories and greenhouses are specially made to withstand the damp conditions and are usually made of aluminium and waterproofed. To obtain sufficient heat without too high a surface temperature drying the air, they have to be rather large and are usually 5cm (2in) in diameter in lengths of from 60cm to 3.6m (2 to 12ft). The electrical loading is usually standardised at 60 watts per foot length, so it is necessary to install the tubes in banks in order to obtain sufficient wattage. The lowest tube should be 15cm (6in) from the ground and, where tubes are installed under staging, there should be a 15cm (6-in) gap between the staging and the wall to allow the hot air to rise and circulate round the greenhouse. The heaters may be floor-mounted or attached to the side wall or back of the conservatory, as convenient. They are not double-insulated like lawnmowers and must be properly earthed.

Thermostats

A separate thermostat will be needed to control the heaters and this will usually be of the rod type situated somewhere near the plant area so that it monitors the air round the plants. To avoid incorrect readings due to local overheating it should, if at all possible, be mounted out of the way of the morning sun. Usually there is a differential of ±2 or 3°C, which can give a temperature swing between switching on and off, of as much as 6°C. This means that to be absolutely sure that the temperature never goes below 4°C (40°F) the heaters will not be switched off until the air temperature has reached 7°C (45°F).

This is wasteful of electricity and, in the long term, it may well be more economical to buy an aspirated thermostat, although it is more expensive. With this type of thermostat, a small fan draws in air which is monitored and the thermostat will keep the air temperature within about 1 deg. F. of the setting. For most plants, such accuracy of setting is not important, but it may be important if you are aiming at frost protection only.

Night Storage Heaters

These are usually coupled to a special meter to take advantage of the low night time tariff when the cost of electricity is competitive with gas and cheaper than most other fuels. If you already use night storage heating, it is certainly worthwhile adding a heater in the conservatory to give the basic background heating at night. It can be 'topped up' on cold nights with a thermostatically controlled electric fan heater which will be charged at the same rate. If storage heaters are not already used, it will hardly be worthwhile to use them for the conservatory. The installation cost would be high and temperature control is not easy.

Fan Heaters

Although fan heaters are the most popular form of heating in greenhouses, they are not ideal in a conservatory that is used for relaxing in because they create a draught – especially the type that has the fan running continuously. However, they have their uses since they take up very little room, can be moved about into any convenient part of the room and can be plugged into any convenient power socket. The moving air from the fan is ideal for plants so it is best to buy one which allows the selection of cool air (fan only) or fan with heat. You can then leave the fan running when you are not using the conservatory or for cooling the air during the summer.

The biggest advantage of a fan heater, apart from space saving, is the fact that there are no installation costs. Even the thermostat is built into the heater, although you can place another thermostat in the electrical circuit if your want greater accuracy. There are various sizes, but always buy a heater with sufficient heat output to cope with the worst conditions of wind and frost. Because of the action of the thermostat it costs no more to heat the room with a powerful heater than a smaller one; the larger heaters just cost a little more in the first place. Generally speaking a fan heater is placed on the floor at the far end from the door to achieve the best air circulation, although in a conservatory it will probably have to be moved around quite a bit to suit the manner in which the room is being used at the time. Wherever you put it, make sure that there is plenty of room for the air to enter at the back of the heater.

Calculating the Size of Heater

Whether you use a fan heater or tubular heaters the same formula is used to establish the rating of the heater required to maintain a given temperature. It will suffice to use a greenhouse formula, although in actual practice a conservatory stays warmer than a greenhouse because the brick wall of the dwelling actually radiates heat during the night. The greatest loss of heat is through the glass, but if double glazing is used the heat loss is greatly reduced, probably by as much as half.

Generally it is assumed that the minimum outside temperature is not likely to fall below –7°C (20°F) for any length of time, so, in order to maintain a tempera-

This diagram shows the method of measuring and calculating the size of a conservatory in order to establish the size of heater required.

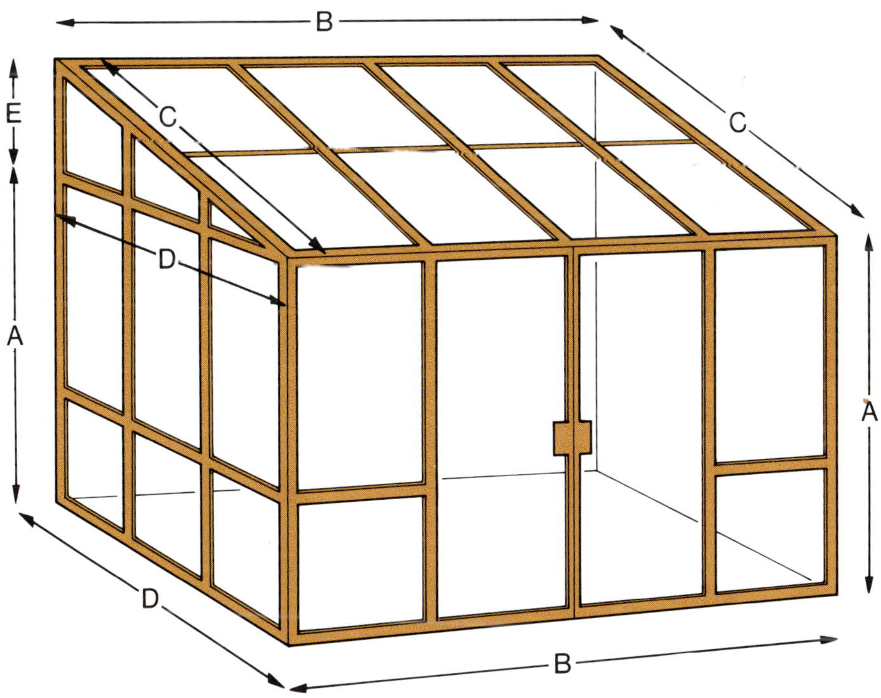

Equivalent Glass Area

Roof B×C
+ Sides D×A (twice)
+ D×E (once)
+ A×B
+ Floor ⅓×D×B

Left, some form of shading is essential on hot days and these striped blinds are effective and decorative.

ture of +7° (45°F), a temperature rise above ambient of 14°C (25°F) will be needed. The procedure is to measure the length, width, and height to the eaves and height to the ridge of the conservatory, and then, from these figures, calculate the total glass area and 'equivalent' glass area of the sides, ends and roof sections. If any sides or ends are constructed of timber, brick or concrete, or double glazing, through which heat loss is less than through glass, add one half of their area to the total glass area to give the total 'equivalent glass' area. The house wall of the conservatory can be ignored, but add one-third of the floor area which accounts for some heat loss. Finally, multiply the 'total equivalent glass' area in metres by 100 or, if in feet, by 9.3, to find the number of watts needed to raise the conservatory temperature by 14°C (25°F) above the outside temperature. If the answer comes to, say, 2½ kw, you will need to buy a 3-kw heater to be safe, although with tubular heaters that are rated at 120 watts per unit there will not be any need to go far above the actual calculated figure.

Electricity Consumption

Our winter climate is so variable that it is virtually impossible to predict what the consumption will be, but the Electricity Council has produced some 'average' figures showing that the weekly consumption during October to April inclusive per 1000 watts of calculated heating requirement could be expected to work out at 14 units in South and West England and West Wales, 25 units in South-west Scotland and Northern Ireland and the rest of England and 28 units in North and East Scotland. They cite as an example, a structure needing 2.6 kw to maintain 7°C (45°F) would use an average of about 37 units per week over the seven months period in the South of England.

Within the parameters of heating there are one or two suggestions that will help to reduce the risk of failure. For instance, a good maximum/minimum thermometer is a 'must' in the conservatory. This will enable you to relate the actual minimum temperature recorded with the numerical setting on the heater or thermostat. Never rely on the temperature settings on the equipment: always check their operation first.

Another very important fact to bear in mind is that consumption of electricity or indeed of any other fuel – will virtually double if the thermostat setting is increased from 7 to 10°C (45 to 50°F). As most plants will grow at a night temperature of 7°C (45°F) it is not worth the cost of providing extra heat.

All the figures in this chapter are based on aluminium structures. There is a good deal of evidence today that timber framing will cut energy consumption by anything up to 20 per cent. This is largely due to the cooling effect of the aluminium glazing bars, which act as fins during windy weather.

SHADING

Even if you do not need shading against the mid-day sun, plants most certainly do, otherwise they are going to lose moisture faster than they can take it up and so dry out. The domestic solution would be to use curtains or vertical slatted blinds, and very attractive they are too, but they are not really suitable for a growing room. True, most indoor plants will accept this type of shading and so will plants that are only brought into the conservatory on a temporary basis, like pot chrysanthemums.

There is a real problem here, however, because plants growing in the conservatory, other than shade-loving ones, will not put up with high density shading, unless it is of a temporary nature just while you are sitting in the room. Under these conditions slatted blinds, curtains and those delightful external blinds that roll back into a box above the roof are fine, but you must remember to open them up when you are not using the room. This is why the choice of furniture is so important in a sun lounge which is also used for growing. (See page 36.)

Having established that shading is needed, there remains the problem, what kind? Let us first of all consider how shading works, insofar as the plants are concerned. Plants grow through a process called photosynthesis, which uses light, although not the whole spectrum. Plants use mainly the visible light – the yellow to far-red as well as some blue light. Infra-red rays are invisible heat rays and these need to be cut out as far as possible during the summer. Ideally, a material is needed that will cut out most of the infra-red heating rays but still allow the visible rays through. Unfortunately, there is nothing available that has this filtering effect, although a proprietary powder for application to the outside of the glass of greenhouses performs well on this count.

Interior Shading

Most shading is designed for internal use. Unfortunately, although this cuts out glare and scorching, it does not do a great deal to reduce the air temperature because the sunlight is absorbed by the shading material and re-radiated as long-wave heat radiation which will not pass back through the glass to the open air. It has to be dissipated by good ventilation.

The various forms of greenhouse

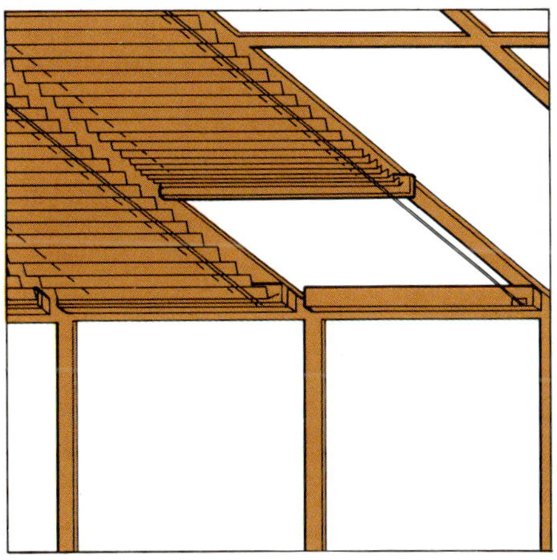

Pleated fabric blinds on each roof panel allow shading over different parts of the conservatory to be adjusted easily.

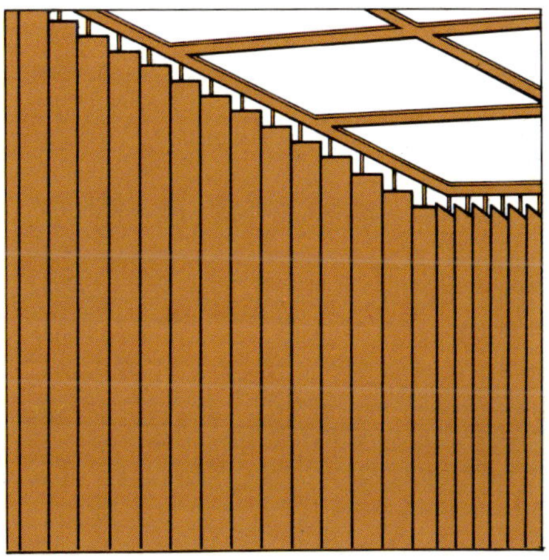

Vertical venetian blinds are worth looking at because they can be set to cut glare without darkening the room.

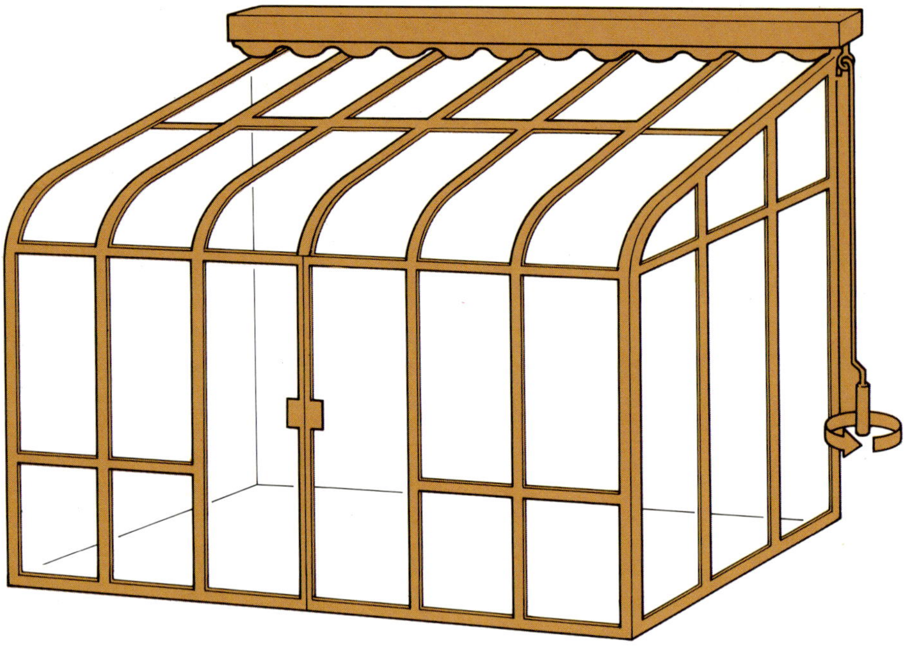

An exterior roller blind which is operated by a removable handle.

shading can also be used in a conservatory, although they will not improve the appearance and cannot be quickly taken down. Woven or knitted netting is available in different densities according to the plants you are growing, but it needs to be a make that is ultra-violet light stabilised; there are semi-rigid plastic meshes that might be easier to fix, especially if you do not have any glazing bar slots, and there is also flexible twin-walled polypropylene in white or green. This provides quite good infra-red reduction, but it is advisable not to use the green type or the green roller blinds that used to be so popular, because green filters out the yellow-red light needed for growing and allows through the green light which is of no value for photosynthesis.

A strong cross-laminated fabric is available which cuts out glare, while still giving decent growing light; the higher the light intensity the greater the percentage light reduction. In addition a white translucent material made of polyester gives a light transmission of 45 to 55 per cent.

Any form of internal shading, to be effective, needs really good ventilation to dispel the heat. But most of the materials available, although allowing some passage of air, will cover the ventilators and make the build-up of heat even worse. Perhaps it is best to lay shading material over the plants and use this in conjunction with adjustable curtains or blinds.

Exterior Blinds

Having established that outside shading is best, what is there on the market? There are roller blinds and a more decorative form of blind that rolls back into a box on the wall of the house, similar to house blinds. These are all efficient because they cut out the heat rays before they enter the conservatory, but the sort that rolls back into a box cannot be used under very low eaves, such as those of a bungalow. Another snag from a growing point of view is that the material is often so dense that the blinds should only be used for a few hours after mid-day, otherwise the plants will be starved of light and become leggy. This also applies to plastic and wooden lath blinds.

WATERING

Watering in a sun room or leisure room is likely to be the simplest, since the plants will all be in plant containers or flower pots or self-watering pots, or maybe in a hanging basket or two.

Watering Cans

For watering flower pots it is well worth while to invest in a really good quality watering can that is nicely balanced and has a long spout so that you can reach plants at the back without making a mess. Although a 7.5-litre (2-gallon) can is ideal in the garden, a 4-litre (1-gallon) size is much handier to use indoors. It is worth mentioning one unusual can which has the hole under the spout, the actual end being blocked up. Instead of a violent rush of water out of the end when you tip it up, there is a gentle trickle of water in a downward direction which provides easier control.

Another recent innovation is a special pump-up watering can for hanging baskets and high shelves. It has a long vertical tube at the end of which is an inverted U outlet. You just pump up the plastic container to send the water scurrying up the delivery spout.

Capillary Watering

Many plant holders and jardinieres today are self-watering by capillary action, that is, they have a reservoir in the base and the water is transferred to the

Different kinds of water-holding crystals can be used to keep individual pots well watered.

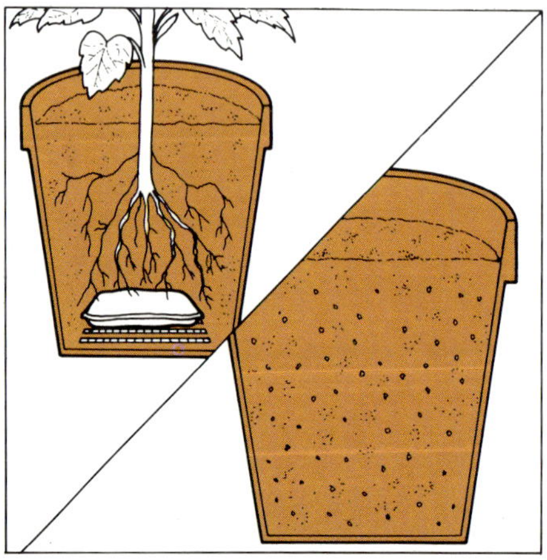

An alternative is the self-watering pot, which works by capillary action, using a reservoir and wick.

potting medium by capillary action through a wick or sand or something similar. It is a very efficient and labour saving way of keeping plants happy, but there is the likelihood that the plants will remain too wet for their own good during the winter, even indoors, and root rot then becomes a problem. It is advisable, therefore, to treat self-watering pots like ordinary flower pots during the winter and only use the self-watering facility from May onwards. Self-watering pots are available in all manner of shapes and sizes, but the better ones are more efficient and less likely to let you down than inferior grades.

If you decided to use part of your conservatory as a greenhouse, using staging or shelving, other options are open to you. There are plenty of self-watering trays on which to stand the pots, a sheet of capillary matting on the tray being used to transfer the water from a trough which may be filled by hand, or from a 7.5-litre (2-gallon) plastic bag hung up above the staging, or from a tank through an automatic float device which maintains the correct level in the reservoir. The reservoir itself can easily be made out of a short length of plastic guttering stopped at each end. The water level must not be as high as the matting but, on the other hand, the water will not rise more than 5cm (2in) from the trough to the matting.

Pots more than about 10cm (4in) high cannot be watered very satisfactorily by the capillary matting method as the water will not rise high enough in the pot, unless a thick wick of soft wool, or a proprietary wick, is used inside the pot. Capillary watering also lends itself to watering seed boxes, especially as overhead watering, other than spraying, can wash the seeds about. The idea of capillary watering is not new. Old-time gardeners achieved the same objective with a thick bed of sand, but this led to a problem of weight and very solid staging was needed.

Although not strictly capillary watering, an extremely useful new development is a type of crystal. These, when mixed with the potting compost, absorb water and swell up to become little reservoirs. Personal trials have shown that when control pots needed watering every week, those with the crystals survived for three weeks between waterings.

With no running costs, the capillary mat system, capable of liquid feeding as well as watering, is a good buy.

Trickle Watering

Where all the plants are grown together on staging, but in pots – even very large ones – automatic watering can be achieved by another system called trickle watering. This is a system by which water is supplied through an arrangement of small-bore tubes fed either directly from the mains or, more frequently, from a reservoir which may, itself, either be fed from the mains through a conventional ball valve, or be topped up by hand. These tubes are fitted with small adjustable nozzles from which the water drips, and one or more nozzles is placed on each flower pot. The nozzles are adjusted by hand to suit the amount of water required.

The trickle system is a method that works rather better in theory than in practice. Setting up takes a great deal of time and patience, the nozzles do tend to become blocked, especially in hard water areas, and siphoning systems, where used, sometimes develop air locks and stop working.

Trickle watering is best for large pots where the individual requirements of a number of plants can be met.

You can, of course, set the system up on a hit or miss basis and adjust the nozzles by screwing them in or out if the pots are getting too much or too little water. However, the correct way to set up the installation is to find out just how much water is being delivered. This can be done by placing margarine or yoghurt pots under each nozzle. Turn the system on and set the nozzles so that each one delivers the same amount of water, at the same time clearing any that are blocked. The nozzles can be readjusted later to suit the water demands of individual plants. For example, azaleas will need much more water than the average plant.

Most trickle systems are supplied as separate parts consisting of lengths of tubing, the nozzles and a reservoir; there are some, however, that connect direct to the mains without a reservoir. It may be as well to prepare a drawing of the system as it relates to your installation so that you know exactly how you are going to run the water line and where you are going to put the reservoir tank. If it is mains fed you may not have much choice; if it is hand filled you will have more choice but it must be easily accessible so that you do not spill the water when topping it up.

It is almost impossible to install a reliable fully automatic system for a reservoir-fed layout, but it can be done if the watering system is fed directly off the mains, particularly if an electricity supply is available. There is a clock-type timer and another system controlled by evaporation, and a third by sunlight, wherein a photo-electric cell operates an electro-magnetic water valve. There is also a non-electric timing system, but all these control methods are relatively expensive. By contrast, there are two different makes that embody a moisture monitor placed in the soil near one of the plants and this opens and closes a water valve controlling the feed to the nozzles.

In general, trickle systems will work well if you can monitor them all the time, and they will save a great deal of time and labour. However, relatively low-priced amateur versions are not yet a hundred per cent reliable.

Seeping Hose

There is yet another system of watering which, although mainly designed for the greenhouse beds, can also be used to irrigate sand-gravel beds on the staging where capillary matting is not used. This is a seeping hose. Most are designed for outdoor use, but one, in particular, is suitable for greenhouse use and consists of micro-porous PVC tubing. Water fed from a tank oozes out all along the tube, which can be laid on the ground, on a bench or run over the tops of pots. Control of the amount of water fed is by a valve which responds to changes in soil moisture. It is not suitable for mains pressure.

An aspect of watering that needs to be considered is the spare water that drips through if you are using slatted staging. To avoid flooding the conservatory floor, place waterproof trays filled with gravel under the staging and place pots of ferns on them to obscure the trays and give a decorative appearance. In general, all the watering systems, once adjusted, will save you a great deal of time, work and probably mess, against hand watering with a can. Most are not yet in a stage to be relied upon to work automatically for long periods of time. If this is required, a timer-clock-operated valve would be the least expensive choice, but a light or moisture sensitive controller would be better.

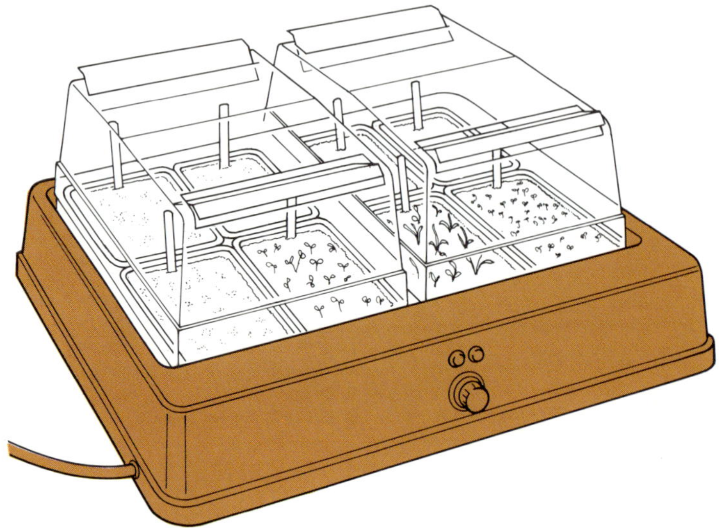

Electrically heated propagators are valuable for germinating seeds, rooting cuttings and nurturing young plants.

PROPAGATING EQUIPMENT

One of the greatest joys of owning a conservatory or a greenhouse is being able to do your own propagation, both sowing seeds and taking cuttings. In the warm conditions of the conservatory and with the aid of a small propagator you can produce plants for the garden as well as decorative items for the conservatory itself.

The range of propagators is vast: from cold propagators which are virtually seed trays with a plastic cover, to mini-greenhouses with bottom heating, air heating and an air circulating fan.

Cold Propagator

The cold propagator relies on the conservatory for all its heat but is a propagator by virtue of the fact that the plastic top maintains a moist atmosphere conducive to good seed germination and root action in cuttings. However, the fact that the night temperature will fall to the level of what is probably an unheated conservatory will severely limit the range of cuttings you can take while many of the more interesting seeds need at least 21°C (70°F) for good germination.

Heated Propagator

Better by far is the propagator with a small built-in electric heater. Some of these are only the size of a conventional seed tray and are really intended for use indoors on the windowsill. For any form of serious growing you are sure to want much more than this – at the minimum a propagator that will take two trays and preferably one that will hold three trays. It is cheaper and less bulky to buy the size you will want rather than buy an extra one later on. These propagators will usually raise the temperature by about 11°C (20°F) above the conservatory temperature, which is sufficient except in the severest weather.

In order to keep the price down, some makers offer electrically heated propagators without a built-in thermostat. Whilst this may be satisfactory for a north-facing kitchen windowsill, it is unrealistic for a conservatory, because the heating element will stay on, even when the propagator is sitting in the hot sunshine. The temperature inside will rise to well over 38°C (100°F), at which point most seedlings will want to curl up and die and seeds certainly will not germinate. It is better to buy a unit with a built-in thermostat which will cut off the heater at somewhere around 24°C (75°F). The best type of propagator will have a variable thermostat that will allow you to set the temperature according to the plants you want to grow. There is an optimum figure for various seeds and cuttings and you can set it accordingly.

The larger proprietary propagators are designed to take standard seed trays and may have a single cover or a separate one for each tray. The advantage of the latter system is that seedlings can be hardened off at different times. Some seeds are slow to germinate and it is useful to be able to keep these covered when another batch have germinated and need plenty of ventilation. When there is only one cover for the whole propagator, small sliding vents are often provided. This is nowhere near enough and you will have to prop the cover up to let in more air.

The best propagators, and of course, the most expensive, have a high dome and sliding 'windows', usually of plastic, so that the amount of ventilation can be adjusted very quickly to suit the conditions. Right at the top of the market and costing as much as a small greenhouse, is a unit that not only embodies the usual base heating and variable thermostat but many other luxury refinements as well. These include a small thermostatically controlled blower for blowing warm or cool air into the propagator. It also has its own built-in lighting system for illuminating houseplants.

A very valuable use of the high-top propagators with variable heat control is

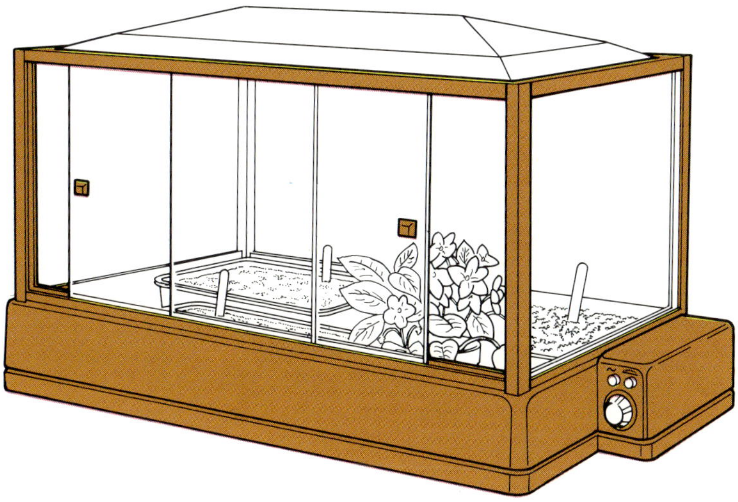

Extra headroom and sliding doors in this design facilitate ventilation and ease of handling. Thermostats are essential to prevent overheating.

that they can be used during the winter to keep delicate plants free of frost. If you set the thermostat on the lowest setting, the heater will switch on automatically at about 7°C (45°F). To save space the plants can be boxed up first or they can stay in their pots, according to the room you have. Typical examples that come to mind are fuchsias and geraniums.

There is an accepted procedure when you bring the propagator into use. Although it is possible to stand flower pots and seed trays directly on the base of the propagator, this is not the best way. Instead, put in 2.5cm (1in) or so of washed gravel or river sand. Keep this moist and then place the pots and trays on top. It is not advisable to use builders' sand. The moist sand will not only distribute the heat evenly but will provide moisture for the roots and a humid environment for the plants.

There is on the market something called a 'Hot Bench'. It consists of a staging framework to which are bolted trays which contain a flat heating element of conductor-coated material, encased in an insulated envelope and laid on polystyrene pads to reduce loss of heat downwards. The electrical rating is 30 watt per foot length of bench and thermostatic control can be built in.

Mist Propagation

If you are really keen on propagating difficult subjects like azaleas, rhododendrons and evergreens, you will find a miniature misting unit invaluable. Although you can build one yourself over your propogating bench by using proprietary parts, a lot of time and trouble can be saved by using a circular unit that has been specially designed for amateur use. It takes the form of a 75-cm (30-in) diameter propagator base, heated and thermostatically controlled. A pillar in the centre contains a misting unit which covers the whole area and the spray mist is contained by a transparent plastic 'wall' that fits round the unit. Control of misting is by pressing a plunger at the side but much better results can be obtained by using a light-sensitive control mechanism that operates an electromagnetic water valve at regular intervals.

Care needs to be taken when 'weaning' the cuttings away from the misting. Too rapid a transition results in losses due to drying out.

Although the duration of misting always remains the same (about a couple of seconds) the frequency of operation will change according to the amount of light and the setting of the automatic controller. The unit can be fed from the water mains through ordinary garden hose or an adaptor can be obtained to allow it to be operated from a large pressure spray. Misting, incidentally, prevents desiccation of cuttings, so that there is less need for shading and the greater amount of light will encourage photosynthesis and thus more rapid root growth.

Just a word of warning. Possessing an electrically heated propagator will encourage you to sow more seeds and take more cuttings, so do leave room for them to harden off. You can't take them staight out of a propagator and put them in a cold frame!

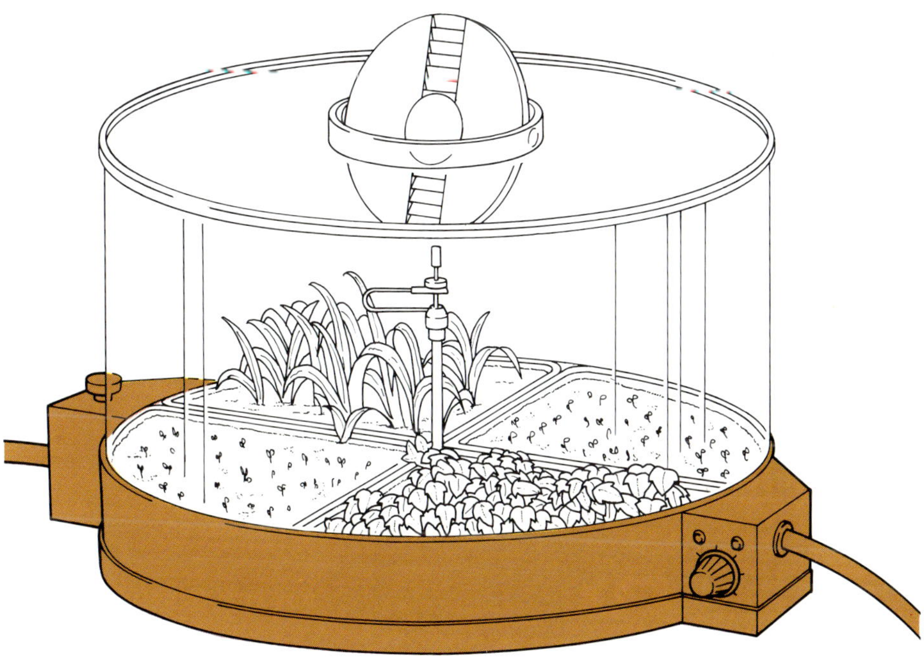

Provided there is sufficient air flow to prevent fungal growth, mist propagators give young plants an ideal micro-climate.

STAGING AND SHELVING

Staging for a greenhouse, where only practical considerations need to be taken into account, is one thing, but staging for a conservatory, where appearance counts just as much, is a totally different story.

The dual-purpose conservatory that acts as a sun lounge but also has a section for bringing on plants will need the combination of a practical bench and decorative staging. Because young plants need good light, the growing or propagating bench really ought to be down one side of the conservatory, so that the opposite side is clear for sitting in. For plant display, tiered staging is the best, and again it should be kept out of the way of the walking and sitting area. It really looks best against the rear wall.

Before choosing the staging it is absolutely essential to decide upon how you are going to use the conservatory. If you intend to do serious propagation and greenhouse work then you must have something very substantial and you are very unlikely to want to move it. If, on the other hand, you only want to bring on mature plants to the flowering stage, or frost-sensitive house plants during the winter, it will be an immense advantage to have foldaway staging that will allow maximum living room during the summer.

Rigid Staging

For the propagating area, don't be tempted to buy cheap flimsy staging. It is essential to have something that will carry a fair weight – say 51 kg (1 cwt) of wet soil without collapsing or swaying about. This means it has either to be very strongly made or it must have adequate bracing bars. The bench height is fairly standard at about 75cm (30in). Almost all the staging is made of aluminium but you can buy wooden staging and this, as well as the aluminium staging, can be made to order so that it can actually be designed to fit the requirements of your own conservatory.

Whether you are concentrating on the display of plants or their propagation, staging is an important consideration. Tiered shelves do justice to cascading plant arrangements, while benches provide work surfaces. Smaller units are versatile if part of a modular system.

One maker produces a special conservatory plant bench in brown plastic which is nearly 90cm (3ft) high.

Quite often the staging frame is designed to accept a second shelf about 23cm (9in) above the ground; this is extremely useful for storing accessories out of the way or for growing decorative ferns which do not require a great deal of light. However, this second layer is only of any real advantage when the top tray is a solid one. If you have a slatted or mesh top tray, every time you water the plants at the top, the water drips through on to the plants or equipment underneath.

Trays

Unfortunately solid plastic trays are no longer obtainable and so most are made of aluminium. Usually these are about 2.5cm (1in) deep, which is sufficient to hold enough gravel to provide moisture and humidity for pot plants. Many, but not all, trays are reversible, and this is to be recommended, to provide either a flat working area or to provide a surface for matting for capillary watering (see page 30). Usually the trays are not sealed at the corners to allow for drain-

age, but where the gravel bed is intended to provide watering, they can easily be sealed with Bostick or Araldite. This is quite important in a conservatory where drips of water on the floor would be most unwelcome. Incidentally, it is possible to obtain aluminium trays made up to size, if you already have some existing staging you want to use.

Although capillary watering with light-weight matting is very popular today, there still are keen gardeners who prefer to use a gravel bed in place of matting and for this the 2.5-cm (1-in) deep tray is unsatisfactory. Instead it is best to buy the 5-cm (2-in) deep aluminium trays which are readily available, although more expensive.

Slatted Staging

Some plants, especially in the winter, need a good airflow round them to ward off disease. For these, slatted staging – or mesh – is essential. Fortunately you can buy movable aluminium slats as well as slatted wooden staging. A new development is plastic-coated mesh staging, which usually folds away and looks attractive.

Movable Staging

The staging considered so far is rigid with the frame units bolted together, but tubular staging in aluminium is also available in modules that allow a very high degree of personal layout. It is very light and is designed so that it can be dismantled very quickly and easily, although in practice, it can be quite tricky to separate the tubular aluminium bars from the plastic corner pieces that hold them together. A mallet has to be used for the job. Cross bracing is fitted at the back and at the side, but even so it is not as rigid as a substantial bolted structure. The manufacturers offer reversible solid trays in aluminium and alternative slatted trays in untreated wood. It is advisable that the wooden slats be treated with a horticultural grade preservative, such as Cuprinol, and then weathered before use. This will defer rotting for a very long time.

Reverting back to the question of removable staging so that the conservatory can be converted into a sun lounge in the summer, this can be achieved in a number of ways. Even the bolted staging is not all that difficult to dismantle, but where requirements may vary from week to week, or even month to month, hinged staging is a much more practical approach. It is not only quick to operate but it is tidy to look at. Unfortunately, it is not all that easy to find as it is only made by certain greenhouse manufacturers, so it will be necessary to check the fitting and the width against the make of conservatory you have. Being designed to fit at the rear into greenhouse glazing bars, it will not be suitable for use with conservatories that have box or square section frames instead of slotted glazing bars. The front of the staging is suspended on chains from the roof glazing bars (again only possible if the bars are slotted), or in the case of another make, supported on legs. The wire mesh is either plastic coated or coated in epoxy resin. It certainly looks attractive. A suspended hinged shelf is also available in the same style.

Hanging shelves, using space under the roof, keep plants away from the glass.

Shelves can be attached to the wall by brackets.

Width

Incidentally, staging is made in a number of widths to suit different sized houses. A width of 60cm (2ft) is probably the optimum to avoid taking up too much room in the conservatory, although 75cm (30in) would probably suit the keen grower better. Anything wider than this makes it difficult to reach the plants at the back, as a result of which they tend to become neglected. Remember, too, that the weight per 6 sq cm (1 sq in) pressing on the conservatory floor via the staging legs will be very considerable, so unless the floor is concrete, quarry tiles or something similar, spread the load. Proprietary staging foot plates in aluminium are available.

Shelving

Most suppliers of staging will also supply shelving, usually about 20cm (8in) deep and designed to bolt on to brackets that fit into the glazing bar slots – the problem arises again if your conservatory does not have these slots. The shelves need to be positioned about 45cm (18in) or more above the staging otherwise they will interfere with the plants in pots. Modular tubular staging is available with shelves that actually fit to the top of the staging, independent of the conservatory structure.

Every conservatory should have a set of display staging, the kind of thing you see in garden centres, department stores and florists. The staging consists of a set of aluminium trays, usually about 23cm (9in) wide, set on a modular tubular frame set up from the floor like a staircase. According to whether there are two, three or four steps, so the projection varies from 50 to 100cm (20 to 40in), and the 'staircase' of plants uses up to 90cm (3ft) in lengths which are multiples of 56cm (22in) or so. Because of the simple modular construction, the display staging can be supplied to suit any size of conservatory. To simplify management watertight liners can be supplied for the trays, which can then be fitted with water mats to reduce the frequency of watering.

Furnishing the Conservatory

The decor of the conservatory will be mostly a matter of personal taste, but any fabrics used must be resistant to deterioration through sunshine. It is, therefore, best to furnish the room with specifically designed garden furniture.

Unless the conservatory is mainly a 'growing room', there are two main uses for the space, and which one is chosen will influence the choice of furniture. There is a great deal of fun to be enjoyed by having meals 'out in the garden' but under cover, and this choice means installing a fair-sized table and some upright chairs. If, on the other hand it is your intention to eat indoors and use the conservatory for relaxation only, then a coffee table and lounger chairs are more likely to fit the bill.

Eating in the Conservatory

If your choice is to eat out in the conservatory, you may be tempted to use the dining room table and chairs, but the combination of heat, light and humidity is likely to play havoc with them. Far better to buy something designed for the job. Although rather expensive, a cast aluminium Victorian style table and similar chairs look very decorative indeed and are comfortable enough, provided you fit the chairs with pads or cushions. Similar chairs and tables are also available in cast iron, but it is heavy to move around. All these Victorian reproductions have intricate castings which can collect dirt and be difficult to keep clean. There will still be room in most conservatories for a reclining chair.

Somewhat softer, and certainly more modern in appearance, are the widely available white plastic tables and chairs. These are made in various sizes and shapes and have the merit that they can be matched up with the lounger chairs. They are easily wiped over to keep them clean. Check that the width of the gap between the table slats will not allow the salt cellar to disappear on to the floor during a meal!

Relaxation

Every owner of a conservatory will want to relax in the sun room and comfortable reclining chairs are a 'must'. They are available in all manner of colours with frames that may be all plastic or plastic coated. Sun beds may be suitable for the garden but they are not really the right

Furniture for the Conservatory
Comfort, practicality and aesthetics will determine your choice from a range of hardwood, plastic, and tubular steel-framed furniture now available.

furniture for the conservatory. They take up too much room when extended and are not a comfortable seat when folded. Furthermore, you are not likely to use them to get an attractive tan because much of the ultra-violet that causes the suntan is filtered out by the glass. Far better are the adjustable recliners, which offer a selection of about five backrest positions through a ratchet mechanism. In some models there is a built-in leg rest which comes up as the back of the seat goes down, to provide a comfortable, not quite horizontal, relaxing position. All these chairs will fold and so save space.

The degree of comfort, the amount of padding and the quality of fabric used varies according to how much one is prepared to pay. Bear in mind, however, that there is a pretty hefty mark-up on garden furniture, so it is well worthwhile to shop around in the local garden centres, department stores and 'cash and carry' stores. Of interest also is the ancillary furniture often made to match, such as coffee tables, trollies, stools and cocktail tables.

Some people like teak. Although this type of furniture, which includes tables, chairs and padded 'relaxers' is primarily intended for outdoor use, if you like it there is no reason why it should not grace the conservatory. Since it will not have to withstand the weather, it will retain its colour and continue to give that subtle feeling of solid warmth. However, for indoor use you really do not necessarily have to go to the expense of buying teak or iroko, as cheaper woods will suffice.

Finishing Touches

Well, what of the remaining decor? If the plant growing is subsidiary, what about curtains to tone with the chairs? Alternatively, vertical slatted blinds look well. Although these are rather expensive, they can be adjusted to any angle or pulled to one side out of the way and are really much more adaptable than curtains. Lighting plays an important part in decor, but this has its own chapter. Hanging baskets of flowers are just the thing to give colour and, if you choose the right plants, scent as well (see page 41). Remember, though, that in the summer they will have to be watered every day and they must be situated where the drips will not do any

Tiles make an elegant and durable flooring for a conservatory, as they will withstand water and humidity. Rugs can be added for cosiness in the winter.

damage. One make is provided with its own drip tray.

Where the conservatory is fitted with slotted glazing bars it is easy to hang up the flower baskets and also any other hanging decorations like macrame. If the bars do not have slots they will have to be drilled to take hanging baskets.

FLOORING

What you put on the floor will depend upon the use to which the conservatory is to be put. For a sun room with pot plants in containers, an underlay and carpet can be used, but for a growing room you need something that will withstand water and high humidity. Quarry tiles are a favourite flooring and lend themselves to the addition of rugs in the central area. There are also many forms of decorative brick.

A new and very attractive wooden floor is called Checkerboard, consisting of 50 cm (20in) square slatted paving blocks. It is made in African hardwood and pressure impregnated pine. Carpet tiles are another alternative because they are easily taken up for cleaning or replacement.

LIGHTING

Conservatory lighting falls into three groups, namely general lighting, decorative lighting and plant lighting.

General Lighting

There is no reason why a conservatory should not be treated the same way as a room. Central pendant lighting is particularly easily arranged where the roof glazing bars have slots along which the cables can run, but the serious disadvantage of this type of lighting is the fact that it is going to get in the way of any interior roof shading. If you have a tinted roof, blinds will not be needed

QUARRY TILING

Check the height of battens marking the first area to be tiled with a spirit level, and adjust with wedges.

Spread mortar with a dragging board which has notches 9mm (3⁄8in) shallower than the thickness of the tiles.

Check that a line of tiles will fit into the space bordered by the batten. Dust the mortar with dry cement.

Lay the tiles, making sure they are correctly spaced, and tamp down with wooden block for an even surface.

Run a trowel along the joints to straighten any displaced tiles. Move battens to the next area to be tiled.

Twenty four hours after the whole area has been tiled, mortar the joints, wiping away surpluses with a wet cloth.

and roof lighting can be used without any problems. For even lighting, warm-white fluorescent tubes can be used, but they are rather stark compared with pendant lights and coloured shades.

Aesthetically there is much to be said for wall lights mounted on the house wall. They are out of the way, can be easily installed and can be used with coloured shades to give a warmth to the conservatory. At the same time they do not interfere with any additional decorative lighting.

Decorative Lighting
There are a number of special garden fittings designed for appearance rather than illumination. For example, there are attractive lighting spheres which hang on either side of a vertical tube. This tube or stand can be passed through the centre of a meal table or alternatively mounted on a pedestal to form a neat standard lamp that does not take up too much room.

Lamps can be arranged to illuminate particular displays of flowers or individual pot plants. This can be done by using one of the readily available spot lamps for domestic use, or the coloured spot lamps made for garden illumination.

There are also special plant illuminating lamps with tungsten carbide filaments to produce a light very similar to daylight. One firm supplies a complete illuminated hanging garden comprising a brass-finished plant bowl and hanging chains suspended below a 75 watt tungsten carbide lamp. For displaying your African violets, kalanchoes and similar house plants, there is a 'light box' or illuminated plantarium which is somewhat like a propagator in appearance but has two 20-watt fluorescent tubes in the roof of the 'box' to illuminate the plant tray. Sometimes ordinary white tubes are fitted but special 'Grolux' tubes bring out the colours much more vividly as they have a high output in the red and blue spectrum. For this reason they are ideal for lighting fish tanks. The way they bring out the colours of the fish needs to be seen to be believed.

Plant Lighting

Lighting to improve the growth of the plants is particularly necessary in conservatories fitted with a tinted roof. Used correctly during the early part of the year, the effect on growth can be dramatic.

Light is required by plants in order for photosynthesis to take place. This is the process by which plants convert water from the soil and carbon dioxide from the atmosphere into glucose by means of chlorophyll, the green coloured substance in the leaf. This glucose then provides the raw material for the plant's growth processes. Without adequate light there is no chlorophyll and no photosynthetic process. Research has shown that red and blue light produce the greatest effect, and as green shading filters out both these colours, plants will never do well under permanent green shading.

Although most plants will benefit from additional lighting on dull days and also evening lighting, all plants must have a rest period at night. Plants vary in their light requirements and are called long-day plants or short-day plants according to the day length required to induce flowering. For example, if chrysanthemums (short-day plants) are subjected to a long-day length by artificial lighting, they flower later in the year. Conversely, heavy shading to reduce the day-length is used to bring chrysanthemums into flower early.

In practice lights can be used for fully grown plants to make them flower or to bring on seedlings, but surprisingly powerful lighting is needed to have any material effect. To cater for all plants a 400-watt system is required, usually in the form of a special horticultural mercury-vapour lamp, but this needs expensive control gear and is only likely to be used in the conservatory by the plant enthusiast. This kind of lamp is powerful and produces 20,000 lumens, covers 2.75sq m (30sq ft) and has an adjustable chain suspension so that the intensity of light can be varied. The metal halide lamp is more efficient than the straight mercury lamp, and this, again rated at 400-watts, produces a third more light and has a very good light spectrum for plant growth.

There are also small, 125-watt mercury lamps giving 5800 lumens of light to cover an area of 0.6sq m (7sq ft) which will normally be sufficient for bringing on seedlings in a conservatory or to keep larger plants growing well. For house plants (which do not require the higher light levels) there is a much cheaper blended lamp, consisting of a mercury vapour lamp (to provide the blue) and built-in tungsten filament (to provide the red). It produces nearly 1000 lumens of light without the need for control-gear. A more powerful 160-watt/2600 lumens version is also available and is particularly suitable for cuttings.

A word of warning! Many of the ordinary grow bulbs on sale in garden centres are basically ordinary incandescent lamps, although this is not readily apparent from looking at the packaging. A filter is incorporated to correct this type of lamp's unbalanced spectrum. This results in an enormous loss of energy and a reduction in the light output and this type of bulb cannot be recommended for serious growing. Incandescent grow-bulbs also have a very much shorter life than mercury-discharge and filament dual bulbs, as well as providing much less light per bulb, so in the end the cost would be much higher.

Fluorescent tubes can, of course, be used and indeed often are when only a small plantarium or fish tank is to be illuminated, but for propagation a minimum of some 15-watts per 929sq cm (1sq ft) is needed with the light source about 30cm (12in) above the plants to avoid scorching. For seedlings a light period of 12 to 16 hours each day should be aimed at, including the daylight period. Unfortunately it is here that fluorescent tubes are at a disadvantage because the very bulky reflector above the tubes keeps out so much of the daylight. Remember, too, that just as heat without light produces poor etoliated (drawn) plants, so light without heat has little benefit. Try to maintain a temperature of between 13-21°C (55-70°F) together with humidity, which, in the case of pots, can be obtained by putting the pots in moist peat or on trays filled with moist pebbles.

Spotlamps concealed in foliage or attached to house walls bring out special qualities in plants and enhance the conservatory as a living space.

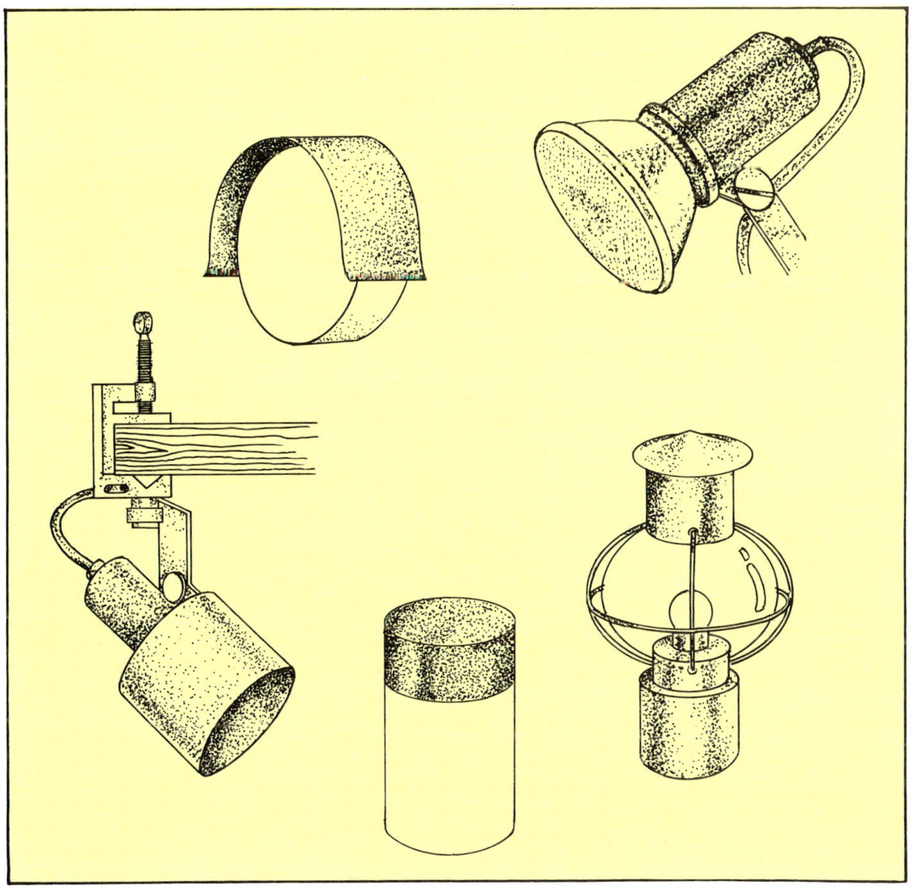

CONTAINERS

There are plant containers for all tastes and any big garden centre will carry a wide range. Some are plastic, others are wood or ceramic. They can be round or oblong or in the form of troughs or tubs, or even in the form of barrels. A simple thing, a container, but it is possible to run into trouble which will result in either a waterlogged plant or a wet floor. Most containers are designed to hold flower pots and the containers themselves have no drainage holes. Never plant directly into these. Others have drainage holes and are intended to replace the flower pot. They often have matching saucers to hold the water that drains out of the pot.

There are also self-watering pots and troughs (see page 30), in all manner of shapes and sizes, and usually in white plastic to tone in with any decor. Some of the cheapest do not work all that efficiently but they are very useful in the summer when you go away on holiday.

Left and below, the use of decorative lamps alters the atmosphere of a conservatory by creating pools of light, which illuminate the plants in the immediate vicinty.

Hanging Baskets

Hanging baskets add an extra dimension to the conservatory, extending greenery and blossom upwards into space that could easily be wasted. Horticulturally, hanging baskets provide ideal homes for climbing and trailing plants, and epiphytes, such as many orchids, forest cacti and bromeliads. Ferns, too, can often be best displayed in hanging baskets, in which their naturally arching habit can be given full reign. Using hanging baskets liberates valuable horizontal space – floor and staging – thus increasing the number of plants that can be grown.

Types of Hanging Basket

Hanging baskets come in several types, designs and materials. Most traditional is the close-meshed wire basket, nowadays plastic-coated or galvanized. They are traditionally lined with damp sphagnum moss, then filled nearly to the rim with compost and planted. Small young plants – lobelia, for example – can be tucked into the sides of the basket, as it is being filled with compost, to create a more luxurious, verdant effect. Modern equivalents to moss include foam liners, available in several sizes, and black polythene – effective but not very pretty. If you use black polythene, punch several holes in it to allow excess water to escape.

Similar to wire hanging baskets are wrought-iron baskets, or their modern-day equivalent in plastic-coated steel. These, too, need lining before being filled and planted.

More recently, solid plastic hanging baskets have come on the market, fitted with drip trays to catch any over-spill of water. The drip trays are an important feature if you have carpeting or matting underfoot, less important if you have brick, quarry tile, cork or vinyl. Some solid plastic hanging baskets have built-in water reservoirs, reducing the need for frequent watering. Against this, solid plastic sides mean that small plants cannot be tucked in to grow and conceal the pot.

A quick word about colour. Although colour is a matter of taste, many people buy green plastic in the mistaken belief that the container will 'blend' with the plants or somehow look more natural. In fact, green plastic never looks natural, and its artificiality is exaggerated and intensified by the comparison with living green foliage. White plastic can be very startling, and compete for your attention with the plants; additionally, few things look sorrier and more dejected than dirty white containers. For unobtrusive colour, stick to black, terra cotta, or dark grey.

Real terracotta hanging pots are available, with holes through which chains or straps can be fitted. Particularly pretty are those imported from Spain or Italy, with ornate fluted or scalloped trim. Just as plastic brings with it the problem of colour, terra cotta (and glazed terra cotta) baskets introduce the problem of weight.

A large hanging basket containing a full-size plant and damp compost can be very heavy, and must be securely fixed. Swivel hooks with plates and locking nuts are available, to take up to 22.5kg (50lb) in weight. Alternatively, use a plastic-sleeved heavy-duty workshop

hook. Always secure overhead supports to a strong beam. Wall brackets are also available; make sure the bracket is long enough to keep the hanging basket free of the wall. Raffia and cane wall brackets can be very pretty, but cannot take heavy weight. Use wall plugs and screws to fix wall brackets. Never fix a hanging basket to an overhead hook or wall bracket before testing it first.

At the expensive end of the market are reproduction Victorian and Edwardian hanging glass planters. Fully enclosed ones act as terrariums or Wardian cases, and are ideal for plants, such as maidenhair ferns, needing a constantly humid environment.

Partially open glass planters allow trailers to trail, climbers to climb, and also give instant access.

Last but not least on the hanging container scene are the 'convertible' plastic flower pots, which have snap-on saucers that act as drip trays, and snap-on hangers to turn the pots into instant hanging baskets.

Wall Planters

Half-way between hanging baskets and conventional pots are wall planters. Usually half rounded, they are available in all the materials – plastic-coated and galvanized wire, plastic-coated steel, wrought iron, solid plastic, terra cotta and glass – described for hanging baskets. Consider the materials in your conservatory before choosing a particular wall planter; not only can it drip onto the floor, but it can also drip down the wall. Waterproof wall planters are available, but the plants need careful watering if they are not to become waterlogged.

You can also get single or multiple wall pot holders. These are steel strips which screw into the wall, with circular steel bands into which small pots are slipped.

Depending on the height of the hanging basket or wall planter, watering and maintenance generally can be a problem. You may wish to consider a pulley system for raising and lowering baskets.

Left, some of the many plant pots available. These range from the usual clay kinds to antique jardinieres.

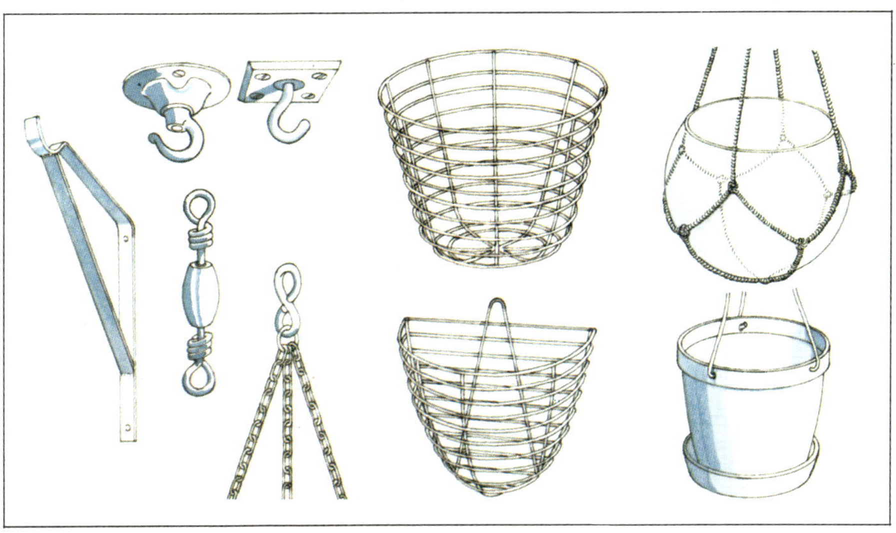

Wire, glass and plastic containers for hanging. Ceiling hooks and wall brackets provide firm attachments.

Otherwise a sturdy chair, step ladder and watering can with an extra-long spout should suffice.

SUPPORTS

Supports are essential for most climbing plants and those with top-heavy flowers and brittle, thin or very tall stems. Ideally supports should combine effectiveness with a pleasant, or at least unobtrusive, appearance. Trellises fixed to a conservatory wall or free standing, provide large-scale support if stiffened and braced. Treated wood is the traditional material, either in fixed panels with a square pattern of trellising, or extending panels in a diamond pattern. There are now plastic-coated wire and PVC trellises; tightly stretched flexible nylon mesh fulfils the same purpose as trellising. Trellising should be fixed to 2.5cm (1in) wooden battens or blocks before being attached to a wall. This protects the wall and allows the air to circulate freely around the plants, as well as providing space for twining plants to twine.

A system of parallel, horizontal, plastic-coated or galvanized wires can also be fixed to a conservatory wall. Space the wires 30cm (12in) apart and use wall nails or vine eyes for brick walls, or metal eye hooks to attach the wires to wood.

For single plants, bamboo canes are useful. They are available from 60cm-2.4m (2-8ft) in height. If one cane seems unstable, use three canes, well pushed into the compost, and tied together at the top, wigwam-fashion, instead.

Old-fashioned twiggy hazel sticks can be pushed into the compost around a bushy plant needing support; this should grow through and over the twiggy wood, eventually concealing it. Smaller still are the green-dyed or natural split canes, usually 30-45cm (12-18in) high. Use them singly or several together, to form a 'cage', surrounded with twine, around a floppy plant. As a general rule, canes and sticks should be slightly shorter than the plant they are supporting.

Cyperus, ivy and peperomia in this semi-circular wire basket make a strong focal point against a plain wall.

To attach a plant to its support, use

split wire rings, natural or plastic raffia, soft garden twine, or paper-covered wire plant ties. The object is to provide firm fixing, but not to strangle the plant. With raffia or twine, a figure-of-eight tie is often recommended, for support without constriction. For a single-stemmed plant, tie at 10-15cm (4-6in) intervals. For a multi-stemmed plant, if you aren't using hazel sticks, take twine or raffia around and between the stems, loosely attaching them to several cane supports.

There is a proprietary support which doesn't need ties; it consists of a circular wire mesh frame on three legs which are inserted in the compost. The plant grows through the frame, concealing it – or nearly so. In some cases, proprietary supports have 'stolen the show' from the plants they are meant to serve. Bamboo and rattan supports contorted into peculiar shapes – hearts entwined, for example, or double helixes – even the old-fashioned wire rings around which hoyas are traditionally trained – somehow present living growth in an artificial form. Once again, it is a matter of taste, a hugely subjective factor.

'Self-clinging' climbers can be a misnomer, or at least misleading.

Moss Poles

Ivies and some philodendrons produce aerial roots that in nature cling to tree trunks, rocks or other damp, rough forms of support. The smooth, dry surfaces of a conservatory are not conducive to clinging, and a bit of help is usually needed. A form of support that mimics nature, and encourages self clinging, is a moss pole. This can be easily made, using as a core a hollow plastic tube or wooden pole, pushed firmly into a compost-filled pot. Wrap the tube or pole first in wire mesh, to form an outer tube, then pack the mesh with damp sphagnum moss. Alternatively, omit the mesh netting and secure the moss directly to the tube or pole, using plastic-coated wire or nylon string. The pole can also be used for epiphytes, their roots wrapped in moss before being wired to the pole.

A variation in the structure of a moss pole will allow you to grow ferns vertically; make the diameter of the wire mesh outer tube about 5cm (2in) larger than the inner support. Pack the mesh loosely with damp sphagnum moss, leaving the space between the wire and support free of moss. Fill this with damp compost, then gently insert the roots of small ferns through the moss and into the compost. Keep the plants and the pole well watered.

An extreme variation on the moss pole is wire-mesh topiary. Globes, pyramids, even animal shapes, can be fashioned out of wire mesh and sphagnum moss, and ferns, epiphytes or climbers, such as ivy, trained over them. Results can range from the elegant and impressive to near kitsch, again, depending on your taste.

Plant Tree

Lastly, there is the epiphytic tree: choose a small dead tree or large branch, depending on the space available. Anchor it securely – a large piece of driftwood attached to the conservatory wall might be nice – before attaching the epiphytes, their roots wrapped in damp sphagnum moss and secured to the tree with plastic-coated wire or nylon thread.

COMPOSTS

There is an old saying, 'Never bring outdoor soil indoors'. Although garden soil, especially fertile soil, may seem an instant and free alternative to potting compost, it brings with it the problems of soil-borne pests, diseases and weed seeds, which outweigh any savings. You can sterilize good, slightly acid, fibrous loam and use it for the basis of loam-based compost; the recipes and that for peat-based compost, are given at the end of this section. On a large scale, making your own compost saves money, but most people are content to pay extra for ready-made composts, available from garden centres, nurseries, and larger chain stores.

Loam-based compost or peat-based compost, which is best? Both have good and weak points. Most plants will grow in either, provided their needs are met, though in many ways, loam-based com-

Providing a focal point to this arrangement of superb foliage plants is a plant tree, on which is grouped a collection of bromeliads, including a variety of cryptanthus, neoregelia and guzmania.

posts are easier for the non-professional to handle.

Peat-based Composts
To begin with peat-based composts: they are standardized, free draining, light-weight, relatively clean and easy to work with. They are much favoured by commercial growers for these reasons, where the scale of growing means that weight is a very real consideration. On the negative side, the nutrients in a peat-based mixture are quickly expended, and regular feeding is vital. Additionally, unless you are using a capillary system of watering (see page 30), it is easier to go wrong with watering. Peat-based composts dry out more quickly than soil-based ones and, once dry, are difficult to get thoroughly wet again. There are various commercial formulae for peat-based composts. All contain peat and fertilizers; some have coarse sand, perlite or vermiculite added as well.

Loam-based Composts
These are heavy, relatively 'dirty' and extremely variable in composition and quality, simply because loam itself is infinitely variable. Weight is unlikely to be a problem in domestic conservatories, though, and often the weight is necessary to counterbalance the heavy-top growth of tall plants: *Sparmannia*, for example, or large *Ficus* or *Monstera*. Additionally, soil-based composts retain their nutrients and moisture longer and are easier in terms of watering; mistakes in that area can usually be quickly and totally rectified.

John Innes Composts
John Innes loam-based composts are made according to specific formulae, and vary in the proportion of sterilized loam, peat and sand, and the fertilizer content. John Innes seed compost is used for sowing; John Innes potting compost No. 1 has a low nutrient content, and is used for growing on young seedlings or for plants with minimal nutritional needs. John Innes potting compost No. 2 is richer in nutrients, and is sufficient for most plants. Richest of all is John Innes potting compost No. 3, and suitable for 'greedy feeders', such as chrysanthemums. There is also a John Innes lime-free compost for plants, such as azaleas, which cannot tolerate lime; this compost is often labelled 'Ericaceous'. There are orchid composts and cacti composts.

All commercially available composts come in bags of various sizes. It is generally more economical to purchase large-size bags, but if storage is a problem, then the economy is a false one.

Adapting Basic Composts
Though the following recipes are quite specific, there are other, equally good recipes for peat-based composts, and you may find that you wish to improvise with the John Innes composts. Adding some extra peat, or even peat-based compost, to a loam-based compost, will give it a more open, free-draining texture, while still retaining most of its richness. Adding coarse sand or grit to a loam-based compost for desert cacti and succulents, or adding leafmould to loam-based composts for epiphytes are examples of variations on the compost theme. Knowing a little bit about the plant's origins and native environment is as helpful in getting the compost as well the temperatures right.

Home-made Composts
To make your own John Innes composts, use loam, heated in an electric soil sterilizer to a temperature of 82°C (180°F). Helpful soil organisms that break down organic matter into nutrients for the plants should survive this temperature. Soil-borne pests and diseases and weed seeds however, are much less resistant and you can assume the majority will be eradicated.

John Innes Seed Compost

(parts by volume)

2 parts sterilized, sieved loam
1 part sieved, granulated moss peat
1 part coarse sand or horticultural grit
To each 35.5 litres (bushel) add
40g (1½oz) superphosphate of lime
20g (¾oz) chalk or ground limestone

John Innes Potting Compost No. 1

(parts by volume)

7 parts sterilized, sieved loam
1 part sieved, granulated moss peat
2 parts coarse sand or horticultural grit
To each 35.5 litres (bushel) add
100g (4oz) John Innes base fertilizer (available from garden centres)
20g (¾oz) chalk or ground limestone

John Innes Potting Compost No. 2

(parts by volume)

as for John Innes potting compost No. 1, but double the amount of base fertilizer and chalk or ground limestone per 35.5 litres (bushel)

John Innes Potting Compost No. 3

(parts by volume)

as for John Innes potting compost No. 1, but triple the amount of base fertilizer and chalk or ground limestone per 35.5 litres (bushel)

General Purpose Peat-based Compost

(parts by volume)

2 parts sieved, granulated moss peat
1 part perlite, vermiculite or coarse sand
To each 35.5 litres (1 bushel) add
15g (½oz) ammonium nitrate
75g (3oz) chalk or ground limestone
15g (½oz) fritted trace elements
75g (3oz) magnesium limestone
25g (1oz) nitrate of potash
50g (2oz) superphosphate of lime

POTTING

The language of gardening, like any specialist language, can be worrying to the non-specialist. The activities that gardening terms describe can be even more worrying, but, in fact, potting up, potting on and re-potting are governed largely by common sense. Disturbing a plant, like a person moving house, can be ultimately beneficial, but traumatic at the time, and should only be done when necessary.

When, exactly, is it necessary? This depends on a plant's rate of growth, its nature, and its state when purchased. Quick-growing annuals may need to be moved three or four times into larger pots, in the course of their brief existence. Cuttings of fuchsias and geraniums (*Pelargonium*) are quick growing and need similar treatment. Some plants – clivias and hippeastrums, for example – prefer restricted root conditions and need larger containers only when their present ones are in danger of bursting. Lastly, though most newly purchased long-term plants should have at least a year's grace before needing a larger container or fresh compost, some may be in need of moving immediately (see below).

Potting Up

This refers to the initial move of a rooted seedling, rooted cutting, open-grown plant or bulb into a container. (Bulbs are covered in detail under individual entries.) The container should be just large enough to hold the plant's (or plants', if you are potting up several to a container) roots. A pot that is too large will contain more compost than the roots can penetrate, and the compost is liable to become waterlogged, or 'sour'. Clay pots need soaking for several hours in water, and 'crocking' with bits of broken clay flower pot placed concavely over the drainage hole; plastic pots need no initial preparation. Both clay and plastic pots need to be absolutely clean, and old pots should be disinfected and rinsed thoroughly before re-use.

Cover the crock, or bottom of a plastic pot, with a layer of compost, then gently place the plant in the middle; if potting up several plants to a container, space them evenly apart. Add more compost, tap the pot several times on the floor or work surface to settle the compost, then firm it with your fingers if it is loam based. Omit the final firming for peat-based compost. You should have a 13-20mm (½-¾in) space between the surface of the compost and the rim of the pot, to allow for watering; large pots need relatively deeper spaces, 2.5cm (1in) or more. Water gently, then place the pot out of direct light for a day or two, to allow the plant to recover.

Potting On

A term which refers to the moving of an established potted plant into a larger pot – usually one size larger – because its present pot is too small. Potting on is usually an annual exercise done at the beginning of spring, when plants are likely to be starting into growth and about to send out new roots. However, it is best to avoid potting on a plant in bud or flower; besides the possibility of physically damaging the flowers, a plant in flower is already working hard, and is less able to cope with the stress of potting on. Additionally, annuals sown in late summer or early autumn will be potted on in autumn; those sown in spring will be potted on in late spring and summer. Some flowering bulbs begin growing in autumn, and should be potted on then. Always give the needs of a particular plant precedence over theoretical schedules and dictums.

To find out if a plant needs potting on, tap the side of the pot against a work surface to dislodge the root ball, then spread your fingers over the surface of the compost on either side of the plant, and turn the pot upside down. The plant and its root ball should come away freely. If not, repeat the exercise; pushing a pencil or dowel through the drainage hole(s) sometimes helps. If no or few roots are visible, gently return the plant to its pot. If roots have thoroughly filled the compost, especially if they are winding around the compost or have become so tightly packed that they are moulded into the shape of the pot, potting on is generally necessary.

Prepare the larger pot as before; remove any crocks which may have become entangled in the root ball, and

Tuberous begonias and streptocarpus are easily grown to produce this brilliant display of colour.

Checking a plant to see if it is potbound. Note the network of roots covering the rootball.

Place the plant in position in a large pot and fill in around the roots with fresh compost.

Tap the pot lightly on the table to settle the compost around the root and firm gently.

carefully unwind encircling roots. Scrape away some of the old potting compost and place the plant centrally in the pot. Fill the space between the root ball and the sides of the pot with new compost, and any spaces between the roots. Adjust the levels so there is still space above the surface of the compost for watering, and the plant is at the same level, in relation to the surrounding compost, as it was in its previous pot. Firm and water, as before, and protect from strong sunlight.

Re-potting

This is a similar exercise, except the same pot, not a larger one, is used. It stands to reason that you can't go on potting plants into ever larger containers, indefinitely. Re-potting, like potting on, is usually done annually in spring. Plants which have reached their maximum size or maximum reasonable container size, plants which are slow growing, and plants which are being deliberately kept small by 'underpotting' are candidates. Decant the plant, as for potting on, but carefully remove as much of the spent compost from the root ball as you can. Examine the roots at the same time, and prune away any that are dead, rotting, or otherwise damaged.

Clean the pot, then re-crock, if clay, and place a layer of compost in the bottom. Replace the plant and work fresh compost in and around the space between the roots, tapping the pot to settle the compost and fill any large air pockets.

An alternative to re-potting, especially for very slow-growing plants or those in very large pots or tubs, is topdressing. Remove the top 2.5cm (1in) of compost – a bit more if it can be done without disturbing the roots – and replace it with fresh compost.

Do's and Don'ts

Fresh compost should always be at conservatory temperature, to avoid shocking the plants. Watering a plant just before moving is sometimes advocated, but in the case of plants with large root balls growing in loam-based compost, the additional weight can cause some of the roots to shear off. Also, dryish compost is easier to shake off, when re-potting, than wet compost, and the plant receives a thorough watering at the end of the move in any case. Still, it is not a matter of major importance and what works best for you is fine.

WATERING

There are so many variables in watering, and so many seemingly contradictory rules, that it is hard for the beginner to know where to start. Start with the particular plant first: *Cyperus*, for example, needs continually wet compost, while *Lithops* needs almost continually bone-dry compost. Most conservatory plants have less extreme requirements, but when buying a plant, find out its basic inclinations. Within that framework, all of the following factors are relevant.

When to Water

Plants that are growing visibly – producing new leaves, buds or flowers – need more water than when they are starting into growth, have just been potted or re-potted, or have just finished flowering. Least water is needed when a plant is dormant. The active growing period is usually, but not always, in spring and summer, when high light levels and temperatures encourage transpiration (loss of water through the leaves) and growth, thus increasing water needs. In the low light levels and low temperatures of a cool conservatory in winter, watering needs of plants are minimal. Those plants in flower at this season need careful watering: enough to keep them from wilting, but not so much that they rot.

Plants that are well established in their pots, and those kept deliberately pot bound, need more frequent watering than newly potted plants.

All other things being equal, compost in small pots dries out more quickly than that in large pots. Because clay is highly absorbent, compost in clay pots dries out more quickly than that in plastic pots. Peat-based composts dry out more quickly than loam-based ones.

Compost already moist does not need more water. Damp compost is usually darker in colour and heavier than dry compost. Traditionally, a clay pot is knocked with the knuckle to determine the water content of the compost; a dull thud indicates sufficient water, a ringing sound indicates dry compost. Or press the surface of the compost with your fingers; if it feels dry to a depth of 6mm (¼in) or more, it is dry, and an actively growing plant will probably

need watering. Peat-based composts can be deceptive; incorrect watering often results in the top few millimetres appearing nicely moist, with the bulk of the compost beneath being bone dry.

Hard or Soft Water

Water should be at room (i.e. conservatory) temperature. In an ideal world, rainwater, stored free of algae and other debris, would be used for watering. In the real world, most people use tap water, which varies in quality between acid, or soft, and alkaline, or hard. If you are growing lime-hating plants and use alkaline tap water, counteract the build up of lime with applications of iron sequestrene, according to the manufacturers' instructions.

Watering Techniques

There are several ways to apply water manually. The easiest is to fill the space above the compost, up to the rim, with water. Dried-out composts, though, tend to shrink away from the pot and water will quickly run down the sides

This collection of individually potted Cyclamen persicum is effectively grouped on unusual glass staging.

and out the bottom. If this happens, stand the pot in a larger container of water and leave it there until bubbles stop rising to the surface. Some plants – cyclamen, rosette-forming succulents, and African violets, for example – are best watered from below. Stand the pot in a saucer or bowl of water and leave for 10-15 minutes, then remove any remaining water.

The best time to water is in the morning, when temperatures are rising. Water given in the evening, when temperatures are falling, is taken up less quickly and encourages fungal diseases. (If, however, you find a plant wilting from lack of water, don't wait until the next morning to water it. Use common sense.)

Damping Down

It is the usual practice in greenhouse management to 'damp down'. This simply means spraying or sprinkling the floor with water several times a day in order to increase the humidity and provide the kind of atmosphere that is the most acceptable to a large number of plants. Some plants, of course, notably those like cacti which grow naturally in hot, arid regions, do not need humid conditions, but those of jungle or humid, warm climate origin usually grow better if the humidity of the atmosphere is increased along with the naturally occurring rise in temperature. On the whole, the warmer the temperature, the higher the degree of humidity is needed. At low temperatures, as in winter, the atmosphere should be kept dry otherwise, you may create the worst possible conditions for plants – damp coldness.

However, damping down the floor of a conservatory may not be possible. It will depend on what flooring material has been used. If it is impossible to damp down, then it is necessary to pay close attention to ventilation and shading in order to keep temperatures to acceptable levels for you and the plants.

In hot weather, it is helpful to mist the plants with clean water from a hand sprayer. This will increase the humidity in their immediate vicinity, but this treatment should not be used on plants with hairy or succulent leaves or on any plant while it is standing in direct sunshine.

FEEDING

As with watering, the plant's need for food is dependent on its character. Bromeliads, cacti and orchids, for example, generally need less food than annuals raised from seed, which have to make a great deal of growth and fulfil all their life's functions in a single year. That having been stated, there are still many useful guidelines and generalities applicable to most plants.

When to Feed

Plants in active growth (usually in spring and summer) need feeding, while plants that are dormant (again, usually autumn and winter) do not.

Newly bought plants, or those which have recently been potted or re-potted, should not need feeding initially; the compost should provide nutrients to start with. But after 10-12 weeks with soil-based composts, or 6 weeks for peat-based composts, the nutrients will be used up, if the plant is actively growing. For all but 'disposable' plants, supplementary feeding then becomes necessary.

Types of Fertilizer

The traditional recipe for plant food was a bag of cow manure steeped in water until the resulting liquor was the colour of weak tea. Today, few people have the necessary raw material, space or inclination to make their own plant food, and commercially available substitutes have become universally acceptable. These are made in several forms. Liquid and water-soluble fertilizers should be diluted and used according to manufacturers' instructions. There are also nutrient-impregnated pads for placing under plant pots, and fertilizer tablets and spikes for inserting in the compost, all of which slowly release food over a long period, up to six months or a year.

Dry fertilizers can be sprinkled over the surface of the compost, again applied according to the manufacturers' instructions.

Foliar feeds are sprayed directly on to a plant's leaves; the absorption rate is much quicker than for nutrients taken up through the roots. It is a sensible way to feed bromeliads and other epiphytes which have relatively small, weak root systems, or a plant which has been starved of food and needs a quick pick-me-up.

There are different recipes as well as different forms of fertilizers. An ordinary, general-purpose fertilizer will have roughly equal proportions of nitrogen(N), phosphorus(P) and potassium(K), and usually additional trace elements, such as iron, manganese, magnesium and zinc. For the one-fertilizer conservatory, this is fine. But there are special recipes, with varying proportions of elements, that have been devised for particular plants or types of plant. Potash-high fertilizers are most commonly used to get heavy tomato crops, but they are also good for long-term flowering plants – perennials, shrubs and bulbs – that have finished flowering and need to build up vigour for future displays.

Fertilizers rich in nitrogen are good for leaf and stem growth, and so are particularly suited to ferns and other foliage plants. Remember, though, that too much nitrogenous fertilizer can encourage soft, vulnerable growth, and leafy growth at the expense of flowers. Annuals are a good example – use nitrogenous fertilizer with restraint, especially once sufficient leafy growth has been made. For production of buds and flowers, phosphorus is especially important.

For the specialist, there are chrysanthemum fertilizers, as well as others for roses, carnations, orchids, and plants, such as azaleas, requiring acid compost.

Do's and Don'ts

Never apply fertilizer to dry compost and, above all: underfeed rather than overfeed, if you're not sure. Overfeeding results in a build-up of salts in the compost that can burn the roots and, in the extreme, kill the plant.

Finally, let common sense prevail. If instructions say 'Feed fortnightly in spring and summer' and, on March 21st, it is winter, not spring, and the plant in question is showing no sign of coming out of dormancy, don't reach for your bottle of fertilizer. And if autumn is a particularly hot and sunny one, don't put the bottle away on September 21st. Respond to the plant first, then the calendar and reference books.

Many of the clump-forming plants, such as sansevieria, are easy to propagate by dividing the roots.

PROPAGATING PLANTS

In nature, propagation takes place for the survival of the species. In commercial horticulture, it is done, unsentimentally, for profit. Within the confines of your own conservatory (or greenhouse, if you are lucky enough to have both) propagation should be done primarily for pleasure. Unlike other aspects of cultivation – watering, feeding, and so on – propagation is an optional extra, and you can stock and maintain an entirely successful conservatory without ever becoming involved in propagation.

On the other hand, you may want more of a plant you particularly like, or to replace an old and worn-out specimen with a young one, without spending a lot of money. It is often easier to get seed of certain plants – including some very beautiful annuals – than the plants themselves. And part of the ongoing routine care of some plants will leave you with 'babies' on your hands, whether you particularly wanted them or not.

For those who become addicted to plant propagation, there are many specialist books, but try to keep propagation in perspective: there is no point propagating plants you don't have room for in your conservatory or can find homes for. (Many conservatory plants make equally good house plants, though, and you could use your conservatory to supply an endless stock of house plants. As a last resort, there are always plant stalls at fetes and bazaars.)

Division

This is the easiest method of propagation, and is usually done in spring, as part of the potting-on or re-potting exercise. Most rosette, clump, or carpet-forming plants are the usual candidates, especially if they have grown too big for their containers. Remove the plant from its pot, shake off or otherwise dislodge as much of the compost as possible, then gently prize the roots apart into two or more sections. Each should have sufficient roots to support the top growth. If you can't easily separate the sections, use a sharp knife to slice through the roots, then dust the cut surfaces with a fungicide to prevent rotting. Pot up, with fresh compost, into suitable sized pots (see page 46), water, then keep out of direct sunlight for a few days. If there is insufficient root, cutting back the above-ground growth can help to re-create the balance.

Offsets

Offsets – miniature versions of the parent plant – are often produced by desert cacti, bulbs, succulents and bromeliads. These can be detached, again when potting on or re-potting. Hyacinths can be induced to produce bulbils; in the dormant season remove the basal portions of bulbs and keep the bulbs in warm, moist sand through the summer. Roots may have already formed, in which case the offset can be planted directly into fresh compost identical to that of the parent plant. If there are no roots, use a mixture of peat and coarse sand; perlite or vermiculite to encourage rooting. Keep the offset warm and out of direct sunlight, and the compost barely moist. Pot once the roots have formed.

Layering

Plantlets – miniature versions of the parent plant – are produced on the ends of runners or on mature leaves. *Saxifraga sarmentosa* and *Tolmeia menziesii* are good examples. Again, if roots have already formed, treat them as adults, providing a suitable pot and compost. If there are no roots, encourage roots to form by pegging down the plantlet into a suitably open compost, while it is still attached to the parent. This is a form of layering, and can be done successfully with many trailing plants; roots are sent out from the leaf nodes if the stem is in contact with a suitable compost.

Ivy, rooting as it grows in the garden, is a perfect example. Indoors, use unbent paper clips or hairpins to peg down the stem, while it is still attached to the parent plant. Keep the compost moist, but not sodden, and the temperature warm. Once roots have formed, detach the new plant, or plants from the parent, and pot up separately.

Air Layering

The principles of air layering are the same as for layering, except the nodes cannot be brought into contact with the compost, because of the rigidity of the stem. Therefore, the rooting medium is brought up to the nodes. Old leggy rubber plants spring to mind for this treatment; other candidates include *Dracaena, Monstera* and *Dieffenbachia*. Make a 2.5-cm (1-in) long sloping cut, – not cutting completely through the stem – where you want roots to form. Cut no higher than 45cm (18in) from the top of the plant. Coat the wound with hormone rooting powder, then pack it with damp peat or sphagnum moss. Use a sheet of transparent plastic, tied tightly at both ends to form a tube, for keeping the rooting medium in place. When roots appear, cut the stem directly below the roots, remove the plastic tube, and pot the new plant up, providing a stake for support if necessary. The parent plant should sprout from below the cut. Air layering, like most forms of propagation, is sensibly done during the spring.

Seed Sowing

Propagation from seed can only be dealt with here in the most general terms. Use seed compost evenly thick and firm, in scrupulously clean seed trays or small pots. Distribute the seed evenly over the surface. Mixing fine seed with sand and sowing it slowly, first in one direction and then in the other, helps. Large

Propagating a succulent plant from an offset produced at the base. This is readily detached and repotted.

Chlorophytum is another example of a plant which can be layered, a plantlet being rooted in a pot of compost.

Right, air layering rejuvenates an old, leggy plant. Make a cut at a convenient point, and pack it with moss. Wrap the wound in more moss and polythene and wait for roots to appear.

Sow seed thinly on the surface of a pot of seed compost. Cover with a thin layer of sieved compost.

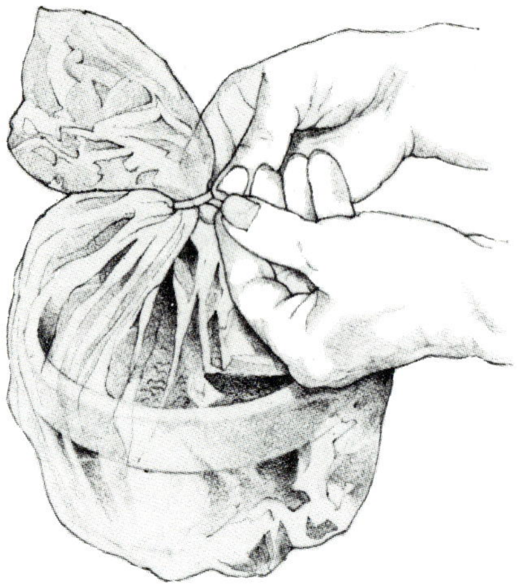

Water the pot and place it in a propagator. Alternatively put the pot into a plastic bag with the top sealed.

Once the seedlings have germinated, they will need to be 'pricked out', or moved, to give them more space.

seeds and pelleted seeds can be sown exactly where you want them. After sowing, cover the seed with finely sieved compost, no more than twice the thickness of the seed. Do not cover fine seed at all.

Watering the compost from above will probably disturb the seeds; instead, place the tray or pots in a sink or other container shallowly filled with water. When the surface of the compost changes colour, remove the tray or pots and place them in a suitably warm spot, draining them for a minute or two first. Cover the prepared trays or pots with a sheet of glass, or place them in a propagator (see page 32) and cover with a sheet of paper or black plastic. Remove the paper or plastic once germination has occurred and provide bright indirect light.

When the seedlings are large enough to handle, prick them out into pots or trays of low-nutrient compost. Make holes in the compost first, with a pencil or dibber. Then, holding the seedlings by their leaves, gently lever them out of the seed tray, using a kitchen fork. Plant them quite deeply, with their leaves just clear of the compost, then firm and water with a watering can fitted with a fine rose. Provide bright indirect light for a few days, then begin to acclimatize the young plants to their optimum environment according to kind.

Cuttings

Propagation from cuttings encompasses several techniques: root, leaf and stem cuttings. The latter are subdivided into soft, semi-ripe and hardwood cuttings. Root cuttings are normally taken from hardy plants – perennials and shrubs – with thick, fleshy roots, and the process doesn't usually apply to those plants grown in a conservatory.

Leaf Cuttings

These are more relevant to conservatory plants. It is always amazing to see a complete young plant form from a leaf or even a piece of leaf. Success is most likely in spring and summer, and an electric propagator will provide the heat and controlled humidity needed (see page 32).

Always choose healthy leaves. Those that are used whole – African violet and peperomia – should have their leaf stalks cut cleanly from the parent plant, dipped in hormone rooting powder, then inserted in a mixture of damp peat and coarse sand or damp peat and vermiculite. Insert the leaves vertically or at a slight angle, but don't crowd them, and make sure the whole stalk is buried in compost.

A leaf cutting of Begonia rex. In time young plants form from the slits in the main leaf veins.

Rhizomatous-rooted begonias, *Streptocarpus, Sinningia* (*Gloxinia*) and *Sansevieria* work best when their leaves are cut into sections. Long thin leaves are cut crossways into 2.5-5-cm (1-2-in) pieces, the lower edge dipped in hormone rooting powder and inserted (right way up!) in the above compost. Large broad leaves, such as those of *Begonia rex*, are removed from the parent plant, and several slits made across the veins, on the leaf undersides. The prepared leaf is then rested, right-way up, on the compost, with pebbles or hair pins stuck through to ensure that the cut veins are in contact with the compost. New plantlets should form at each cut. Alternatively, cut the leaf into 2.5-cm (1-in) squares, each with a section of vein, and rest them on the surface of the compost.

Some leaves will produce plantlets if their stalks are submerged in water, African violets are an example. The roots formed in water sometimes die when transferred to compost, and rooting leaf cuttings in compost is less risky.

Stem Cuttings

The method of taking stem cuttings is basically the same, whether softwood, semi-ripe or hardwood. A healthy shoot is severed from the parent plant and encouraged to form roots. Softwood cuttings, from current growth, are usually taken in spring and early summer; semi-ripe cuttings are taken later in the season, when the wood begins to ripen but isn't fully hard. Hardwood cuttings are usually taken of fully ripe current growth, in autumn, but the procedure applies most often to hardy shrubs growing outdoors, and isn't really relevant here. Lastly, cuttings of plants that are always soft stemmed – *Tradescantia*, for example, or *Zebrina* – can be rooted at any time of the year.

When taking softwood cuttings, you are working against the clock, as the cuttings quickly wilt. Have ready prepared trays or pots of compost, as for leaf cuttings. Use non-flowering side shoots, cut with a razor just below a leaf node, and from 8-10cm (3-4in) long. Remove the leaves from the lower half of the shoot, dip into hormone rooting powder, and insert the lower half of the stem into the compost. Use a dibber or pencil to make the holes. Make sure no leaves are touching the compost, then firm and water with a can fitted with a fine rose. As with leaf cuttings, the warmth and high humidity that can be provided by an electric propagator are the ideal environment.

Procedure is the same for semi-ripe cuttings, though timing is not so desperate. Both types need bright, indirect light, and plenty of patience, until new growth appears. (Sadly, any flower buds that form on the young cuttings should be removed, as they sap energy and, once faded, encourage fungal infections.) Cuttings that are sending out new leaves and shoots have rooted and can be potted on into a low-nutrient compost.

Finally, whatever the method of propagation, plants that start life in an electric propagator need gradual hardening off, to the lower temperatures and drier atmosphere normally found in a conservatory.

PESTS AND DISEASES

Unfortunately the warm, humid conditions that many plants appreciate, and which often prevail in conservatories and sunrooms, are the ideal breeding ground for a range of pests and diseases. And the fact that the conservatory is usually adjacent to the house and used as additional living space makes the control of pests and diseases something of a problem, because it is necessary to be cautious for safety's sake,

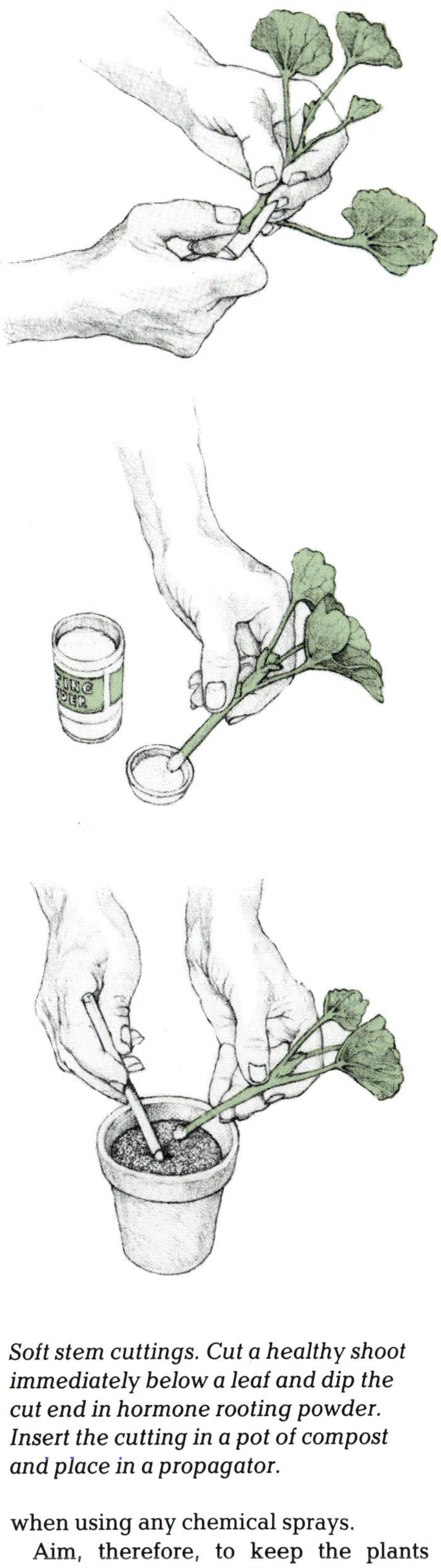

Soft stem cuttings. Cut a healthy shoot immediately below a leaf and dip the cut end in hormone rooting powder. Insert the cutting in a pot of compost and place in a propagator.

when using any chemical sprays.

Aim, therefore, to keep the plants growing well by paying attention to correct watering, feeding and potting on, as well as ensuring adequate shading and ventilation.

Examine carefully any newly acquired plant for the presence of pests and diseases and, if necessary, treat it before you introduce it into the conservatory. Look particularly on the underside of the leaves and in the joints between leaf and stem.

Inspect all the plants in the conservatory regularly and take prompt action at the first sign of any attack. It is sometimes possible to control pests such as greenfly, by washing the plant in a bucket of mild soapy water, then rinsing and allowing it to dry away from direct sunshine. If you need to resort to chemical control measures, use only those insecticides and fungicides which have been specially formulated for use in the house and read the manufacturers' instructions carefully. Wear rubber gloves when mixing and applying the chemical and keep it well away from children and pets. One manufacturer has produced pesticide-impregnated cardboard 'pins' which, when inserted into the soil, release the chemical so that it can be taken up by the plant's roots and translocated to the point of attack. These are effective and safe.

The following are the pests and diseases you are most likely to encounter.

PESTS

Most of the pests listed are easily recognised. Examine all plants regularly as a preventive measure.

Aphids (Greenfly, Blackfly)
Small, plump winged or wingless insects found mainly on the young shoots or underside of leaves. They suck the sap, causing discoloration of the leaf tissue and weaken the plant. They also secrete a substance called honeydew which often becomes infected with a fungus called sooty mould.

Control by washing in mild soapy water or use an insecticide.

Mealy bugs
Also sap suckers and causing much the same damage as aphids, these small insects are covered and protected by a coating of white wax. They can be controlled by touching each one with a paintbrush (or matchstick tipped with cottonwool) dipped in methylated spirit. Check carefully before using chemical sprays as those which are effective against this pest may damage plants such as ferns and succulents and could possibly kill predators which take the bugs.

Red Spider Mite
Minute pests which are just visible to the naked eye as reddish-coloured pinheads. They are sap feeding and attacked foliage develops a yellow speckling which later becomes bronzed. Some species produce silken webs.

Mites are rather difficult to control but a liquid derris will help if sprayed at regular intervals. As they thrive in dry, overcrowded conditions, keeping a humid atmosphere around the plants will help control them.

Scale Insects
Small, louse-like insects that are covered by a waxy shell and look rather like miniature limpets. They suck sap and weaken growth and also produce sticky honeydew which becomes infected with sooty moulds.

Scale insects are difficult to control because of their protective coating. If the infestation is not too heavy the adults can be removed with a matchstick tipped with cottonwool soaked in methylated spirit. They can also be wiped off the leaves and stems with a wet cloth.

Thrips
These are tiny, dark-coloured winged insects that feed on the undersides of the leaves by scraping the surface and then sucking the sap. This results in a mottling of the leaves, while infected flowers develop white streaks.

This pest can become a serious problem indoors where its breeding is encouraged by hot, dry conditions. Control by using a suitable insecticide at regular intervals.

Whitefly
Small, white, moth-like insects that fly up in a cloud when a badly infected plant is touched. The eggs are laid on the underside of the leaves and these hatch into green larvae which feed by sucking the plant's sap and causing damage similar to that of greenflies.

They can be difficult to control and will need regular treatment with a suitable insecticide.

Artificial grass is an unusual choice of flooring which makes a good complement to some of the more delicate flowering plants.

DISEASES
It is sometimes difficult to decide the cause of plant damage. Most diseases are due to poor growing conditions.

Botrytis (Grey Mould)
A common problem, usually associated with cool, damp growing conditions and excessive moisture. Its common name, grey mould, is very descriptive of the fluffy, grey growths on the leaves, stems and flowers of infected plants. It usually enters a plant through damaged or diseased tissue, and dead leaves or flowers left on the plant are especially vulnerable. Poor growing conditions can lead to a severe attack.

The best way of controlling the problem is to make sure that the plants are not overcrowded and that air can circulate freely around them. Raise the temperature, if necessary, and give more ventilation. Remove and destroy all infected growth and spray with a fungicide, repeating the application if necessary.

Damping Off
This is caused by a group of fungal diseases which attack seedlings, and occasionally older plants, at or just above soil level. The stem bases wither and turn black and the plant will keel over and die. Like botrytis, this disease flourishes in damp, stuffy conditions and is most likely to attack seedlings which have become etiolated through lack of light.

Control by sowing thinly and avoid overwatering. Water affected plants with Cheshunt Compound.

Mildew
A plant disease which shows as a surface coating of powdery white or greyish fungus on the leaves, shoots and sometimes flowers.

Plants that are growing in poorly ventilated, moist conditions are especially vulnerable and also those that are too dry at the roots. Remove and destroy the infected parts and spray the plants with a fungicide. It is also essential to improve the growing conditions.

PESTS AND DISEASES

A Conservatory is an ideal environment for a variety of pests and diseases which, if left unchecked, will flourish in the warm, humid atmosphere. Check all plants regularly for signs of damage and take prompt action if necessary, but do remember to use all pesticides and fungicides with care, especially if the conservatory is used as a living area.

Botrytis is caused by excessive humidity. Remove infected leaves, spray plant with fungicide.

Mildew is a white, powdery fungus, the result of poor ventilation. Cut off infected parts and apply fungicide.

Scale insects, responsible for sooty moulds on plants, can be removed with a tooth brush or alcohol soaked swab.

Mealy bugs also suck sap, and should be removed with swabs soaked in alcohol or methylated spirits.

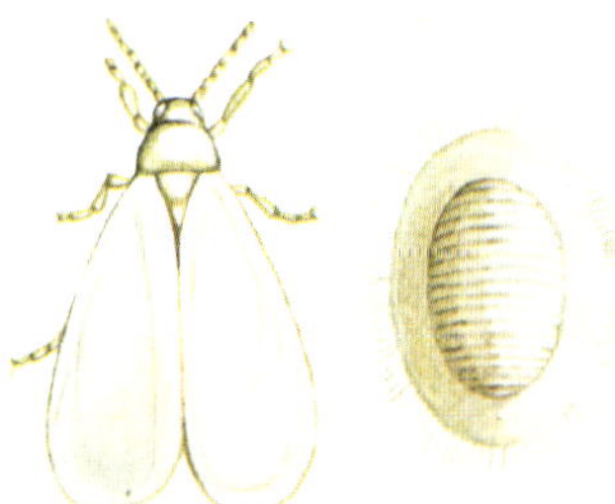

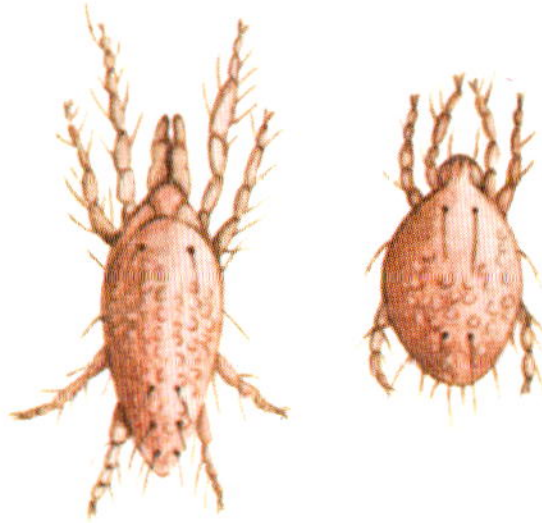

Aphids are green, black or red insects which damage leaves and young shoots. Wash off with soapy water.

Whiteflies' eggs laid on the underside of leaves hatch into larvae which suck sap. Control with an insecticide.

Red spider mites suck sap, weakening plants, shrivelling leaves and turning them yellow.

Thrips attack flowers, buds and leaves, leaving a silvery sheen and speckled markings on the plants.

Flowering Plants

Flowers have a universal appeal, bringing as they do a welcoming touch to interior environments. They also bring with them a certain challenge. This can vary from that of keeping short-term flowering plants, such as chrysanthemums, cinerarias or poinsettias, blooming for weeks rather than days, to the challenge of keeping long-term plants, such as jasmines or camellias, flourishing and flowering year after year.

Taste in flowering plants, like taste in anything, is largely subjective. It is sensible, however, when choosing flowering plants for conservatories, to consider the flower as part of a larger whole. Particularly in small conservatories, the shape of a plant, its gracefulness (or lack thereof), the quality and presence (or seasonal absence) of its foliage, are as visually important as its flowers, particularly if the flowering season is a short one. You may be willing to tolerate an unattractive plant for 50 weeks of the year, in return for its glorious floral display the other two weeks, but a conservatory 'planted' entirely according to this philosophy is unlikely to be attractive.

Plants with modest but dependable flowers, a long season of display, and attractive foliage may well offer better value for space. Plants which produce flowers according to a seasonal schedule can often be more rewarding than those, such as chrysanthemums, that can be had in flower at any time of the year, without any reference to the seasons.

If you are a keen gardener, plants that you bring into flower, having raised them from seed, can be more enjoyable than the most flamboyant flowering plant, bought in flower and 'ready made' from a shop. You may, on the other hand, have minimal horticultural commitment, and want a flowering plant that looks beautiful from the start, to be replaced with a fresh one when its charms begin to fade. Success with flowering plants depends, to a large extent, on the time, commitment and environment you can give them.

Abutilon

Flowering Maple

Abutilons are slightly tender shrubs with attractive, pendulous bell-shaped flowers appearing from spring to the autumn. The maple-shaped leaves give the plant its common name.

Cultivation

Abutilons are ideal for sunny conservatories with a minimum temperature of 7°C (45°F). Fast growing, abutilons can reach a height and spread of 1.8m (6ft) or more, if grown in a large pot. They can get very spindly, though, and need regular pinching out of the growing tips and cutting back in early spring, by about a quarter. Feed fortnightly during spring and summer, and water freely while growing; the rest of the year, water just enough to keep the soil from drying out completely. Abutilons are showy, but not long lived, and are best replaced after two or three years.

Types to choose

Abutilon × hybridum has rather dull leaves but flowers in a wide range of colours and a pretty, arching growth habit. 'Boule de Neige' has white flowers; 'Canary Bird' and 'Golden Fleece', yellow flowers; and 'Ashford Red' has red flowers. *A.pictum* 'Thompsonii' is grown as much for its strikingly attractive, yellow-variegated leaves as for its orange and yellow flowers. It has a slender, upright, growth habit. *A.megapotamicum* is good for growing against a wall, trained to wires. The hanging, lantern-shaped flowers are red and yellow, and the form *A.m.*'Variegatum' has yellow-mottled leaves.

Acacia

Wattle, Mimosa

These sun-loving Australian evergreen trees are fast growing, and make huge specimens in the wild. Grown in a large pot or tub, they make attractive shrubs up to 3m (10ft) high for a cool conservatory.

Cultivation

Though a temperature of 5°C (40°F) will suffice, acacias will produce their fluffy yellow flowers earlier in spring – or even towards the end of winter – if a slightly warmer temperature is provided. What they do need is plenty of ventilation and sunlight; standing the pots outside in a sunny, sheltered spot during the summer months helps ripen the wood, and encourages the production of flowers.

Acacia longifolia

In the wild, acacias grow in poor, well-drained soil; in a conservatory, use John Innes potting compost No. 2, and feed fortnightly in spring and summer. Water generously during the growing season, and moderately the rest of the year. Acacias that have outgrown their allotted space can be cut back by up to a half after flowering.

Types to choose

Acacia armata, or kangaroo thorn, has fluffy yellow globe-shaped flowers, singly or in pairs, all along its branches, and is 'armed' with formidable, spiny leaf shoots. Better known is *A.dealbata*, sometimes called silver wattle or florist's mimosa. Its silvery green, fern-like leaves make an attractive foil for the panicles of fragrant, fluffy flowers. *A.longifolia*, or Sydney golden wattle, has long, lance-shaped leaves and upright spikes of bright-yellow flowers.

Acalypha

Copperleaf

These fast-growing shrubs need high temperatures and humidity to thrive, but their long, bright-red, hanging flowers make them worth a try if you can provide a minimum temperature of 16°C (60°F) all year round.

Cultivation

As with many fast-growing plants, acalyphas can quickly become spindly, a problem remedied by cutting them back by half in spring, or renewing them annually from cuttings. Though acalyphas need good light to flower, and to produce highly coloured leaves in those forms grown for foliage direct sunlight can be harmful and some shading should be provided.

In the growing season, keep the compost continually moist, but not waterlogged. In autumn and winter provide only enough water to keep the compost from drying out. Use John Innes potting compost No. 2, and feed fortnightly during the growing period.

Types to choose

Acalypha hispida, sometimes called the chenille plant, or red-hot cat-tail, has rather ordinary looking foliage, but produces petal-less, drooping flower spikes, up to 45cm (18in) long, in summer and autumn. There is a white-flowered form, *A.h.*'Alba'.

Achimenes

Cupid's Bower, Hot Water Plant

Achimenes are tender, deciduous perennial plants grown for their richly coloured, trumpet-shaped or tubular flowers, which are produced in summer or early autumn.

Cultivation

As with hardy perennials, achimenes have a dormant period as well as an active one, so you need a cool, frost-free place to store the plant during its rest period. You can buy plants in flower, or buy the scaly, acorn-shaped rhizomes and plant them in early spring. Plant four or five rhizomes in a 10cm (4in) pot filled with a peat-based compost or John Innes potting compost No. 2, with vermiculite or coarse sand added to improve drainage. Provide a minimum temperature of 16°C (60°F) and give a steady supply of water. As young shoots appear, increase the watering and feed fortnightly until flowering is finished, in autumn. Achimenes need strong light, but protection from direct sunlight. The taller-growing forms benefit from small supporting twigs in the compost.

Achimenes 'Little Beauty'

When flowering has finished, gradually reduce the supply of water. Once the plant is dormant, withhold water until the following spring, then carefully extract the rhizomes from the old compost and plant them in fresh compost, as above. The plant will probably have formed additional new rhizomes, which can be potted up separately.

Types to Choose

Achimenes erecta is a trailing form with red flowers, ideal for hanging baskets. The stems can reach a length of 45cm (18in) or more. *A.grandiflora* is much the same size, but with erect stems and large, rosy purple and white flowers. *A.longiflora* is another trailing form with huge, blue and white flowers. There are numerous named hybrids, including the white-flowered 'Ambroise Vers chaffelt' and the pink-flowered 'Minuet'.

Aechmea

Urn Plant, Living Vase

Aechmeas could equally well be listed under foliage plants, as their evergreen leaves, arranged in typical bromeliad rosette fashion, are as attractive as their tall flower bracts. These, and the tiny flowers they carry, are only produced by mature rosettes, after which the rosette usually dies. Before it does so it produces young offshoots from the base, which will eventually produce flower bracts of their own.

Cultivation

Most aechmeas are epiphytes and use their roots more for anchorage than for drawing up nourishment and moisture. These they obtain from the hollow, vase-like centre of the plant, which should always be kept topped up with fresh water.

Grow aechmeas in small pots filled with a peat-based compost, or a mixture of equal parts peat, leafmould and coarse sand. They can also be grown, as they appear in the wild, on a branch, with their roots wrapped in moss and fixed in place with wire. Water the compost or moss regularly, but allow it to dry out between waterings, and feed with liquid fertilizer monthly in spring and summer. Apply the fertilizer to the compost and the central 'vase'. Full sunlight is necessary, high humidity and a minimum temperature of 10°C (50°F) if kept fairly dry.

Types to choose

Aechmea chantinii, with dark-green leaves, an orange flower bract and tiny, red and yellow flowers, can reach a height of 90cm (3ft). *A.fasciata* is slightly smaller, with grey and white striped leaves and a pink flower bract with small blue flowers that turn red.

Aechmea fasciata

Agapanthus

African Blue Lily

These clump-forming perennial plants produce attractive, strap-shaped leaves and large, round heads of blue or white trumpet-shaped flowers. The flowers are carried on tall, graceful stems in late summer or autumn.

Cultivation

Bright light is necessary for the plants to flower, but not much artificial heat, as long as they are not exposed to extended frost. Grow in pots filled with John Innes potting compost No. 2. Feed fortnightly and water generously in spring and summer; water sparingly while the plants are dormant. Agapanthus flower best when slightly pot bound, but once the roots become overcrowded, either pot on to a larger-size pot or small tub, or divide and re-plant in several small pots.

Types to choose

The hardiest form is the deciduous *Agapanthus* 'Headbourne Hybrids', with a height of 60-90cm (2-3ft) and flowers from pale to deep blue. Less hardy ones include the evergreen *A.africanus*, of similar size but with violet-blue flowers; the deciduous *A.campanulatus* 'Isis' with deep-blue flowers, and the evergreen *A.orientalis* 'Snowball', with white flowers and a height of up to 1.2m (4ft).

Allamanda

Golden Trumpet

Allamandas are not easy plants, but their spectacular yellow, trumpet-shaped flowers in summer and autumn make the challenge of growing them worthwhile.

Cultivation

Provide a minimum temperature of 13° (55°F), full sunlight and high humidity. In the wild, they are evergreen climbers, reaching a height of 4.6m (15ft) or more; in a conservatory, they can be kept to reasonable proportions by being grown in large pots filled with John Innes potting compost No. 3 and pruned back by half, if necessary, in late winter. Water moderately and feed fortnightly in spring and summer; the rest of the year water sparingly.

Types to choose

There is a compact form available, *Allamanda cathartica* 'Grandiflora', with pale yellow flowers; *A.c.*'Hendersonii' has deep-yellow flowers.

Aloe

Aloes are succulent plants grown as much for their rosettes of thick, tapering leaves as for their long-stemmed, pink, orange or red flowers. Though some can grow to huge proportions in the wild, in cultivation they are usually small-scale, slow-growing plants. There are hundreds of species, and many are available commercially.

Cultivation

All require maximum light and ventilation, minimum humidity and a minimum temperature of 5°C (40°F). A free-draining compost is essential, as waterlogged conditions quickly lead to rot. John Innes potting compost No. 2 with an equal quantity of coarse sand or grit added is ideal. Water generously in the growing season; keep barely moist the rest of the year.

Aloes benefit from a spell outdoors in the summer, with protection from strong sunlight. They are easily propagated from offsets removed from the base of the plant in summer and potted up as above. Shade from direct light until fully established.

Types to choose

Aloe arborescens, sometimes called the candelabra plant, has loose rosettes of long, narrow, grey-green leaves on woody stems and red flowers sometimes produced on long stems. The lace aloe, *A.aristata*, is a stemless plant, with 8-10cm (3-4in) long, tightly packed leaves and bright orange flowers on long stalks in summer.

The short-leaved aloe, *A.brevifolia*, is a similar size but the rosettes, of wide, prickly-edged leaves, eventually trail over the edge of the pot, and its flowers, again on tall stalks, are light-pink. One of the most commonly available aloes is the partridge-breasted aloe, *A.variegata*, with tightly packed, white-striped leaves and pink flowers.

Anthurium

Flamingo Flower, Tailflower, Painter's Palette

These popular evergreen tropical plants produce showy 'flowers' – actually inflorescences – made up of a flat, brightly coloured spathe and tail-like spadix, in spring and summer.

Cultivation

Anthuriums require a minimum temperature of 13-16°C (55-60°F), high humidity and bright, but indirect, sunlight. Free-draining compost is essential; use either a peat-based compost or equal parts of John Innes potting compost No. 2, sphagnum peat and coarse sand. In spring and summer, keep well watered and feed fortnightly; water moderately the rest of the year.

Types to choose

Anthurium andreanum has attractive, large, heart-shaped leaves and bright-red flower spathes, each with a creamy yellow spadix. There are hybrid forms available with white, pink or rosy-red spathes, all reaching 45cm (18in) in height. *A.scherzerianum* reaches a height of 23cm (9in) and has glossy, narrowly pointed leaves and bright-red flower spathes, each with a curiously twisted spadix.

Aphelandra

Zebra Plant, Saffron Spike

The strikingly variegated green and white leaves and the bright-yellow flower bracts make this a doubly valuable plant for a conservatory with high humidity and a temperature of 13-18°C (55-65°F).

Cultivation

Bright light, but not direct sunlight, is best. Water generously and feed once a week in the growing season; water sparingly the rest of the year. John Innes potting compost No. 2 is acceptable. Aphelandras can get leggy, so cut back to just above a pair of leaves in spring to promote bushy growth.

Types to choose

Aphelandra squarrosa 'Louisae' is a compact form, up to 45cm (18in) high, with naturally drooping leaves; *A.s.*'Brockfield' is even more compact, with darker-green leaves and dramatic leaf markings. Both produce their short-lived, tiny flowers in spring, though the bracts remain attractive for some time afterwards, eventually turning from yellow to green.

Begonia

There are three basic types of begonia: fibrous rooted, tuberous rooted and rhizomatous rooted. All are flowering plants, but some have equally attractive foliage and flowers while others are grown primarily for their flowers or foliage alone. Though any division is bound to be slightly arbitrary, rhizomatous begonias and some fibrous-rooted begonias are covered in the section on foliage plants (see page 93).

Tuberous-rooted forms

Cultivation

Start the tubers into growth in spring by placing them in shallow trays of moist peat, placing the tubers so that the concave-side is uppermost. Provide indirect light and a minimum temperature of 18°C (65°F). Once growth appears, transfer them into pots or hanging baskets of peat-based compost, or John Innes potting compost No. 2, with peat or leafmould added. Provide bright light but shade from direct summer sunlight, and high humidity in high tempera-

Anthurium andreanum

Begonia 'Sweet Dreams'

tures. Water moderately and feed fortnightly in spring and summer.

After flowering, gradually reduce the amount of water given and when the leaves have died back, stop watering and allow the compost to dry off. Shake the tubers from the compost and store them in a layer packed with dry sand or peat. Keep over winter at a minimum temperature of 4°C (39°F); in spring, start into growth as above.

Types to choose

Tuberous-rooted begonias include the popular summer-flowering plants, *B.x. tuberhybrida.* There are many named forms, with flowers ranging from shades of pink, yellow, white, red or orange; some have a second contrasting colour. Flowers are usually double, though there are single-flowered forms; the flowers can be large, up to 15cm (6in) across, or quite small.

Lorraine begonias (*B.cheimantha* hybrids) are semi-tuberous rooted. The plants, which are up to 45cm (18in) tall, have large, round shiny leaves and single pink flowers up to 5cm (2in) across. Similar are the 'Elatior' hybrids (more correctly, *B.hyemalis* hybrids), though their flowers are slightly larger and are available in yellow, orange, white and red as well as pink. Both are sold in flower at Christmas time, and although they are technically perennials, are usually discarded after flowering. They require the same cultivation as actively growing *Begonia* × *tuberhybrida* (see above).

The Rieger Hybrids can be bought in flower at any time of the year. These are also semi-tuberous and need reasonable warmth and good light.

Fibrous-rooted forms

Cultivation

All fibrous-rooted forms need exposure to direct sunlight, but some protection from strong summer sun, a minimum temperature of 13°C (55°F), and high humidity when the temperature is high. Water moderately and feed fortnightly in spring and summer; water sparingly the rest of the year.

Though wax begonias are technically tender perennials, they are usually discarded after flowering, and new plants either bought in or grown from seed the following year. Other fibrous-rooted begonias can be kept for several years, though they tend to get leggy with age. Re-pot in spring, using compost as for *B.* × *tuberhybrida* (see above), and prune back by up to half, if necessary, to encourage compact growth. Pinching out the growing tips from time to time also helps.

Propagation

New plants are easily propagated from 8cm (3in) cuttings taken in spring. Remove the lower leaf and insert in a mixture of peat and coarse sand in a pot. Water lightly, enclose the pot in a clear plastic bag, and place in a semi-shaded, warm spot. Once roots have formed and new growth appears, pot up as described earlier.

Types to choose

The most popular flowering fibrous-rooted begonia is probably the wax begonia (*B.* × *semperflorens cultorum*). These are often used in bedding-out schemes, but make admirable conservatory plants as they flower throughout the year. They have a height and spread of 10-30cm (4-12in), white, pink or red flowers and shiny round leaves which are usually green but bronzy-red in some forms.

Begonia fuchsioides, or the fuchsia begonia, is less well known but equally valuable, with a more graceful habit of growth. Reaching a height of 90cm (3ft) or more, *B.fuchsioides* carries delicate clusters of pink or red flowers from autumn through spring.

Begonia 'Lucerna' is taller growing still, up to 1.8m (6ft). Its leaves are large and pointed, white-spotted on the upper surfaces and dark red underneath. Huge, hanging clusters of pink or red flowers are produced usually in summer, but occasionally at other times of the year. *Begonia coccinea* is a bamboo-like plant with red flower panicles.

Beloperone
Shrimp Plant

The main attraction of this tropical shrub is not its leaves or flowers, but the pink and white, shrimp-like bracts which hold the flowers. These are produced from late spring through early winter on the ends of the growing tips. *Beloperone guttata* is now more correctly called *Justicea brandegeana*.

Cultivation

A minimum temperature of 7°C (45°F) is needed, and plenty of light, though some protection from direct sunlight in summer. A fairly rich compost, such as John Innes potting compost No. 2 is suitable. Water generously from spring through autumn; water sparingly in winter. Feed fortnightly in the growing season.

The main drawback of this plant is its tendency to become spindly and leafless at the base. To remedy this, cut back by half in spring, and pinch out the growing tips of young shoots to encourage bushy side shoots. Mature plants can reach a height of 90cm (3ft), if unpruned.

Billbergia
Queen's Tears

Billbergias are bromeliads, with narrow, evergreen leaves forming loose or compact rosettes, according to the species chosen. The short-lived flowers vary in size and colour, but tend to be tube shaped and displayed on arching stems. Most of the species are epiphytic.

Beloperone guttata

Cultivation

Billbergias are easy plants, requiring a minimum temperature of 7°C (45°F) and bright light. Provide an even, steady supply of water, allowing the compost to dry out slightly between waterings, and fill the 'cups' of those forms with watertight rosettes. Feed fortnightly in spring and summer. Billbergias have small root systems, so provide small pots, using John Innes potting compost No. 2, with peat or leafmould added. Billbergias can be easily propagated by dividing the plant into several rosettes and potting them up separately in spring or summer.

Billbergia x *windii*

Types to choose

Billbergia nutans, or queen's tears, is the most commonly available form; its dark-green leaves can reach 45cm (18in) in length, and the small pink, green and blue flowers appear at the ends of bright-pink bracts. *B. x windii* has broader leaves and broader pink bracts to the flowers. Less common is *B. pyramidalis*, a smaller plant with a central rosette of wide, greeny-grey leaves. Its pink flower bracts hold the scarlet and blue flowers.

Bougainvillea
Paper Flower

In the wild, this subtropical climber can reach 9m (30ft) or more; grown in a large pot or tub, it assumes smaller and bushier proportions. Bougainvillea's main attraction is the colourful bracts that surround the tiny, insignificant flowers in spring and summer, and may last for several weeks. When not in flower, bougainvillea is quite dull looking, with small, mid-green leaves and a slightly rigid habit of growth.

Cultivation

Bougainvilleas need bright light, cool conditions in winter, but with a minimum temperature of 7°C (45°F), and plenty of humidity in the warm summer months. John Innes potting compost No. 3 and weekly feeds in spring and summer will provide the nourishment needed for flowering and growth. In the growing season water generously; water sparingly the rest of the year, decreasing the amount of water once the bracts fall. Bougainvilleas are deciduous, and shed their leaves in winter. Larger specimens can be trained round wire hoops or tied in to wires or trelliswork. Any pruning necessary should be done in early spring, when up to half the growth can be safely removed.

Types to choose

Bougainvillea × *buttiana* hybrids can be had in orange, copper, yellow, crimson and red forms, all relatively slow growing and suitable for a small space. Far more vigorous is *B.glabra* 'Sanderana', with bright-purple bracts.

Browallia

These tender, sun-loving plants are relatives of the petunia, and produce wide, starry blue flowers in summer or winter, according to time of sowing.

Cultivation

Provide steady even temperatures, not

below 13°C (55°F), and bright sunlight. Water moderately and feed fortnightly when in flower. Though technically perennials, they are best treated as annuals, and discarded after flowering.

Types to choose

Most browallias grown today are cultivars of *B.speciosa*, which can reach a height of 1.2m (4ft). The cultivars are far more compact, and range in height from 25-50cm (10-20in). They include *B.s.*'Major', with large, bright-blue flowers; *B.s.*'White Troll', and *B.s.*'Marine Blue', with dark-blue flowers. Browallias are suitable for hanging baskets as well as small pots.

Brunfelsia

Yesterday, Today and Tomorrow Plant

The young flowers of this rather narrow, evergreen shrub are dark blue-purple. As they age, they gradually become paler, until they are nearly white when they die. Brunfelsia's common name comes from this curious feature. The large, fragrant flowers are carried in clusters, though they open one at a time, and a well grown specimen may be in flower from spring to the autumn.

Cultivation

Although it can reach a height of 90cm (3ft), given confined conditions and regular pruning, brunfelsia can be kept to more modest proportions. Provide as much light as possible, a winter temperature of 10°C (50°F) or slightly higher, and good ventilation and plenty of humidity in summer. Water moderately in the growing season, when fortnightly feeds are appreciated, and water sparingly the rest of the year. Grow in John Innes potting compost No. 2 or No. 3, with peat or leafmould added. It is not terribly quick growing, and seems to flower best when pot bound. Any pruning necessary should be done in spring, and pinching out the growing tips will encourage compact, bushy growth.

Types to choose

The two most commonly available forms are *Brunfelsia pauciflora* (*B.calycina*) 'Floribunda', a dwarf, compact plant, and *B.p.*'Macrantha', with flowers 5cm (2in) or more in diameter. Both have lance-shaped, shiny leaves.

Calceolaria

Slipper Flower, Pouch Flower

Though technically tender perennials, calceolarias are treated as biennials by commercial growers, to be enjoyed for several weeks, then discarded. Their common name comes from the colourful, pouch- or slipper-shaped flowers, which can be yellow, orange, red or crimson, often spotted or blotched with a second colour. These are carried in clusters above the large, rather dull, heart-shaped leaves; the plants range in height from 20-45cm (8-18in), according to the form chosen.

Cultivation

Provide bright light but some protection from direct sunlight and a cool temperature – 10-16°C (50-60°F) is ideal with a minimum of 7°C (45°F). Keep the compost thoroughly moist, but not waterlogged, and provide plenty of ventilation. Plants in bud are available in late winter or spring, but calceolarias can also be grown from seed sown in early summer to flower the following spring.

Types to choose

Seedsmen offer several different strains of *Calceolaria* × *herbeohybrida.*

Callistemon

Bottle Brush

Though it can reach tree-like proportions in the wild, this evergreen shrub can be kept to a more modest size in a large pot or tub in a conservatory, where it may eventually reach 1.8m (6ft). Its main attraction is the bright-red, cylindrical spikes of flowers, although the petals are actually insignificant and the colour comes from the stamens. These are produced on the tips of the branches in summer.

Cultivation

Provide maximum light and a winter temperature of 7-10°C (45-50°F). Grow in John Innes potting compost No. 2. Water generously and feed fortnightly during the growing season; water sparingly the rest of the year. If the plant becomes straggly, or outgrows its allotted space, prune it back hard after flowering. To ripen the wood, and thus encourage future flower production, stand the pot outdoors in a sunny, sheltered spot after flowering, returning it to the conservatory when frost threatens in autumn.

Types to choose

The best form to grow is *Callistemon citrinus* 'Splendens', with brilliant-scarlet flowers and narrow, lemon-scented leaves.

Callistemon citrinus

Camellia

These glossy-leaved, evergreen, flowering shrubs range from the moderately hardy to the very hardy, and don't need the protection of a conservatory to thrive. Still, in autumn, winter or spring, their large, single, semi-double or double flowers, in shades of white, pink or red, make a lovely show in an unheated or slightly heated conservatory. Additionally, you are more likely to get perfect flowers – weather conditions outdoors can brown or otherwise disfigure the waxy blooms.

Cultivation

Though camellias can reach tree-like proportions in the wild, growth is curtailed in containers. Commercially, sizes range from quite small plants, suitable for 13-cm (5-in) pots, to those needing large tubs. Provide bright light, a maximum winter temperature of 16°C (60°F) and a rich, soil-based, lime-free compost, with leafmould added. Water generously and feed fortnightly while plants are actively growing or flowering; water sparingly the rest of the year but never allow plants to become really dry at the roots.

Camellias are not house plants and, ideally, they should spend summer and autumn in a sheltered position in the garden, with their pots buried in the soil, then brought into the conservatory to flower. If this is not possible, then keep the plants cool and provide humid growing conditions if the temperature rises.

Types to choose

There are hundreds of named varieties, usually of *Camellia japonica*, but *C.* × *williamsii* hybrids and forms of *C.reticulata* are also available.

Camellia sp.

Campanula

Italian Bellflower

Though campanulas are usually thought of as plants for the perennial border or rock garden, *Campanula isophylla* is ideal for hanging baskets or training up trellis work in a cool conservatory.

Cultivation

Campanulas need a minimum winter temperature of 5-10°C (40-50°F), maximum light and rich growing conditions: John Innes potting compost No. 2 or 3, and fortnightly feeds during the growing period. Water generously and regularly in spring and summer, and water sparingly while dormant – only enough to keep the compost from drying out completely. These campanulas are tender herbaceous perennials; their aboveground growth dies back in autumn, and re-appears in spring. Very warm temperatures in winter prevent dormancy, and weaken or kill the plant; summer temperatures above 18°C (65°F) can be equally damaging, unless high humidity is provided. Think of it as a garden plant, needing frost protection but not cosseting, and all will be well. Increase by division in spring.

Types to choose

In summer and autumn, the small, heart-shaped leaves and thin, rather brittle stems of *Campanula isophylla* are completely hidden by large, pale-blue, star-shaped flowers. There is also a white-flowered form, *C.i.*'Alba', somewhat less stunning than the pale blue of the species. The trailing stems can reach 30cm (12in) or more in length, so the plant is also ideal for growing along the edge of staging or simply allowed to trail over a small table.

Capsicum

Ornamental Pepper, Christmas Pepper

It is not for the insignificant flowers that *Capsicum annuum* is grown, but for its glossy, colourful fruit, which can be round or pointed; and yellow, orange, red, green or purple according to the variety chosen. The plants are small and bushy, rarely reaching a height and spread of more than 45cm (18in).

Cultivation

Provide a sunny, cool growing environment, ideally 13-15°C (55-60°), water generously and feed fortnightly. Once the fruit begins to shrivel – after two or three months' display in suitable environments – discard the plant. Although technically a perennial, it is short lived and difficult to bring into fruit again. Propagate from seed.

Catharanthus

Madagascar Periwinkle

This tender evergreen shrub is sometimes sold as *Vinca rosea*, its former botanical name. It is grown for its periwinkle-like, pale-pink flowers which are freely produced from late spring through autumn. The shrub has an upright habit of growth, and may reach a height of 60cm (2ft), rather less across. The leaves, which are shiny and pointed, make an attractive foil for the flowers.

Cultivation
Provide maximum light and a minimum temperature of 10°C (50°F). Grow in John Innes potting compost No. 2. Water generously and feed fortnightly in spring and summer; water moderately the rest of the year. To encourage compact, bushy growth, pinch out the growing tips once or twice in summer. The plant can be kept over winter and then cut back to within 5cm (2in) of the base in early spring, but it is usually treated as an annual and discarded at the end of the flowering season.

Types to choose
Catharanthus roseus 'Albus' has white flowers; *C.r.*'Little Bright Eyes' has white flowers with deep-pink centres.

Chrysanthemum

A huge category, chrysanthemums for the conservatory range from pot plants to be enjoyed for several weeks and then discarded, to annual and perennial autumn, winter or summer flowering-plants, in a wide range of sizes, flower shapes and colours. The following two kinds make good pot plants for the conservatory.

Cultivation of Pot Chrysanthemums
The popular chrysanthemums sold as pot plants are complex hybrids based on *C.* × *morifolium*. They are commercially dwarfed with chemicals and forced into flower by a special regime of exposure to varying amounts of light and darkness over several weeks. They are available at any time of the year (buy them in bud but with some colour showing) and are usually under 30cm (12in) high. Provide bright but indirect light and cool growing conditions – 5-16°C (40-60°F) is a good range; flowers are longer lasting at the lower temperatures. Provide high humidity at the higher temperature range. Water generously while in flower, but no feeding is necessary.

When flowering is over, the plants can be cut back and cuttings taken from the new growth produced, but the resulting plants are likely to be much taller, and also flower only in autumn or winter. It is usually more sensible to replace your stock with new plants.

Cultivation of Marguerites
Marguerite, also called Paris daisy *(C.frutescens)*, is a charming, tender perennial covered in white, daisy-like flowers in summer and autumn. Young plants are available in spring, usually as small, multi-stemmed specimens, reaching a height and spread of 45cm (18in), but occasionally as standards, up to 1.2m (4ft) high.

Marguerites need a minimum temperature of 10°C (50°F) and bright, well ventilated growing conditions. Feed fortnightly and water steadily but moderately in the growing season. When flowering is over, the plants are best discarded, though standards can be kept for several years. Water sparingly in late autumn, winter and early spring, then increase watering and cut back the bushy 'head' by half once growth starts.

Citrus

Lemon, Calamondin Orange
Citrus trees, with their shiny, evergreen leaves, heavily scented white flowers and orange or yellow fruit make year-round features in a conservatory, and are certainly worth including if you can provide a minimum winter temperature of 7°C (45°F).

Cultivation
Provide as much light as possible and, to ripen the wood and encourage flowering, place the pots outdoors in a sunny, sheltered spot in summer. Grow in John Innes potting compost No. 2. Water generously and feed fortnightly in the growing season, when the plants will need high humidity and maximum ventilation. When dormant, keep the compost on the dry side. To prevent sparse, leggy growth, prune the branches back by up to half in spring, and pinch out growing tips to encourage bushiness.

Citrus plants can be easily grown from seed, but the seedlings may take years to flower and fruit. Cuttings give more predictable results.

Types to choose
Citrus limon 'Meyeri', or Meyer's lemon, makes a small tree, 90-120cm (3-4ft) high. Its purple-tinged, white flowers appear in late spring and, in ideal conditions, are followed by small lemons. *C.mitis*, the Calamondin orange, is similar and produces its clusters of small, sour oranges when quite young. Technically, this plant is × *Citrofortunella mitis*, a hybrid between mandarin orange and kumquat. While the mandarin orange is not usually available as a pot plant, the kumquat (*Fortunella japonica*) is.

Citrus mitis

Clianthus

Glory Pea, Lobster Claw, Parrot's Bill

This sprawling, evergreen shrub has attractive, fern-like leaves and clusters of large, brilliant-red, claw-shaped flowers in spring and summer.

Cultivation

Clianthus is a good plant for growing in a large pot or tub, filled with John Innes potting compost No. 3. In time, it can reach a height and spread of 1.8m (6ft) or more, and may need tying in to wires or trellis-work for support. Clianthus is a nearly hardy plant, so a winter temperature of 5°C (40°F) is ideal: just enough to keep frost off, but not too warm. In spring and summer, water generously and feed fortnightly; the rest of the year water sparingly. In high summer temperatures, provide high humidity, misting the plant daily but also keeping it well ventilated. Bright light is essential for flowering.

Clianthus puniceus

Types to choose

Clianthus puniceus is the red-flowered species. There is also a white-flowered form *C.p.*'Albus', which is somewhat less dramatic.

Clivia

Kaffir Lily

Clivia miniata is a striking plant in leaf and flower. Its evergreen, glossy, strap-like leaves grow from tightly packed, thick, bulb-like bases. The leaves, which can be 60cm (24in) long, arch gracefully and provide a sculptural setting for the clusters of large, trumpet-shaped, orange flowers, which are carried on tall stems in spring and summer.

Cultivation

Clivias are tough, undemanding plants, with few requirements. Provide light, but protection from direct sunlight, and a minimum winter temperature of 7°C (45°F) or a bit lower. No additional artificial heat should be necessary the rest of the year, but low temperatures during the winter months are essential for future flowering. A low-nutrient compost, such as John Innes potting compost No. 1, is sufficient, generous supplies of water and occasional feeds during the growing season, once the flower buds appear. Water sparingly the rest of the year.

Clivias flower best in pot-bound conditions, and should only be re-potted if the roots break the existing containers. If necessary, pot on after flowering, in autumn, when the plant can also be propagated by division of offsets. An established specimen, grown in a large pot or small tub, is most attractive and, unless it has reached unmanageable proportions, it is worth keeping a clivia intact.

Columnea

These plants are epiphytes, with trailing or arching habits of growth and brilliant red or orange flowers produced from leaf junctions all along the stems. The tubular flowers are long lasting, and produced on and off through the year. Columneas are not easy to grow, but a large plant in flower can be quite breath-taking and if you can provide the specific conditions needed, it is worth 'having a go'.

Clivia miniata

Cultivation

Bright but indirect light is necessary, and a minimum temperature of 16°C (60°F). Spray plants daily with tepid water; those grown in pots should be stood on pebble-filled dishes kept topped up with water. Potting compost is needed more for anchorage than for nourishment. Grow in small pots or hanging baskets filled with a mixture of a peat-based compost and coarse sand; pot-bound plants tend to flower best. Water moderately, allowing the compost to dry out slightly between waterings, and water sparingly when not in flower. During the spring and summer months feed fortnightly using a weak solution.

Types to choose

There are many species and named forms available. Among the most popular are *Columnea* × *banksii*, with red flowers in autumn, winter and spring on 75cm (2½ft) long stems; *C.gloriosa* 'Purpurea', with yellow-centred red flowers and velvety purple leaves on stems up to 1.2m (4ft) long; *C.microphylla*, with stems up to 1.5m (5ft) long and orange flowers, produced in all but the summer months; and the hybrid *C.*'Chanticleer', a compact, arching rather than trailing plant, with orange flowers.

Crinum

Spider Lily

Crinum is a large, bulbous plant with clusters of impressive, pink, trumpet-shaped flowers but terribly messy evergreen leaves. To keep older specimens looking nice requires constant care, a point worth keeping in mind.

Cultivation

Plant the bulbs, with their necks exposed, in John Innes potting compost No. 2. Use relatively small pots, as crinum flowers best when pot bound; it also resents root disturbance. Provide bright light but shade from strong summer sunlight, and water generously in the growing season. In winter, when a period of dormancy is needed, keep the temperature at about 10°C (50°F) and the compost on the dry side. Judiciously trim away the brown portions of leaves as they die; new leaves will then soon replace them.

Types to choose

Crinum × powellii is the form most often grown, but there are other crinums available for keen growers, including the white-flowered *C.moorei* 'Album'. Both of these grow to a height of 90cm (3ft). There is a smaller form, *C.bulbispermum*, growing half as high, with white and pink flowers. All flower in late summer and autumn.

Crocus

Crocuses, a welcome sight in the garden, are even more welcome in a cool conservatory, where they make a colourful presence during the winter and early spring.

Cultivation

Plant corms in the autumn, in shallow containers filled with John Innes potting compost No. 1 or special bulb fibre, available from garden centres. Plant the corms just below the surface and about 2.5cm (1in) apart. Water lightly. Ideally, the prepared container should be placed outdoors, covered in peat, ashes or sand, and brought into the conservatory once the shoots are 2.5cm (1in) high. Otherwise, keep them indoors, in a dark, cool but frost-free spot.

Once they are in the conservatory, provide bright light but some shade from strong sunlight, and a moderate supply of water. Be careful if the container has no drainage holes, as the growing medium can easily become waterlogged, and bulb fibre is preferable in this case. After flowering, plant outside in the garden, as they are unsuitable for forcing again under glass.

Types to choose

There are many species and hybrids of crocus available, in colours ranging from white to lavender, purple, yellow, orange, blue and pink; some are bicoloured. Whichever types you choose, plant only one type to each container, to ensure a good display.

Crossandra

These evergreen shrubby plants need a minimum temperature of 13°C (55°F) and constantly high humidity. If you can meet the demands, crossandras are worth growing for their impressive, long-lasting flower spikes in spring and summer.

Cultivation

Grow in John Innes potting compost No. 2. Provide maximum light in late autumn, winter and early spring, but shade from direct sunlight at other times. Water generously and feed weekly when in full growth; water sparingly the rest of the year. If the plants become straggly, cut them back by up to half in early spring.

Types to choose

Crossandra nilotica carries spikes of bright-red flowers, usually in summer but occasionally in spring or autumn. It reaches a height of 60cm (24in). *C.infundibuliformis* (formerly *C.undulifolia*) is similar, but larger; it can reach a height of 90cm (3ft), and its pink or red flowers are also larger-scale. Both species have attractive, shiny, dark-green leaves.

Cyclamen

Among the most popular of pot plants, especially in the winter months, cyclamen is also one that is very often killed by kindness. It is not at all difficult to care for in a cool conservatory, and a well grown plant can go on flowering for years.

Cultivation

Cool temperatures and careful watering are the keys to success. A constant temperature of 10-18°C (50-65°F) is best, with high humidity provided at higher temperatures. Plenty of light but protection from direct sunlight is necessary, and a steady supply of water. Water must never lie on the tuber, or it is liable to rot, and it is safest to water from below. Fill a shallow dish with lukewarm water and place the pot in it

Cyclamen persicum

for several minutes, to allow sufficient water to be absorbed through the drainage holes. Do this once a week, more often in high temperatures or if the flowers go limp, a sign of dryness at the roots.

Once flowering is over and the leaves begin to yellow, gradually dry off the tuber and place it, still in its pot, in a cool, dry spot. The following autumn, re-pot it in John Innes potting compost No. 2, with a bit of leafmould, peat and coarse sand added, if possible. Water sparingly; once growth appears, gradually increase watering.

Types to choose

The plants, varieties derived from *Cyclamen persicum*, can be acquired in a wide range of colours, from white, pink, rose, crimson, red, mauve and deep magenta to purple. The leaves are often attractively marbled. Most have a height and spread of 23cm (9in), but there are miniature forms available.

Cytisus

Florists' Genista

Cytisus canariensis is a gracefully arching evergreen shrub, covered with bright-yellow, sweetly scented flowers in spring and summer. Though it can grow to a height and spread of 1.8m (6ft) in the open ground, in a pot in the conservatory it will rarely exceed a height and spread of 45cm (18in).

Cultivation

Provide bright light but shade from strong sunlight, and a winter temperature of 7°C (45°F). Grow in John Innes potting compost No. 2. Water generously and feed fortnightly in spring and summer; water sparingly the rest of the year when the plant is dormant.

After flowering, cut back the old flowered stems to within 8cm (3in) of the base and, if possible, stand the pot outdoors in a sunny, sheltered spot in summer and early autumn to ripen the wood. Return it to the conservatory before the first frosts, and in late winter, raise the temperature slightly to encourage the formation of flowers. Cytisus resents root disturbance, and should be potted on with great care, after pruning. It is safer to topdress than to re-pot mature specimens.

Datura

Thorn Apple, Angel's Trumpets

Members of the potato family, daturas are semi-hardy shrubs, annuals or perennials grown for their huge, fragrant, drooping, trumpet-like flowers in summer. The plants themselves are rather coarse looking, and not worth the space in a small conservatory; in a large conservatory, their rich fragrance (usually strongest in the evenings) makes them worth including.

Cultivation

Grow daturas in large pots or tubs filled with John Innes potting compost No. 3. They need bright light, but some shade from direct sunlight in summer, good ventilation and high humidity in high temperatures. Water generously and feed fortnightly in spring and summer; the rest of the year, water sparingly and provide a minimum winter temperature of 7°C (45°F). Each spring, prune back to within 20cm (8in) of the base; daturas are quick growing, and some species can be trained as standards.

Types to choose

The naming of daturas is quite complicated; *D.innoxia* (*D.meteloides*) is a short-lived perennial usually sold as an annual. It has a height and spread of 90cm (3ft) and white or lavender flowers. *D.metel* is similar sized, with white or bright-red flowers. *D.sanğuinea* is an orange-flowered, evergreen shrub with a height and spread of up to 1.8m (6ft). *D.suaveolens* is equally large scale, with white flowers. The seeds and flowers of daturas are poisonous.

Datura

Dianthus

Perpetual-flowering Carnation, Florists' Carnation

Though not particularly difficult to grow, carnations are not first-class candidates for a conservatory. They can flower all year round, but few flowers are produced at any one time, and the plants themselves are tall – 1.2m (4ft) or more – leggy and not particularly attractive. Carnations also need a drier atmosphere than many other conservatory plants. Still, you may be determined to 'have a go.'

Cultivation

A minimum winter temperature of 5°C (40°F) is needed, though 10°C (50°F) is essential for winter flowering. Provide maximum light and good ventilation all year round, as the plants are prone to rotting. In high summer temperatures, increase the humidity during the day (humid conditions at lower, night-time temperatures can cause rotting). Grow in pots of John Innes potting compost No.2, with coarse sand and a sprinkling of carbonate of lime added.

Pinch out the growing tips of young plants to encourage the production of side shoots and pinch out the growing tips of side shoots to encourage the formation of flower buds. Water moderately and feed fortnightly in the growing season; water sparingly the rest of the year. Provide supports in the form of canes and strong twine. Perpetual-flowering carnations are usually grown for two years and then replaced with rooted cuttings, taken from non-flowering side shoots in autumn, winter or spring.

Types to choose

There are many named cultivars of *Dianthus caryophyllus,* the perpetual-flowering carnation, with colours ranging from white, yellow, salmon, orange and scarlet to crimson, purple and cerise. There are also bicoloured forms.

Dipladenia

This is not an easy plant, but a beautiful one when in flower, and worth trying if you can meet its exacting requirements.

Cultivation

Provide a well-lit spot, but shade from strong sunlight. The optimum winter temperature is about 13°C (55°F), with warmer temperatures the rest of the year and ventilation and high humidity provided in summer. Grow in John Innes potting compost No. 3. Water generously and feed weekly in the growing season, water sparingly the rest of the year. If necessary to keep the plant within bounds, cut back the old flowered growth hard in autumn. As dipladenias flower only on new wood, this also encourages heavy production of flowers.

Types to choose

Dipladenia splendens (*Mandevilla splendens*) is a large-scale, evergreen, climbing or twining shrub, capable of reaching 4.6m (15ft) if grown in a tub and trained to trellis work or wires. Smaller specimens can be grown in small pots and trained round a circular wire framework or canes. The plant produces clusters of deep-pink, fragrant, trumpet-shaped flowers during the summer months.

Dipladenia splendens

Erica

Heather, French Heather, Cape Heath

Heathers in flower are often sold as pot plants at Christmas time, and most come to grief in centrally heated rooms shortly thereafter.

Cultivation

These small, lime-hating shrubs need very particular growing conditions: a temperature of 7-10°C (45-50°F), bright but indirect sunlight, continually moist but never waterlogged growing conditions. A slightly heated conservatory is a far more accommodating environment than a heated living room, but even here the plant is likely to be short lived, and is best discarded once the flowers fade.

Types to choose

There are two main species offered for sale; both grow to about 45cm (18in) in height. *Erica gracilis* has dark-pink flowers, white in the form *E.g.*'Alba'. *E.hyemalis* has more delicate foliage and larger, white and rose-pink flowers; hybrids derived from it are available in several colours.

Eucharis

Amazon lily

Not a true lily, but a relative of hippeastrum, *Eucharis grandiflora* is a bulbous plant producing intriguing, narcissus-shaped flowers in summer. They are heavily fragrant, white with pale-green centres, and up to 12.5cm (5in) across. The leaves are also impressive: evergreen, shiny and broadly strap shaped.

Cultivation

It is a demanding plant in terms of environment, needing a minimum winter temperature of 13°C (55°F), with 23-25°C (75-80°F) and maximum humidity in the growing season. Pot up the bulbs, 6 to a 25cm (10in) pot, and do not cover completely until growth starts. Grow in John Innes potting compost No. 2, with a bit of peat and sharp sand added. Water generously and feed weekly in spring and summer, and water sparingly the rest of the year.

Eucharis can reach a height of 60cm (24in) when in flower and can be increased by offsets that are produced at the base of the bulb. Though summer is the main season of flowering, blooms may be carried nearly all year round.

Eucomis

Pineapple Flower

These large-scale bulbous plants are members of the lily family and produce tightly packed spikes of small, starry flowers in summer. The common name comes from the curious tufts of leaf-like bracts that are carried – pineapple-fashion – above the flowers. The true leaves are strap shaped and attractively arching, and form a basal rosette from which the flower spike grows.

Cultivation

Plant the bulbs singly in spring, in pots of John Innes potting compost No. 2, with the tops of the bulbs visible above the surface of the compost. Provide a minimum temperature of 5°C (40°F). Water lightly until new growth appears, then increase watering and once growth is well under way, water generously and feed fortnightly. Provide bright light, but shade from strong summer sunlight, and good ventilation.

After flowering is finished, gradually decrease the amount of water given and allow the compost to become almost dry in winter. Re-pot in fresh compost in spring, when any bulbils produced at the base of the plant may be detached and potted up separately.

Types to choose

Eucomis bicolor reaches a height of 60cm (24in). Its leaves are wavy edged and its flowers are light green, edged in violet. *E.b.*'Alba' is a white-flowered form. *E.comosa* is a similar size, but has pointed, crimson-spotted leaves, and light-green flowers each with a dark-purple 'eye'.

Euphorbia splendens

Euphorbia

Poinsettia, Crown of Thorns

The genus *Euphorbia* is a huge one, including biennials and herbaceous perennials as well as succulents and shrubby plants. Only two are suitable flowering plants for conservatories; as their cultivation needs differ, it is best to treat them as separate entries.

Cultivation of Euphorbia pulcherrima

Euphorbia pulcherrima, or poinsettia, is a Christmas pot plant far too well known to need description. The 'flowers', though, are actually colourful bracts which surround the tiny, dull-green 'proper' flowers. Originally, plants with only red bracts were grown, but there are now named forms with pink or elegant, creamy-white bracts. Though the wild form reaches a height of 1.8m (6ft) or more, commercial growers have succeeded in producing dwarf strains that rarely exceed 45cm (18in) in height. Plants bought in 'flower' should be given bright light but shade from direct sunlight, a minimum temperature of 13°C (55°F) and a thorough soaking with water at room temperature whenever the leaves start to droop. No feeding is necessary. It is possible, but difficult, to produce new plants from cuttings taken in late spring. It is also possible to cut back flowered poinsettias and grow them on for a second year, but generally it is better to buy in new plants on a yearly basis.

Cultivation of Euphorbia milii

Euphorbia milii (*E.splendens*), or crown of thorns, is a sparsely leafed but densely spined shrub, up to 90cm (3ft) high, but usually much smaller as it is slow growing. The 'flowers', again colourful bracts surrounding the tiny flowers, can be red or yellow. They appear in spring and summer, though it may flower all year round in ideal conditions. Grow in John Innes potting compost No. 2 with grit added to improve drainage. Provide maximum light, a minimum temperature of 7°C (45°F) and a dry, well ventilated atmosphere. Water moderately when in flower, sparingly the rest of the year. Feed fortnightly in spring and summer. The plant's root system is relatively small and it can remain in the same pot for several years. When necessary, re-pot in spring.

All euphorbias exude a milky substance when pruned or damaged. This can cause skin irritation, and the plants should be handled with care.

Freesia

The great drawback with freesias is their long, narrow ungainly leaves, which give the plant a distinctly sloppy look. The flowers, though, are exquisite: fragrant, waxy, tubular blooms, single or double, in shades of white, pink, yellow, red, orange, mauve or purple. Given a bit of judicious support, in the form of twiggy sticks inserted among the leaves and flowers, or an outer 'cage' of twine and canes, freesias can be made presentable.

Cultivation

Plant the corms in summer, in John Innes potting compost No. 2, spacing them about 2.5cm (1in) apart. Water lightly and leave outdoors until mid-autumn, then bring them into the conservatory. Provide plenty of light and a minimum temperature of 7°C (45°F); cool or warm, rather than hot, growing conditions suit them. Water moderately and, once the flower buds appear, feed fortnightly.

After flowering, decrease watering and gradually allow the bulbs to dry off completely. Re-pot in fresh compost the following autumn and treat as above. For a long season of display, from late winter through spring, prepare several pots and bring them into the conservatory at fortnightly intervals. (Remember to keep those for later displays cool but frost free.)

Fuchsia

Some fuchsias are perfectly hardy and can be grown outdoors all year round, but many are tender and enjoy the protection that a slightly heated conservatory can offer. In fact, conservatories are ideal environments, as tender fuchsias dislike the hot dry atmosphere of a centrally heated room as much as they dislike extreme cold.

Cultivation

Provide bright light, but some shading and maximum ventilation in the hot summer months. Use John Innes potting compost No. 2 or a peat-based compost. Water generously and feed weekly in the growing season; provide high humidity in high temperatures. Water sparingly in autumn and winter, and provide a minimum winter temperature of 5°C (40°F). In spring, re-pot in fresh compost, cut back by about a third, increase water and provide slightly warmer growing conditions to bring on new growth.

Fuchsias can be kept for many years, but they can also be easily propagated from cuttings taken in autumn and over wintered at 10°C (50°F), or taken from the new growth produced in spring. Cuttings 7.5cm (3in) long should be stripped of their bottom leaves, inserted in a mixture of peat and coarse sand, watered lightly and placed in a warm, semi-shaded spot. For best results enclose the cuttings and pot in clear polythene to keep the leaves from wilting or place them in a propagator. Once new growth appears, pot them up as above, and pinch out the growing tips to encourage bushy plants.

Types to choose

There are innumerable named forms of fuchsia, all with nodding, bell-shaped flowers. Colours include white, pink, cerise, purple, red, magenta, scarlet, lavender and orange; the flowers can be single coloured or bicoloured, with contrasting sepals and corolla. The leaves of most fuchsias are a rather dull green, but there are variegated-leaved forms, with yellow, white, cream and pink markings.

In the open ground, fuchsias can reach a height and spread of 1.5m (5ft) or more; containerized in a conservatory, they rarely exceed 60cm (2ft). In addition to shrubby fuchsias, there are standards and half standards available and trailing forms suitable for hanging baskets. There are also dwarf fuchsias, 30cm (12in) or less in height. All fuchsias flower in summer and autumn, though the season can be extended in both directions, if the plants are given additional artificial heat.

Fuchsia 'Royal Velvet'

Gardenia

Cape Jasmine

A gardenia in flower is a tempting plant to buy, but a difficult plant to keep healthy and flowering once you get it home.

Cultivation

Gardenias need bright light, but shade from direct sunlight, a winter temperature of 10-16°C (50-60°F) and a temperature no higher than 24°C (75°F) the rest of the year. Temperatures higher or lower than this, or sudden changes in temperature, will cause the flower buds to drop off, as will a dry atmosphere. Watering is equally tricky. Do not water unless the surface of the compost appears dry or the plant is wilting, but never allow the compost to dry out completely; water less frequently in winter than the rest of the year. Grow in a lime-free or peat-based compost; gardenias are lime haters, and, ideally, should be watered with rainwater.

Feed fortnightly during the growing season, especially when the buds are forming. Yellowed leaves are usually

Gloriosa rothschildiana

due to lack of iron (try applying chelated iron) or overwatering (allow the soil to dry out before watering again). Pruning, if necessary, can be done after flowering; pinching out the growing tips will help keep plants bushy.

Types to choose

There are many named forms of *Gardenia jasminoides,* all with attractive, shiny, evergreen leaves and a height and spread, when container grown, of under 60cm (24in). The large, waxy white flowers may be double or semi-double, and usually appear in summer.

Gerbera

Barberton Daisy, Transvaal Daisy

The brilliantly coloured, large, daisy-like flowers of this perennial plant are produced in summer. Grown as pot plants in a conservatory, they provide longer-lasting pleasure.

Cultivation

Grow in John Innes potting compost No. 2, and provide a minimum winter temperature of 5°C (40°F). Gerberas need bright light, but plenty of ventilation and shade from direct sunlight in the hottest summer months. Water moderately and feed fortnightly in the growing season; water sparingly the rest of the year. The plants, which can reach a height and spread of 45cm (18in), are available in flower, but they can also be grown from seed, usually sold as mixed colours. Mature plants can be divided into several smaller plants in spring.

Types to choose

There are forms of *Gerbera jamesonii* with single or semi-double, white, pink, yellow, salmon, orange, red or violet flowers. These are long lasting, and are often sold as cut flowers in florists' shops.

Gloriosa

Glory Lily

Definitely a tricky plant, *Gloriosa rothschildiana,* glory lily, rewards the determined and successful grower with exotic-looking red and yellow flowers, like Turks'-cap lilies, in summer. It is a deciduous perennial climber, reaching 1.8m (6ft) or more in a season, but dying back completely in autumn.

Cultivation

In early spring, plant the tubers in large pots of John Innes potting compost No. 2, and provide a minimum temperature of 16°C (60°F). Water sparingly until new growth appears, then water generously and feed weekly. Provide high humidity in high temperatures. After flowering, when the stems begin to wither, gradually withhold water and store the tubers over winter, at 10°C (50°F) or thereabouts. Provide support for the stems, in the form of wires, trellis work or canes.

Haemanthus

Blood Lily

The common name refers to the blood-red flowers of one of the species of this South African bulbous plant, but there are others with white or salmon-orange flowers. The flowers, most of which are curious rather than beautiful, appear in summer or early autumn. The individual, star-shaped flowers are tiny, but are carried in large, round umbels, often with showy stamens or petal-like bracts. The thick leaves are oval or lance-shaped; some are evergreen, others die down for part of the year.

Cultivation

Provide a winter temperature of 10-13°C (50-55°F) and bright sunlight. Plant the large bulbs, with their necks exposed, in relatively small pots of John Innes potting compost No. 2. Feed fortnightly and water moderately in spring and summer. Gradually dry off deciduous species once the leaves turn yellow, after flowering, and resume watering when the flower spikes start to appear. Water evergreen species sparingly in winter. Haemanthus flowers best when pot bound. Those species that produce offsets can be easily propagated by removing the offsets and planting them up separately in spring.

Types to choose

The flowers of *Haemanthus albiflos* look like an old-fashioned shaving brush, white with a tinge of green. Its evergreen, 30cm (12in) high leaves grow in pairs from the bulb, older, outer pairs dying as newer pairs are formed. The blood lily, *H.coccineus,* is much the same size, but its leaves are deciduous and its flowers and bracts, red. Huge heads of salmon-orange flowers are produced by *H.katharinae* on 45-60cm (18-24in) high stems.

Hedychium

Ginger Lily, Butterfly Lily, Garland Flower

These herbaceous perennials, with their tall spikes of orchid-like flowers in summer, are far more exotic looking than the treatment they require.

Cultivation

Provide full sun, a large pot or small tub filled with John Innes potting compost No. 3, and a winter temperature of

Hedychium gardnerianum

Hibiscus rosa-sinensis

7-10°C (45-50°F). Water generously and feed fortnightly in spring and summer; water sparingly the rest of the year. In late autumn, cut the stems back to just above the surface of the compost. New stems will form in spring.

Types to choose

There are several species available, all with large, lance-shaped leaves and a height and spread of 90-150cm (3-5ft). *Hedychium coccineum* has dark-pink flowers; *H.coronarium* has fragrant white flowers; *H.flavum* has fragrant yellow flowers and *H.gardnerianum* has yellow flowers with red stamens.

Hibiscus

Rose Mallow, Rose of China

This glossy-leaved shrub puts on a dramatic display in summer, when the tips of the branches carry wide, trumpet-shaped flowers up to 13cm (5in) across. Grown in a tub, hibiscus can reach a height and spread of 1.8m (6ft) or more, but small hibiscus flower profusely and can add a splash of colour to staging.

Cultivation

Provide maximum light but some protection from strong summer sun, 10-13°C (50-55°F) in winter, and good ventilation, particularly in warm weather. Grow in John Innes potting compost No. 3. Water moderately and feed fortnightly in spring and summer; water sparingly the rest of the year. Though evergreen in tropical environments, the plant may shed its leaves in winter. In spring, cut plants back by up to half, if necessary.

Types to choose

The ordinary form of *Hibiscus rosa-sinensis* produces single crimson flowers, but there are varieties available with white, yellow, pink, orange and scarlet flowers, in single or double forms. *H.r.s.*'Cooperi' has prettily variegated leaves.

Hippeastrum

Amaryllis, Barbados lily

Among the most spectacular of flowering bulbs for the conservatory, hippeastrums are readily available in flower or as dried bulbs, and are easily cultivated.

Cultivation

Plant the bulb in John Innes potting compost No. 2, with the top half of the bulb exposed. Provide as much direct light as possible, and a temperature of 10-18°C (50-65°F). Water lightly until new growth is visible, then gradually increase watering. Water generously and feed fortnightly in the growing season, then stop feeding and decrease watering towards the end of summer. Rest the dried-off bulb until new growth appears, then treat as above.

Hippeastrums resent root disturbance, and should be left for several years before being re-potted in fresh compost at the beginning of the growing season. Offsets, which are freely produced, can be carefully detached then, and potted up separately.

Types to choose

Hippeastrums available commercially are hybrids, with complex parentage. Their huge, trumpet-shaped blooms may be white, pink, scarlet, red or bicoloured, and are carried in twos, threes or fours on thick stalks up to 60cm (24in) high. Hippeastrums flower

Hippeastrum

in late winter or early spring, usually before the large, arching, strap-shaped leaves, but occasionally both appear together. The leaves continue to grow after the flower stalk dies, until autumn, when the bulb becomes dormant for three months or so.

Hoya

Wax Flower

The waxy, star-shaped flowers give these climbing or trailing plants their common name.

Cultivation

Provide full sun, a minimum winter temperature of 10°C (50°F) and a very well drained growing medium, such as John Innes potting compost No. 2 with peat and a bit of coarse sand added. Water moderately and feed fortnightly during spring and summer; water sparingly the rest of the year. Hoyas flower on spurs on which previous year's flowers were produced, so try to leave these spurs intact when removing faded flowers or pruning. Pruning is not usually necessary.

Types to choose

There are two hoyas useful for the conservatory. The more common is *H.carnosa*, a quick-growing climber which can reach 6m (20ft) or more if grown in a large pot and provided with trellis-work or wires around which to twine. If space is short, the thin stems can also be tied to a circular wire framework or to three bamboo canes, arranged in a tripod.

The clusters of long-lasting flowers are produced freely in summer; these are intensely fragrant, and are light pink or white, with a red 'eye'. The thick oval evergreen leaves appear in pairs along the stems; there are variegated forms available, which tend to be weaker growing than the species.

Hoya bella is a much smaller scale, bushier plant, suitable for hanging baskets or small pots. It has dainty, pointed leaves and small clusters of white, crimson-centred flowers.

Hyacinthus

Hyacinth

With their sturdy stalks topped with fragrant, bell-shaped flowers, hyacinths are great favourites for forcing indoors or under glass, from Christmas onwards.

Cultivation

Bulbs are available in autumn for potting up; those that have been specially prepared will flower earlier than untreated ones. In either case, set bulbs a pencil's thickness apart, and plant one colour to each pot, in shallow containers filled with John Innes potting compost No. 1. Hyacinths in flower are very heavy and special bulb fibre or peat-based composts are unlikely to support the weight. Leave the upper surface of the bulbs exposed. Treat as for crocuses (see page 67), bringing them into the conservatory once the shoots are 5-8cm (2-3in) tall, and keeping the temperature cool but frost free. As with crocus, harden off and plant outdoors after flowering, as they cannot be forced again indoors.

Types to choose

Most popular are the Dutch hyacinths, hybrids of *Hyacinthus orientalis.* They produce tightly packed flower spikes, 15-23cm (6-9in) high, one to each bulb, in shades of white, yellow, pink, red, or blue. Smaller and more graceful are the Roman hyacinths, *H.orientalis albulus*, with several flower spikes to each bulb, consisting of fewer, less tightly packed, flowers in pink, blue or white.

Hoya carnosa

Hydrangea

Hydrangeas are often sold as flowering pot plants in spring but, as with heather pot plants, their days indoors are inevitably numbered.

Cultivation

A cool, well ventilated conservatory, with a temperature of 7-10°C (45-50°F), and bright but indirect light suits them best. Water generously and feed fortnightly while the plant is in flower – six weeks or more – then gradually diminish the amount of water given. Remove the faded flowers and plant out permanently in a sunny, sheltered spot in the garden or discard.

Types to choose

Hydrangea macrophylla 'Hortensia' can be white, pink, red, blue or purple; the colour depends very much on the acidity of the growing medium; blue flowers need acid conditions to remain blue, and will turn pink in alkaline conditions. There are special 'blueing agents' available for maintaining blue flowers, but these are normally used for hydrangeas grown as permanent planting in the garden. Varieties in the *H.m.*'Hortensia' group all have mop headed flowers.

Hymenocallis
Spider Lily, Basket Flower, Peruvian Daffodil

These bulbous plants, related to hippeastrum, produce exquisitely graceful white flowers in spring and summer. They are heavily scented, with central trumpets surrounded by slender outer petals, and are carried above the arching, strap-shaped leaves.

Cultivation

Provide bright light but shade from direct summer sunlight, a minimum winter temperature of 16°C (60°F), and high humidity in high temperatures. Plant the bulbs in John Innes potting compost No. 2 with coarse sand added; the tops of the bulbs should be visible above the surface of the compost. Water generously and feed weekly in spring and summer; water sparingly the rest of the year. The plants resent root disturbance and should only be re-potted every three or four years in spring, when offsets can be detached from the base of the bulb.

Types to choose

There are several species, but one of the easiest is *Hymenocallis narcissiflora* (formerly *H.calathina*), 30-60cm (1-2ft) high, with pale green centred flowers. Altogether larger, with leaves up to 90cm (3ft) long, is *H.littoralis* (formerly *H.americana*), with exotic-looking, pure white flowers; it is slightly more difficult, and requires more space to grow well.

Impatiens
Busy Lizzie

Impatiens gets its common name from the fact that it never seems to stop flowering, from early summer to the autumn. Though technically a tender perennial, it is usually treated as an annual and discarded at the end of the flowering season, when it starts to get leggy and sparse looking.

Cultivation

Provide a minimum temperature of 10°C (50°F) and bright light, but some protection from strong sunlight. Use John Innes potting compost No. 1 or a peat-based compost, and 12.5cm (5in) pots or hanging baskets. Water generously and feed fortnightly when in full growth, and provide high humidity in hot conditions.

Impatiens can be grown from seed, but they root very easily from cuttings – even in water. Pot rooted cuttings up as described above, pinching out their growing tips to encourage compact, bushy growth.

Impatiens 'Ringmaster'

Types to choose

Most forms available are hybrids of *Impatiens walleriana* (formerly *I.holstii* and *I.sultani*). All make bushy plants with pointed, oval leaves and flat, long-spurred flowers. The range of colours includes white, pink, orange, scarlet, crimson and purple; there are bicoloured forms available, splashed with white, and double forms as well as the more usual single flowers. Recent additions to the impatiens scene include forms with green, yellow and red-variegated leaves and red-bronze leaves. Heights and spreads range from 15-60cm (6-24in), according to the form chosen and its growing conditions.

Jasminum
Jasmine

These semi-evergreen, twining or rambling shrubs are exceptionally good value for money and for space. They provide sweetly scented, small, trumpet-shaped flowers from winter to the summer, and require little in the way of specialist care.

Cultivation

Provide plenty of light, and only enough artificial heat to keep the frost off in winter. Use John Innes potting compost No. 3. Water moderately and feed fortnightly in the growing period; water sparingly the rest of the year.

Types to choose

Jasminum mesneyi (*J.primulinum*) is sometimes called primrose jasmine, because of its semi-double, primrose-like flowers in spring and summer. It is a rambling plant that can quickly reach a height of 4.6m (15ft) if grown in a large tub. *J.polyanthum*, Chinese jasmine, is the more familiar, white-flowered climber than can grow to twice that height. It produces its flowers, sometimes tinged pink, in winter and spring, at a welcome time of the year for flowers in the conservatory.

Both of these jasmines can be trained up wire or trellis-work supports, and both should be pruned back hard after flowering. They can also be grown as small pot plants, supported by canes or a wire framework.

Kalanchoe

There are many kalanchoes, most of which are grown for their succulent foliage. One, *K.blossfeldiana*, is grown for its long-lasting, starry flowers, carried in tightly packed clusters in winter and spring. Though technically perennial, it is usually treated as an annual, bought in flower and discarded once flowering is over.

Cultivation

Provide maximum light, a minimum temperature of 7°C (45°F) and water moderately, allowing the compost to dry out a bit between waterings. Feed fortnightly.

Types to choose

There are several named forms, all with

Kalanchoe blossfeldiana 'Red Glow'

glossy, round, thick leaves. *Kalanchoe blossfeldiana* 'Tom Thumb', 15cm (6in) high, has red flowers and bronze-red leaves; *K.b.*'Vulcan' is similar, but with green leaves. A good yellow-flowered form is 'Morning Sun'; it reaches 38cm (15in) in height.

Lachenalia

Cape Cowslip

Equally good in pots or hanging baskets, these unusual members of the lily family produce attractive, strap-shaped leaves followed, in spring, by tall spikes of tubular flowers.

Cultivation

Plant several bulbs, a pencil's thickness apart, in containers of John Innes potting compost No. 2, with a bit of added peat, in late summer. The tips of the bulbs should be just beneath the surface of the compost. Water well, then provide maximum light and ventilation, and a temperature of 7-13°C (45-55°F). Once new growth is visible, begin watering moderately; when growth is well under way, gradually increase watering and feed fortnightly.

After flowering is over, reverse the process, decreasing the watering until the leaves have died down, when watering should cease completely. Ideally, place the pot in a sunny spot outdoors for the summer, to ripen the bulbs. Re-pot in fresh compost towards the end of summer, as described above.

Lachenalias can easily be propagated then, by detaching the small bulbils from the base of the bulbs and potting them up separately.

Types to choose

There are many species and named forms of lachenalia, though you may have to get them from a specialist nursery. *Lachenalia aloides* 'Aurea', with yellow-orange flowers, and *L.a.*'Nelsonii', with green and yellow flowers, are good choices; both grow 25-30cm (10-12in) tall. Much smaller is *L.glaucina*, an unusual, blue-flowered form, with a height of 15cm (6in); it is sometimes called the opal lachenalia.

Lapageria

Chilean Bellflower

The huge, waxy, pink bell-shaped flowers of this semi-hardy twining plant appear in summer and autumn, and a large, well grown specimen can make a stunning display, trained up wires or trellis-work. The thin stems, with their leathery, evergreen leaves, can reach 4.6m (15ft) or more. If space is short, train the stems around bamboo canes or a circular wire framework.

Cultivation

Provide maximum light with some shade from direct sunlight in spring and summer, plenty of ventilation, and a winter temperature of 7-10°C (45-50°F). Lapagerias are lime haters, and need well drained, lime-free growing medium. Feed fortnightly and water generously during the growing season; water moderately the rest of the year. Pruning is not usually necessary.

Types to choose

Lapageria rosea has rosy-crimson flowers and there is a rare, white-flowered form, *L.r.*'Albiflora'. In recent years, new colour forms, including cream and pink have been introduced.

Lapageria rosea

Lantana

Yellow Sage, Common Lantana

Though *Lantana camara* is often seen in summer bedding schemes outdoors, this semi-evergreen shrub is equally useful in the conservatory, where it will flower profusely for months on end. The small, fragrant flower clusters can be white, yellow, orange, pink or red, according to the form chosen, and the flowers tend to darken – even change colour – as they age.

Cultivation

Though lantanas can reach a height and spread of 1.8m (6ft) or more, when grown in small containers and kept compact by pruning and pinching out the growing tips, they will make small shrubs, about 45cm (18in) high. Provide a winter temperature of 10°C (50°F), higher the rest of the year, maximum sunlight, and a humid atmosphere in the summer months. Water generously and feed fortnightly during spring and summer; water sparingly the rest of the year. John Innes potting compost No. 3 is most suitable.

To keep mature bushes compact and free flowering, cut them back to within 15-20cm (6-8in) of the base in spring. A spell outdoors in the summer, in a sunny, sheltered spot, ripens the wood and further encourages flowering.

Lantana camara

Lilium

Lily

There are several semi-hardy, and a few perfectly hardy, lilies that are suitable for conservatory cultivation.

Cultivation

Bulbs are available in autumn or spring. Plant them as soon as possible, either singly in 15cm (6in) pots or 3 in a 23cm (9in) pot of John Innes potting compost No. 2, with leafmould and coarse sand added. Most of the suitable lilies are stem rooting, so set the bulbs half-way down the pot when planting; as the stems grow, gradually add more compost to encourage rooting, until the compost is about 2.5cm (1in) from the top of the pot. Newly planted bulbs should be watered sparingly; those planted in autumn should be overwintered in a dark, cool but frost-free spot.

In spring, when growth appears, raise the level of the compost and gradually expose to brighter, well ventilated and warmer conditions: 7-10°C (45-50°F) is ideal. Keep continually moist, feed fortnightly once the flower buds are visible, and shade from very strong sunlight. After flowering, gradually decrease watering and, once the stem withers, dry off the compost completely. Re-pot in fresh compost the following autumn, when tiny bulbils that have formed at the base of the bulbs can be detached and potted up separately.

Types to choose

Among the most suitable lilies for conservatory cultivation are *Lilium auratum*, the golden ray lily, with 1.5-1.8cm (5-6ft) high stems carrying several sweetly scented flowers, each with gold banding and tiny red spots on the petals. The form *L.a.*'Rubrum' has dark-pink banding, and *L.a.*'Tom Thumb' is a dwarf form, ony 45cm (18in) high.

The madonna lily (*L.candidum*) is not stem rooting, and so needs shallower planting. Its 1.2m (4ft) stem carries several, trumpet-shaped, fragrant white flowers. Unlike the other recommended lilies, the madonna lily does not die down completely after flowering, but produces a low rosette of leaves which remain over the winter. Water sparingly when dormant.

The Easter lily (*L.longiflorum*) is so called because it is often forced for spring flowering; its normal flowering time, like that of other lilies, is summer. The Easter lily reached a height of 90cm (3ft) and produces fragrant, pure white trumpet-shaped flowers.

The Japanese lily (*L.speciosum*) has flowers with reflexed, or turned back, petals on 1.2-1.5m (4-5ft) high stems. The flowers are white, heavily shaded and spotted with pink, and there are many named forms with pure white, crimson, or dark-red flowers.

The many Mid-Century hybrids (derived from *L.tigrinum*, the tiger lily, and *L.* × *hollandicum*, or candlestick lily) also make suitable conservatory plants. Ranging in height from 60cm-1.2m (2-4ft), they include the lemon yellow 'Destiny', the maroon 'Cinnebar' and the bright-red 'Firecracker'.

Mutisia

Climbing gazania

This is a rare climber, worth growing for its large, daisy-like flowers in summer.

The plants are evergreen, and climb by means of tendrils that grow from the leaf tips and twine round supports.

Cultivation

Provide plenty of light but shade from direct sunlight in summer, and give just enough artificial heat in winter to keep the frost off. Water freely and feed fortnightly in the growing season, and provide ventilation in high temperatures. Water sparingly the rest of the year. John Innes potting compost No. 3 is suitable.

Types to choose

Mutisia decurrens grows to 3m (10ft) and has orange flowers, 10cm (4in) or more in diameter; *M.oligodon* grows to half that height and has pale pink flowers. Both need some form of support around which to climb. Too vigorous for all but the largest conservatories is *M.clematis*, which can reach a height of 6m (20ft) or more; its bright-scarlet flowers are slightly pendulous.

Myrtus

Myrtle

Though myrtle can be safely grown outdoors in sunny, sheltered gardens, it makes a pleasing shrub for the cool conservatory. Its glossy, pointed, evergreen leaves are aromatic, and in summer it carries single white flowers with prominent stamens. The shrub can grow to 4.6m (15ft) high, but can easily be confined to a height of 90cm (3ft) or less.

Cultivation

Grow in pots of John Innes potting compost No. 2, provide maximum sunlight and a cool winter temperature, 5-7°C (40-45°F) being ideal. Water generously, ventilate freely and feed fortnightly in spring and summer; water sparingly the rest of the year. A spell outdoors in summer, in a sunny, sheltered spot, helps ripen the wood and so encourages flowering. Pruning is not usually necessary; specimens grown in relatively small pots will remain small.

Types to choose

There is a double-flowered form, *Myrtus communis* 'Flore Pleno'. *M.c.*'Variegata' has leaves edged in creamy white. For small conservatories, *M.c.*'Microphylla' is the best form. It is small scale, in leaf, flower and height.

Narcissus

Daffodil

Daffodils are a familiar sight in the garden in spring, but they can also be forced in a cool conservatory, where they will flower from late winter to the spring, according to the type chosen and preparation given.

Cultivation

Plant the bulbs (one type to a container) as early as possible in autumn, in shallow containers filled with John Innes potting compost No. 1 or special bulb fibre. Containers lacking drainage holes should be well crocked first, with a layer of pebbles or broken flower pots.

Plant the bulbs so that they are almost touching, and their upper surfaces are visible above the compost or fibre. Water lightly, then place in a dark, cool but frost-free spot, ideally outdoors under a layer of ashes, sand or peat. Keep just moist and when about 5cm (2in) of growth is visible, transfer to a cool, dimly lit spot in the conservatory. Gradually increase watering and exposure to light as growth gets under way. The cooler the temperature the better; 5-7°C (40-45°F) is ideal, with maximum ventilation and light as they come into flower. After flowering, the plants can be hardened off and then naturalized in the garden, as they cannot be forced again.

Types to choose

There are five main types of narcissus, 30-45cm (12-18in) high, suitable for conservatories. Some can be bought specially prepared for forcing, which means that they can be started in cool light conditions, as opposed to cool, dark ones. Trumpet narcissi are typically 'daffodil-shaped'. Good forms include the yellow 'Dutch Master' and creamy white 'Mount Hood'.

Large-cupped narcissi have wide, cup-shaped and rather shallow trumpets, often with ruffled edges. Good forms include 'Fortune', with yellow petals and an orange-red cup, and the pale-yellow 'Carlton'.

Small-cupped narcissi have very shallow cups (technically less than 1/3 the length of the petals), and include 'La Riante', with pale-yellow petals and a dark-orange cup, and the all-white 'Polar Ice'.

Double narcissi include the creamy-white 'Cheerfulness', 'Yellow Cheerfulness', a yellow form of the former, and the yellow and orange 'Texas'. Lastly there are the very popular 'Tazetta' narcissi, which have masses of small, fragrant flowers on each stem, such as 'Paper White' and 'Grand Soleil d'Or'.

Nerine

Guernsey Lily

This slightly tender bulb produces its clusters of deep-pink, trumpet-shaped flowers in autumn, when the conservatory might otherwise be sadly lacking in flowers. The strap-shaped leaves appear after the flowers, and remain until they die down the following summer. There are many named forms available, with white, pale pink, red or bicoloured flowers.

Nerium oleander, double-flowered form.

Cultivation

Nerines should be grown in pots of John Innes potting compost No. 2; make sure the neck of the bulb shows above the surface of the compost. As soon as the flower buds start to appear, water regularly but moderately, allowing the compost almost to dry out between waterings. Feed fortnightly once the leaves appear and continue feeding until they start to turn yellow, then gradually diminish the supply of water and allow the pots to dry out until the flower buds appear again. Full light is necessary for the production of flowers, and a winter temperature of 10°C (50°F) or thereabouts.

Types to choose

Although the Guernsey Lily, *Nerine sarniensis*, and it hardier relative, *N.bowdenii*, are the most common members of this genus, there are many other species and cultivars of nerine available from specialist nurseries.

Nerium

Oleander, Rose Bay

Nerium is an old-fashioned shrub, good for filling a large corner in a conservatory. In the wild, nerium can reach tree-like proportions; grown in a container, it may eventually make an upright shrub, 1.8m (6ft) or more high. The long, evergreen, lance-shaped leaves are carried in groups of three, and clusters of single or double, rose-like flowers are carried on the tips of the stems in summer.

Cultivation

Neriums are nearly hardy, requiring full sun and a winter temperature of 7-10°C (45-50°F). Water generously and feed fortnightly in spring and summer; keep barely moist the rest of the year. John Innes potting compost No. 2 or No. 3 is suitable. Provide plenty of ventilation, and standing the pot outside during the summer months in a sheltered, sunny spot helps ripen the wood and encourage flowering. To keep the plant bushy, pinch out the growing tips (being careful not to pinch out the flower buds) and cut the stems back by half after flowering has finished.

Neriums are very easy to propagate, and cuttings will root in a jar of water. All parts of the plant are poisonous.

Types to choose

The flowers are often a deep pink, but there are forms with white, pale pink, red, yellow or purple flowers, and one form, *Nerium oleander* 'Variegata', with cream and green variegated leaves and pink flowers. Some, but not all, neriums are scented; forms sold as *N.odoratum* are usually scented.

Passiflora

Passion Flower

The complicated and exotic-looking structure of the flowers of this rampant climber are said to represent the passion of Christ. The ten white petals and sepals symbolize the Apostles who witnessed the event; the central ring of purple filaments symbolize the crown of thorns; the five yellow anthers symbolize Christ's wounds, and the three central stigmas, the nails.

Cultivation

In spite of the exotic appearance of the flowers, the plant itself is quite tough, and is grown outdoors in mild, sheltered gardens. In a conservatory, provide bright light, good ventilation and just enough winter heat to keep the frost off – 7-10°C (45-50°F) is sufficient.

Grow in a large pot or tub filled with John Innes potting compost No. 3. Water generously and feed fortnightly during spring and summer; water sparingly the rest of the year.

Passion flower clings by means of tendrils, so provide strong trellis-work or wires; it is an ideal plant to train up a conservatory wall and along the roof space. If space is limited, train the stems along wire hoops. Pruning, if necessary, should be done in early spring. Thin out weak or overcrowded shoots and cut back long side shoots to within 15cm (6in) of the main stems.

Types to choose

Besides the common passion flower, *Passiflora caerula,* there is a white-flowered form, *P.c.*'Constance Elliott'. For the specialist, there are even more exotic-looking passion flowers: *P.edulis*, the purple granadilla; *P.quadrangularis*, the granadilla, and *P.mollissima*, the banana passion flower. All produce fruit in ideal conditions.

Pelargonium

Geranium

These well loved shrubs are grown as summer bedding and house plants.

Cultivation

They are also ideally suited to a conservatory with a minimum temperature of 10°C (50°F). Provide full sun, though in the hottest summer months, some shading may be necessary. Grow in small pots of John Innes potting compost No. 2; these plants flower best in pot-bound conditions. Water moderately and feed fortnightly in spring and summer, water sparingly the rest of the year. A dry, well ventilated atmosphere is advisable.

Geraniums are easily propagated by 8cm (3in) tip cuttings taken in spring, summer or autumn. Remove the lower leaves and insert the cuttings around the edge of a small pot filled with a mixture of equal parts peat and sand. Water lightly, provide bright, indirect light and once new growth appears, pinch out the growing tip to encourage side shoots to form.

Types to choose

Most geraniums grown today are of complex parentage, but they can be divided into four main groups: *P.hortorum*, or zonal geraniums; *P.domesticum*, or regal geraniums; *P.peltatum*, or ivy-leaved geraniums; and scented-leaved geraniums, of several species and cultivars.

Zonal geraniums, so called because of the attractive zonal markings on their leaves, can reach a height of 1.2m (4ft) or more, and, with patience, can be trained as standards. They flower continuously over many months, and may flower all year round in ideal growing conditions.

Regal geraniums have larger, showier flowers than the zonals, but they flower only in summer, after which a rest period of several weeks, with minimal watering, is necessary. The leaves, too, are duller-looking than those of many zonals, and regals tend to be harder to grow well. Their usual height and spread is 30-60cm (1-2ft), but if conservatory space is limited, zonals are a better choice in terms of longer-lasting colour and ease of cultivation.

The ivy-leaved geraniums (*P.peltatum*) are trailing plants, up to 90cm (3ft) long, that can be tied to wires to trellis-work, or grown in hanging baskets. Spring is the main season of display, but the occasional flower is produced for several months after that. Handle the stems with care, as they break easily. The leaves are shiny, ivy-like, and sometimes, attractively variegated. Geraniums produce flowers in colours ranging from white, pink, salmon, scarlet, rose, lavender, crimson and deep purple black, and there are bicoloured forms available.

Scented-leaved geraniums produce flowers but these are tiny and of far less value than their attractively scented leaves, which may smell of mint, lemon, rose, cinnamon or nutmeg. They are generally rather upright growing, to a height of 90cm (3ft).

Pelargonium regale

Plumbago

Cape Leadwort

Plumbago is a semi-evergreen, semi-climbing shrub that can reach a height of 4.6m (15ft) or more, if given the support of trellis-work or wires; otherwise, it can be grown as a smaller, rather floppy, shrub.

Cultivation

Provide plumbagos with as much light as possible and, ideally, a winter temperature of 10°C (50°F). Grow in John Innes potting compost No. 3. Feed fortnightly and water generously in the growing season; water sparingly the rest of the year. To encourage flowering, prune hard in spring, cutting back the long stems by half to two-thirds.

Types to choose

From spring to the autumn, *Plumbago auriculata* produces clusters of light-blue, primrose-like flowers on short side shoots all along the current year's stems. There is a white-flowered form, *P.a.*'Alba', available.

Primula

Primrose

Tender primroses start flowering in late winter, providing welcome colour in the conservatory at an otherwise dull time of year.

Cultivation

Provide maximum light and cool, well

ventilated growing conditions; 7-13°C (40-55°F) is ideal. Water generously and feed fortnightly when in flower. After flowering, the plants are usually discarded, although *Primula obconica* and *P.sinensis* can be grown on for another year. To do this, keep the plants cool (but frost free) and water sparingly after flowering, then move to a cool, shady spot in the garden. Before the first frost, re-pot in fresh compost (John Innes potting compost No. 2 or a peat-based compost), remove any dead foliage and bring the plants into the conservatory. Increase watering and begin feeding as new growth appears.

Types to choose

There are hundreds of species of *Primula*, but there are four main types sold as indoor plants, and all are grown annually from seed sown in spring. *Primula obconica* hybrids are extremely popular. Umbels of large pink, white, blue or crimson, single flowers are carried on stems up to 30cm (12in) high. It is a relatively tough and uncomplaining plant, and will flower from winter until late spring, occasionally longer. The leaves and stems, though, are covered with small hairs that can cause skin irritation with some people.

Primula malacoides, or fairy primrose, hybrids are equally popular. They have whorls of star-like flowers, in shades of pink, red, white, lilac or purple, on stems up to 45cm (18in) high. They usually flower from winter through to mid-spring.

Primula sinensis originated from China, as did the previous two species, but it alone is referred to as the Chinese primrose. Its leaves and stems, up to 30cm (12in) high, are fleshy. Whorls of large, single flowers, often with a contrasting central 'eye' are produced in the typical primrose colours: pink, mauve, white, red, lavender, and also bright orange.

The least showy, but the only fragrant, indoor primula is *P. × kewensis*, a hybrid originating from The Royal Botanic Gardens, Kew. The small yellow flowers are produced in whorls on a stem up to 30cm (12in) high.

Punica

Pomegranate

Though the red, many-seeded fruits of this large shrub are unlikely to develop and ripen in a conservatory, pomegranate is worth growing for its showy, scarlet, tubular flowers in summer and autumn.

Azalea indica (Rhododendron)

Cultivation

Provide a bright, sunny spot and a cool winter temperature, about 10°C (50°F) or slightly lower, for the plant's dormancy. It is not evergreen; the glossy, lance-shaped leaves turn yellow before they fall in autumn. Keep on the dry side in autumn and winter; water generously, ventilate freely and feed fortnightly in the growing period. Grow in a large pot or tub of John Innes potting compost No. 2. Though pomegranates can make small trees, containerized specimens do not often reach a height of 1.8m (6ft). Pruning is rarely necessary.

Types to choose

There are several named varieties of *Punica granatum*, *P.g.*'Alba Plena' has double white flowers; *P.g.*'Chico' is a compact, sterile form with double scarlet flowers, and *P.g.*'Nana' is a miniature form, which may eventually reach 90cm (3ft) in height, and may produce small orange fruit in hot conditions.

Rhododendron

Most familiar are the so-called 'Indian azaleas': small evergreen pot plants with pink, white or red flowers, sold in vast quantities in winter and spring. The genus *Rhododendron* is a huge and sometimes unwieldy one: these 'Indian azaleas', or '*Azalea indica*', are more correctly *Rhododendron simsii* hybrids, and are Chinese, not Indian, in origin.

Cultivation

Whatever these azaleas are called, they almost always come to grief in the hot, dry environment of a centrally heated home. In a cool conservatory, with a temperature of 5-16°C (40-60°F), they are far more likely to thrive, and can be kept to flower in subsequent years. Buy plants in bud, with colour showing, and place in bright but indirect light. Watering can be tricky: too much water and the plant rots, too little and the plant collapses. The plants are grown in peat-based compost, which dries out very quickly, adding to the problem. Keep the compost steadily moist but not soggy, using lime-free water (rainwater is ideal) at room temperature. High humidity, especially in warmer temperatures, is essential, as is good ventilation all year round.

After flowering, reduce watering slightly and keep cool but frost free. In late spring or early summer, move the plant outdoors into a sheltered, semi-shaded spot. Bury the pot up to its rim in the ground, increase watering and feed fortnightly. In hot weather spray the foliage and in autumn, before the first frost, return it to a cool greenhouse. Keep cool and slightly drier until the flower buds start to swell, then treat as above. Re-potting, which is necessary every three or four years, should be done after flowering, using a lime-free mixture of peat, leafmould and coarse sand or ericaceous compost.

Types to choose

As well as *Rhododendron simsii* hybrids, which carry trusses of up to six flowers, the true *R.indicum* is occasionally available. This, too, is called 'Indian azalea', though it is actually Japanese in origin, and carries its flowers singly or in pairs, in late spring and early summer. Treat it as above.

Sometimes hardy rhododendrons are offered as pot plants. These include *R.edgeworthii*, formerly *R.bullatum*, with glossy, wrinkled leaves and fragrant white or blush-pink flowers in spring. Unlike the 'Indian azaleas', which rarely exceed 38cm (15in) in height in a conservatory, *R.edgeworthii*, if grown in a large pot, may reach a height of 1.2m (4ft) or more.

'Kurume azaleas', largely hybrids of *R.kaempferi* and *R.kiusianum*, can be brought into flower in the conservatory, then moved outdoors, either permanently, or for the summer months. There are dozens of named forms, all making low-spreading bushes which flower in late spring.

Rosa 'Wee man' miniature variety

Rosa

Miniature Rose

Miniature roses are of complex parentage, but largely based on *Rosa* 'Rouletii', a dwarf form of China rose. Because miniature roses are suitable for edging, window boxes, bedding schemes and small gardens generally, as well as for conservatories, they are immensely popular, and there are many named forms.

Cultivation

The key to successful, long-term cultivation in a conservatory is to provide climatic conditions similar to those in the garden. Miniature roses need maximum ventilation, bright light and high humidity in very high temperatures. They are deciduous plants and also need a dormant winter period, with low temperatures. Ideally, stand the pots outdoors towards the end of autumn, and return them to the conservatory in early spring. Avoid sudden transitions, though; gradually acclimatize the plant to its new conditions, indoors or out.

Grow in pots of John Innes potting compost No. 2. Water moderately and feed fortnightly during the growing season; water sparingly the rest of the year. To encourage flowering, prune back by up to half in early spring, and remove faded flowers regularly.

Types to choose

Miniature roses are usually sold in bush form, 23-45cm (9-18in) high, but there are also miniature climbers, to 1.5m (5ft) high, for training up wires or trelliswork, and miniature standards, grown on short, single stems. All flower over a long season, from spring through to autumn (depending on the conservatory's temperature). The flowers come in the typical range of rose colours, and can be single, semi-double or double.

African Violet

Saintpaulia

Immensely popular as a house plant, African violet can be difficult to grow in well lit conservatories.

Cultivation

In the wild, it is a tropical, shade-loving plant. In a conservatory, it needs light but never exposure to direct sunlight, or disfigured leaves and flowers result. Growing African violets in the light shade produced by larger plants might be one solution. Their temperature requirements are as fixed and demanding as their requirements for light: a steady temperature of 18-23°C (65-75°F), though winter temperatures can safely drop to 13°C (55°F). High and constant humidity is essential.

Watering is tricky, too. The slightly fleshy leaves and flowers are prone to rotting, as is the small, shallow root system. On the other hand, the compost must never be allowed to dry out completely. Water moderately, avoiding splashing water on the plants; at lower temperatures, allow the compost to dry out partially between waterings. Feed fortnightly, except in the winter months. African violets are slow growing, and seem to flower best when pot bound, so re-potting should not be necessary for the first two or three years after purchasing. When re-potting, use a peat-based compost, or a mixture of equal parts peat, leafmould, coarse sand and vermiculite. Use relatively small pots; trailing forms can be displayed to advantage in hanging baskets.

African violets can easily be propagated by leaf cuttings. Insert individual leaves, with their stalks still attached, into a jar of water or a small pot filled with a mixture of peat and sand. Keep lightly shaded and watered, and warm; new plantlets will form at the base of each leaf.

Types to choose

Most African violets commercially available are hybrids developed largely from *Saintpaulia ionantha.* Most form rosettes of leaves, though the trailing form bears alternate leaves along the stems. The yellow-centred flowers can be single or double, occasionally ruffled, and violet, white, lavender, pink, rose, blue or red. Some have bicoloured flowers and others have variegated leaves. The plants are usually 10-13cm (4-5in) tall, twice that in diameter, but there are miniature forms available. As the number of named forms is almost endless, it is pointless to list a small selection here. For the keen grower, there are specialist nurseries which offer hundreds of forms.

Saxifraga

Saxifrage, Mother of Thousands, Strawberry Geranium

Though the white, star-shaped flowers of *Saxifraga stolonifera,* carried in summer, are attractive, the main feature of this old-fashioned and popular plant is its production of many tiny plantlets. These are formed on the ends of thin red runners, like those of strawberries, and make the plant an excellent choice for a small hanging basket, or for trailing over the edge of staging. The plantlets are miniature versions of their parent: stemless rosettes of round, green and white slightly hairy leaves with deep-pink undersides.

Cultivation

This saxifrage is grown outdoors in mild districts; in a conservatory, provide direct sunlight for a small part of the day (especially for the variegated form) but light shade as a whole. Keep the plants at 7-10°C (40-50°F) during the winter months, with normal, unheated conservatory temperatures the rest of the year. Grow in John Innes potting compost No. 2. Water generously and feed fortnightly in spring and summer; water sparingly in autumn and winter.

Propagation could not be easier: either pot the plantlets up while still attached to the parent and cut the runner once roots have formed, or detach the plantlet and root it in a peat-based compost.

Types to choose

There is a variegated form, *S.s.*'Tricolour' with creamy white and pink leaf markings; it is slower-growing and smaller than the species, which can eventually reach a height and spread of 45cm (18in) and produce runners 90cm (3ft) long.

Schizanthus

Butterfly Flower, Poor Man's Orchid

This is a tender but easy-to-grow annual with masses of orchid-like blooms in late winter or spring. The flowers, which are carried above the light-green, ferny leaves, can be in shades of yellow, apricot, pink, red or purple, with gold markings. They are occasionally offered as plants in bud, but it is easy – and economical – to grow them from seed.

Cultivation

Sow in pots or trays, outdoors, in summer. Pot them on singly into John Innes potting compost No. 2, keep well watered and pinch out the growing tips to promote bushiness. Pot on until 15cm (6in) pots are used. Ideally, a cold frame is the best environment at this stage, but a sunny, sheltered spot will also be suitable.

In mid-autumn, bring the pots into the conservatory, which should be kept well ventilated and cool, but frost free; 7°C (45°F) or slightly higher. Provide bright light, a regular supply of water and canes or twiggy sticks for support. Once the flower buds show, the heat can be safely raised to 16°C (60°F), but it is not necessary. After flowering, discard the plants.

Types to choose

Schizanthus commercially available are hybrids, and plants can range in height from compact, dwarf forms, 30cm (12in) high, to giant strains 90-120cm (3-4ft) high, according to the seed strain which is chosen.

Senecio

Cineraria

Cineraria's huge heads of colourful, daisy-like flowers are a welcome sight in late winter or spring. Because they prefer cool, bright conditions – a winter temperature of 7°C (45°F) is ideal – they are perfect plants for the slightly heated conservatory.

Cultivation

Although technically perennials, cinerarias are treated as biennials or annuals by commercial growers, and are best discarded after flowering. Correct watering is important: too dry, and the plants collapse, never to recover or, if they do, with considerably shortened flowering period; too wet, and they succumb to rotting. Keep the compost moist but not waterlogged, and keep the conservatory well ventilated, provided conditions outside are not frosty. Those that flower later, in spring, appreciate a bit of shade from direct sunlight.

Types to choose

Cinerarias are hybrids, varying in height from 30-75cm (12-30in). All have large, rather ordinary-looking leaves, and flowers that range in colour from pink, rose, red, blue, mauve and purple, with white central markings, to single colours.

Sinningia

Gloxinia

The clusters of large, velvety, trumpet-shaped flowers and large, equally velvety leaves makes this Victorian plant a firm favourite. Sinningia is tuberous rooted, flowering in late spring and summer, and is still often known as – and sold as – 'gloxinia', its former botanical name.

Cultivation

Sinningias need a minimum temperature of 16°C (60°F), and higher when in bloom. Pot up the tubers in late winter, in a mixture of equal parts, by volume, of John Innes potting compost No. 2, peat and coarse sand. Use 12.5-cm (5-in) pots and set the tuber in the compost so the top of the tuber is visible. For a longer season of display, pot up the tubers at fortnightly intervals. Water sparingly, provide a temperature of 18°C (65°F) and increase watering once growth gets underway. The leaves are hairy, and water can mark them, so water carefully.

In warmer temperatures, high humidity is beneficial (but do not spray the leaves directly), and shade from strong sunlight. Feed weekly from the time that the flower buds appear until the leaves start to turn yellow, when flowering has finished. When this happens, gradually reduce watering, then dry the tuber off completely, removing any shrivelled-up leaves. Store the dormant tuber in its pot until the following late winter, then start into growth as above.

Types to choose

By far the most popular sinningias are hybrids of *S.speciosa*, with a height and spread of up to 30cm (12in). The flowers, which can be single or double, are available in shades of red, blue, violet, pink and white, and there are forms spotted or edged in a second, contrasting colour. There are also dwarf sinningias available, hybrids of *S.pusilla*, 2.5-8cm (1-3in) high. These can be in flower and leaf all year round, without a winter rest period. Nevertheless, they should be watered less generously in autumn and winter. Feed with weak-strength fertilizer fortnightly throughout the year.

Solanum

Jerusalem Cherry, Potato Vine

As with capsicums, the flowers of Jerusalem cherry (or winter cherry) are insignificant, but its fruit is showy and colourful. Bright orange or scarlet, the round berries are carried on small, rather ordinary-looking evergreen bushes, with a height and spread of 30-45cm (12-18in). The berries start green, then gradually ripen to their final colour.

Cultivation

In the conservatory, provide coolish conditions – 10-16°C (50-60°F) is ideal – and as much light as possible. Water generously and feed fortnightly in the growing season, and keep the atmosphere humid in higher temperatures. Grow on in J.I. potting compost No. 2.

Above, *Solanum capsicastrum*

Below, *Sinningia* (Gloxinia)

Once the berries have fallen off, the plants are usually discarded, but they can be kept to fruit a second year. Cut them back hard, water sparingly for a month or so, then place them outdoors in a sheltered, frost-free, sunny spot until the following autumn.

Types to choose

There are two species offered for sale: *S.capsicastrum* (false Jerusalem cherry) and *S.pseudocapsicum*. Both are much the same, though the latter is slightly more vigorous, with larger, longer-lasting berries. There are also compact forms of *S.pseudocapsicum* available, with large berries carried on tiny shrubs.

Much more a collector's plant, the potato vine or jasmine nightshade (*S.jasminoides*) is a strong growing, evergreen twining shrub, to 4.6m (15ft). Its pretty, pale-blue, star-shaped flowers have bright-yellow centres and are carried in summer and autumn. Provide similar growing conditions to the Jerusalem cherry, and support in the form of wires or trellis-work. There is a white-flowered form available.

Strelitzia regina

Spathiphyllum

White Sails, Spathe Flower

These tropical evergreen perennial plants are for a warm conservatory only, with a minimum winter temperature of 13°C (55°F) and as much heat and humidity as possible in the summer months. The glossy, green lance-shaped leaves are attractive, and the tiny flowers, which grow on spikes surrounded by white, sail-like spathes, appear in spring and summer.

Cultivation

Grow in John Innes potting compost No. 2, feed fortnightly and water generously in spring and summer. In autumn and winter, water moderately, or sparingly if the temperature nears 13°C (55°F), and feed every six weeks.

Types to choose

There are two forms commonly available: *S.wallisii* and the hybrid *S.* × 'Mauna Loa'. The former is smaller, reaching a height of 30cm (12in); the latter can be twice as tall and has correspondingly larger leaves and spathes.

Spathiphyllum wallisii

Stephanotis

Madagascar Jasmine, Wax Flower

Though the fragrant white flowers of this evergreen climber look like a waxy version of jasmine, *Stephanotis floribunda* is a tropical plant requiring much more cosseting to thrive and produce its flowers each spring.

Cultivation

The ideal temperature is 18-20°C (65-70°F), though it will survive slightly cooler conditions in winter. Above all, avoid sudden changes in temperatures. At higher temperatures, provide high humidity, misting daily if necessary. Large specimens can be trained up wires or trellis-work and along the roof of the conservatory; the stems of smaller plants can be trained up canes or around a circular wire frame. In either case, make sure the plant is exposed to bright but indirect light. Grow in John Innes potting compost No. 2. Feed fortnightly and water generously in spring and summer; water sparingly the rest of the year.

Strelitzia

Bird of Paradise

A popular plant in Victorian times, strelitzia is not everyone's idea of beauty. Its exotic, crested, bird-like flower heads are fascinating, with their orange and blue flowers emerging from a long, green bract in spring and summer. In spite of its unusual appearance and rarity, strelitzia is relatively easy to grow and is worth trying if you have the room and want an impressive, 'architectural' effect.

Cultivation

Provide as much light as possible, and a winter temperature of 13-15°C (55-60°F) for the plant's dormant period. Water moderately and feed fortnightly in the growing season; keep on the dry side the rest of the year. Grow in John Innes potting compost No. 3 and, to encourage flowering, keep pot bound.

Types to choose
Strelitzia regina is a clump-forming, evergreen perennial suitable for large pots or tubs; confined in this way, it may grow to a height and spread of 1.2m (4ft), though it grows much larger in the wild. Its thick, oval leaves are carried attractively on long stalks, as are the flower heads.

Streptocarpus

Cape Primrose
The most popular of these old-fashioned, perennial, summer-flowering plants are hybrids, with rosettes of leaves (rather like those of primrose) and funnel-shaped flowers on graceful stems.

Cultivation
Provide a minimum winter temperature of 10°C (50°F), higher the rest of the year and with generous ventilation and humidity in the summer months. Although streptocarpus needs light, it also needs protection from strong, direct sunlight, especially in the summer. Grow in John Innes potting compost No. 2, water generously and feed fortnightly in spring and summer; water sparingly the rest of the year.

Streptocarpus are easy and interesting to propagate by means of leaf cuttings. In spring, detach a healthy leaf, cut it crossways into 2.5cm (1in) sections, and partially insert the sections, base-end down, in a peat-based compost. Water lightly, cover with a pane of glass or clear plastic. Keep warm and slightly shaded; in a month or two, small, new plants will have formed at the base of each leaf section and can be potted up separately.

Types to choose
Most streptocarpus hybrids have a height and spread of about 30cm (12in). Named forms include the extremely common *S.*'Constance Nymph', with clear-blue flowers; *S.*'Wiesmoor Hybrids', with ruffled flowers ranging from white through red and purple; and *S.*'John Innes', long flowering and in a mixed colour range.

Tibouchina

Glory Bush, Spider Flower
The large, rich-blue flowers of this tropical shrub have prominent stamens, shaped like the legs of a spider, hence its common name. Clusters of flowers are produced on the ends of the branches, from mid-summer to the late autumn, making *Tibouchina urvilleana* a valuable conservatory plant.

Cultivation
Provide bright light, but some protection from fierce summer sun, and a minimum winter temperature of 10°C (50°F). In spring and summer, the higher the temperature, the better, though high humidity and good ventilation are also necessary then. Water generously and feed fortnightly in the growing season; water sparingly the rest of the year. John Innes potting compost No. 3 is suitable.

The size of the plant depends very much on pruning and growing conditions. Given a large pot or tub, tibouchina can reach a height of 4.6m (15ft) or more, and can be trained up the conservatory wall and along the roof. Grown in a small pot and pruned hard in spring, it can be kept to a height of 90-120cm (3-4ft).

Trachelospermum

Chinese jasmine
Though this evergreen climber can be grown outdoors in mild localities, it is a good plant for the cool conservatory. Its dark, shiny pointed leaves are attractive all year round, and in summer it produces heavily fragrant, white, jasmine-like flowers.

Streptocarpus 'Tina'

Cultivation
Chinese jasmine is slow growing, eventually reaching a height of 4.6m (15ft) or more, though it can be kept to more modest proportions by pruning in spring. Provide wires or trellis-work around which it can twine, and grow in John Innes potting compost No. 3, with leafmould added. Water moderately and feed fortnightly in spring and summer; water sparingly the rest of the year. Chinese jasmine tolerates a few degrees of frost, but should be protected in the case of long, hard cold spells.

Types to choose
Trachelospermum jasminoides is the species and there are two attractive, but rare, cultivars: *T.j.*'Variegatum' has white leaf markings, tinted crimson in the winter; and *T.j.*'Wilsonii', has heavily veined, narrow leaves.

Tulipa

Tulip
The single and double, early-flowering tulips are the most suitable ones for growing in a cool conservatory, to flower from midwinter through to spring.

Cultivation
Pot the bulbs, almost touching, in shallow containers of John Innes potting compost No. 1, a peat-based compost or special bulb fibre, in autumn. The tops of the bulbs should be visible above the surface of the growing medium. Water

lightly, then keep cool (but frost free) and dark, ideally outdoors, under a layer of sand, peat or weathered ash.

When 5cm (2in) of growth is showing, bring the pots into the conservatory, gradually exposing them to warmer and brighter conditions, and gradually increasing the amount of water given. The flowers will last longest if the temperature does not exceed 10°C (50°F). Once flowering is over, harden off the bulbs and plant in the garden; start with fresh bulbs the following year.

Types to choose

The single earlies range in height from 25-60cm (10-24in) and have, typical, cup-shaped flowers in a wide colour range; some are bicoloured. Particularly good ones for forcing include the scarlet red 'Brilliant Star'; the white 'Diana'; the yellow 'Bellona' and the deep purple 'Van der Neer'.

Double earlies look rather like paeonies, and tend to be slightly shorter growing. Good forms include the bright-red 'Electra'; the deep-pink 'Peach Blossom' and the rich-yellow 'Hytuna'.

Vallota

Scarborough Lily

Vallotas, with their evergreen, strap-shaped leaves and scarlet, trumpet-shaped flowers in summer, look rather like scaled-down hippeastrums. (Both are members of the *Amaryllidaceae* family.)

Cultivation

Vallotas need maximum sunlight, a winter temperature of around 13°C (55°F), and reasonable warmth the rest of the year. In spring, plant the bulbs, one to each 13cm (5in) pot and with their necks exposed, in John Innes potting compost No. 2. Water sparingly to start with, then gradually increase the amount of water given until, at the beginning of summer, you are watering generously. After flowering reverse the process, gradually giving less and less water and keep the bulbs nearly dry over winter. Feed every three or four weeks in the growing season.

Vallotas flower best when pot bound, and resent root disturbance. Large bulbs form offsets, which can easily be detached and planted up separately.

Types to choose

There are named forms of *Vallota speciosa* available with pink or white flowers. Like the ordinary form, the flowers are carried in clusters on stems up to 60cm (2ft) tall.

Zantedeschia rehmannii

Zantedeschia

Arum Lily, Calla Lily

Zantedeschias are moisture-loving, deciduous perennial plants grown for their elegant flower heads, composed of an upright, central spadix and curved spathe, carried on a graceful, long stalk. The leaves are large, shiny and arrow shaped, and the plant in full growth conveys a lush appearance.

Cultivation

Zantedeschias have a particular cycle of growth and dormancy, which should be followed if the plant is to flower in second and subsequent years. Provide bright light (direct or indirect) and a temperature of 10-21°C (50-70°F) during the growing season. Plant the thick rhizomes in autumn in large pots of John Innes potting compost No. 3, and water sparingly until growth appears. As the leaves and flowers develop, increase watering and feed fortnightly. When in full bloom, feed weekly and keep the compost thoroughly moist – zantedeschias are waterside plants in the wild.

After flowering, stop feeding and reduce the amount of water given. The leaves will yellow and die, and the pot should ideally be stood outdoors for the summer months, in a sunny, sheltered spot, with the compost kept dry. Bring indoors in autumn, water sparingly, and treat as above. Propagation is easily done by dividing the rhizomes when re-potting.

Types to choose

Zantedeschia aethiopica is the most commonly grown arum lily, and is often seen as a cut flower. It can reach a height of 90cm (3ft) and has white flowers in late winter and early spring. *Z.a.*'Crowborough' is the hardiest form, tolerant of lower temperatures. The yellow arum, *Z.elliottiana*, is a smaller species, with yellow flowers in late spring or early summer and attractive, white-spotted leaves. The pink arum, *Z.rehmannii* is smaller still, reaching a height of 30cm (12in); its flowers vary from pale pink to deep rose, and appear in late spring or early summer.

Foliage Plants

Many people tend to overlook the rich contribution that foliage makes to the success of a conservatory. Lush foliage creates a feeling of peacefulness, seclusion and natural coherence. It provides a perfect setting and background for flowers, but is equally capable of achieving perfection on its own without the presence of a single blossom. A conservatory filled entirely with flowers might easily border on the garish, while one that takes its cue from nature, predominantly furnished with foliage enlivened with flashes of colour, assumes a quite different, restful tone.

It is important to give green a chance. Give 'greens' a chance is perhaps more accurate, as there are many different shades of this colour, and the contrast of one green to another, of one leaf form with another, is the core of visual interest in a conservatory. When the range of greens is combined with the wide variations in leaf size and shape, and even surface texture – glossy leaves that reflect light like mirrors; velvety leaves; deeply crinkled or corrugated leaves – the creative possibilities are endless.

Brightly coloured leaves can be beautiful, but use them sparingly and do not let them blind you to the qualities other than colour that a leafy plant possesses – scented leaves, however modest looking, have particular delights to offer.

Because most plants have both flowers and leaves, however showy or insignificant, try to see them as a whole when assessing them initially. In terms of bulk, far more of a plant is leaves than flowers, and it takes a very exquisite flower indeed to compensate for accompanying, unattractive leaves.

All this is relevant if you see your conservatory in terms of interior design. You may, on the other hand, see your conservatory as a home for a passionate horticultural hobby – collecting members of a particular family, for example – and plant enthusiasts are not necessarily interested in plant displays. Neither attitude is more correct than the other. For success, both require an honest assessment of the amount of care you can give and the growing environment you have to offer.

Acorus

Grassy-leaved Sweet Flag, Japanese Sweet Flag

A hardy evergreen perennial, *Acorus gramineus* 'Variegatus' is usually grown outdoors, as a pond-side plant, but it makes an attractive and easy-going addition to a cool conservatory. Its narrow, grass-like leaves are striped dark green and white, and form clumps up to 30cm (12in) high. Its insignificant flowers are rarely produced.

Cultivation

Grow in John Innes potting compost No.2, in bright light or semi-shade. Keep the compost permanently moist. Placing the pot in a large outer container kept topped up with water is a good idea or, if you are lucky enough to have a pool in the conservatory, place the pot in shallow water. Feed monthly in spring and summer and propagate by division in spring.

Agave

Century Plant

The main problem with agaves is their ultimate size. A mature agave in the wild can have a diameter of 3.6m (12ft) or more, with a flower spike twice as high. Fortunately, these succulent, evergreen, rosette-forming perennials are very slow growing, and young specimens can be enjoyed for several years in a cool conservatory. Equally fortunately, most produce offshoots from the base, so that new, young, replacement plants are always available, should the parent plant become too large or die. (The main rosette dies after producing its flower spike but agaves rarely flower in conservatories.)

Cultivation

Grow in John Innes potting compost No.2, with peat and coarse sand added for improved drainage. Alternatively, use the special cacti and succulent compost that is available commercially. Provide maximum light and ventilation, and a minimum winter temperature of 7°C (45°F) during the plant's rest period. Water moderately and feed monthly in spring and summer; water very sparingly the rest of the year. Agaves benefit from a spell outdoors in the summer.

Types to choose

There are hundreds of species of agave, but the following are among the most suitable for conservatory cultivation.

Agave americana is called the century plant because of its reputation for taking 100 years to flower. In fact, ten-year-old plants can flower. Its loose rosette of thick, greeny-grey leaves can slowly reach a diameter of 90cm (3ft) or more. The leaves are thick, sharply pointed and edged in hooked spines, and have a slightly arching habit of growth. Variegated forms include *A.a.*'Marginata', with thin yellow leaf margins and *A.a.*'Medio-picta', with a wide yellow stripe down the middle of each leaf.

The thread agave, *A.filifera,* gets its common name from the thread-like fibres that hang from the edges and tips of the stiff, pointed leaves. It is a smaller scale plant altogether, rarely exceeding 30cm (1ft) in height.

Agave victoriae-reginae is smaller still, with a height of 15-20cm (6-8in). Its densely packed rosette is made of almost sculptured, spine-tipped leaves, edged and marked with white. It requires slightly higher winter temperatures than the other agaves mentioned, and does not form offsets.

Agave victoriae – reginae

Aglaonema

Chinese Evergreen, Spotted Evergreen, Painted Drop Tongue

These slow-growing evergreen plants are popular for their prettily variegated leaves. Being members of the arum family (*Araceae*), they carry small, arum-like flowers in summer, followed by a column of red berries, like those of the native 'lords and ladies' (*Arum maculatum*); the flowers and berries, though, are very much secondary attractions. Aglaonemas are perennial plants, but may, with age, develop tough, thick, almost woody, stems, which carry their leaves at the top of the plant.

Cultivation

Grow in John Innes potting compost No.2 or a peat-based compost. Provide a minimum temperature of 16°C (60°F) and bright but indirect light, with definite shade in summer. High humidity and good ventilation are essential. Water generously and feed fortnightly with dilute liquid fertilizer; water sparingly the rest of the year. Propagate by division in spring.

Types to choose
The dark-green, lance-shaped leaves of *Aglaonema commutatum* grow to a height of 30cm (12in) and have pale-grey markings along the veins. The form *A.c.*'Treubii', sometimes sold as *A.treubii*, is a smaller, denser version, with yellow and mid-green leaves.

The spotted evergreen, *A.costatum*, reaches a height of 15-20cm (6-8in), and has broad, fresh green leaves with a white midrib and white spots. Painted drop tongue, *A.crispum*, is the largest of this selection, reaching 90cm-1.2m (3-4ft) in height, with silver-grey and green leaves. The form *A.c.*'Silver Queen' is largely silver.

The Chinese evergreen, *A.modestum*, sometimes sold as *A.simplex*, is the most tolerant of the lot, but with rather plain, mid-green leaves. *A.m.*'Variegatum' is more attractive with yellow and green variegated leaves.

Ananas
Pineapple
These slow-growing terrestrial – as opposed to tree-dwelling – bromeliads are unlikely to bear full size, fully ripe pineapples in a conservatory. They are grown largely for their loose rosettes of variegated leaves, which may eventually reach a length of 1.5m (5ft) or more, but remain small for some years. If a central stalk is produced, with red bracts and small blue flowers followed by a tiny fruit, consider it an additional bonus.

Cultivation
In common with other bromeliads, pineapples have relatively small root systems and so need relatively small pots. Use a mixture of equal parts John Innes potting compost No.2, coarse sand and peat or leafmould, for extra drainage. Pineapples need maximum exposure to sunlight all year round, and a minimum temperature of 18°C (65°F), higher in summer. Continual high humidity is also necessary. Water generously and feed fortnightly in spring and summer; water moderately the rest of the year.

Offsets sometimes formed at a base of the rosette can be detached and potted up separately. Propagating new plants from the cut-off leafy tops of pineapples is easier said than done, with rot usually setting in before roots have formed. If you are determined to have a go, cut the rosette of leaves where it joins the flesh, allow it to dry for several days, then insert in damp, coarse sand. A minimum temperature of 27°C (80°F) is needed, and much luck.

Types to choose
Ananas bracteatus is the wild pineapple, represented commercially in its variegated form, *A.b.*'Striatus', with yellow-edged, green leaves, flushed with deep rosy pink.

Ananas comosus (formerly *A.sativus*), is the pineapple grown commercially for its fruit. It, too, is represented by a variegated form, *A.c.*'Variegatus', with creamy yellow margins to the sharply spined leaves.

Araucaria
Norfolk Island Pine
The genus *Araucaria* was much loved by the Victorians. Outdoors, monkey puzzles (*A.araucana*) were planted in great profusion; indoors in greenhouses, conservatories and living rooms, the Norfolk Island pine, *Araucaria heterophylla*, was grown. Though it can reach an eventual height of 60m (200ft) in its natural environment, in a conservatory the tree is slow growing and may, over many years, reach a height of 1.8m (6ft). Norfolk Island pine has an elegant, almost formal, appearance. Its branches are arranged in whorls of four, at right angles to each other; the branches are carried horizontally, and create a layered appearance as they radiate from the central trunk. (It is sometimes called the Christmas tree plant for this reason.) The needle-like, soft leaves are light green when young, becoming darker with age. The plant is occasionally still sold as *A.excelsa*, its former name.

Araucaria heterophylla

Cultivation
Grow in John Innes potting compost No.2. Provide bright light but some shade from fierce summer sunlight. Water moderately and feed fortnightly in spring and summer; water sparingly the rest of the year. The plant benefits from a spell outdoors in the garden for part of the summer; if it remains in the conservatory, provide maximum ventilation and humidity in high temperatures. A winter rest period is necessary, with a minimum temperature of 5°C (40°F).

Asparagus
Asparagus Fern
These are not ferns at all, but evergreen perennial members of the lily family. (Unlike true ferns, asparagus ferns produce tiny flowers, often followed by berries.) Nor are their delicate, lacy 'leaves' true leaves; botanically, they are phylloclades, or leaf-like branchlets. Asparagus are, however, tough, easy-going plants worth including in a conservatory. They can be grown in pots or hanging baskets, and some twining forms can be trained up wires or along trellis work.
Cultivation
Grow in John Innes potting compost No.2. Provide bright light but shade from direct sunlight in summer. Water generously and feed fortnightly in spring and summer; water sparingly the rest of the year. Provide a minimum temperature of 7°C (45°F). Large plants can be quickly and easily divided in spring. The plants can also be grown from seed, but it is a much slower process.
Types to choose
Asparagus densiflorus 'Sprengeri', or emerald feather, is the most widely available form. Its gracefully arching stems can grow to 1.5m (5ft) or more in length; the form *A.d.*'Sprengeri Nanus' is smaller. Both have bright-green, needle-shaped 'leaves' along the stems. The foxtail fern, *A.d.*'Meyers' (formerly *A.meyeri*), produces 60cm (24in) long plumes of delicate 'foliage'. The habit of growth is upright and unbranched, and its common name accurately indicates its appearance.

Often seen in cut flower arrangements, less often as a pot plant, is *Asparagus setaceus* (formerly *A.plumosus*), the florists' fern. As a young plant (and in the dwarf form *A.s.*'Nanus') it is erect growing and non-climbing. Older plants can climb to a height of 3m (10ft), and need wires or other form of support around which to twine. The feathery fronds, carried more or less horizontally on the slim, wiry branches, give the plant an airy, graceful appearance.

Harder to get hold of is *Asparagus falcatus*, which has woody, arching stems to 1.8m (6ft). The stems are armed with sharp thorns to help it hook onto other plants, which then provide support. The 'leaves' are long and thin, and shiny dark green. It is an elegant-looking plant, with a striking, 'architectural' presence.

Aspidistra
Cast Iron Plant
Another surprising member of the lily family, *Aspidistra elatior* gets its common name from its ability to withstand almost any amount of neglect and generally unfavourable growing conditions. And although neglected aspidistras are fairly depressing looking – dusty and comprised of a few, sparse leaves – a well grown specimen can be quite impressive. The evergreen leaves are shiny and lance-shaped, and grow on long stalks that are produced by the rhizomes, like large-scale lilies of the valley. Aspidistra's own flowers are tiny, browny-purple and carried at soil level. In time, an aspidistra can form a large clump, with leaves up to 60cm (24in) high. There is a variegated form available, *A.e.*'Variegata', with white stripes.
Cultivation
Grow in John Innes potting compost No.2. Provide a minimum temprature of 7°C (45°F) and bright but indirect light; fierce sunlight tends to scorch the leaves. Water moderately and feed monthly in spring and summer; water sparingly the rest of the year. Aspidistras don't like root disturbance and can stay for several years in the same pot. Re-pot, if necessary, every second or third year in March or April. Plants are easily propagated by division at this time. Give established plants not being potted on, a weak summer feed.

Aspidistra elatior

Begonia

This huge genus has been roughly divided into plants grown primarily for foliage and those grown primarily for flowers. In the section on flowering plants (see page 60) are tuberous-rooted and some fibrous-rooted begonias. Those covered here are some fibrous-rooted and the most popular rhizomatous-rooted begonias.

Cultivation

Grow in peat-based compost or John Innes potting compost No.2, with peat added for extra drainage. Provide bright light for good leaf colouring, but protection from exposure to direct sunlight. A minimum temperature of 13°C (55°F) is necessary, and high humidity in high temperatures. Water moderately and feed fortnightly in spring and summer; water sparingly the rest of the year.

Tall-growing plants that become leggy and leafless can be cut back hard in spring, and new plants propagated from cuttings taken from the prunings. Rhizomatous-rooted begonias can be propagated from leaf cuttings, an interesting and easy method. Place a young leaf, with its stalk attached and veins cut crossways in several places, in a pot or shallow tray filled with a damp mixture of peat and coarse sand. Make sure the leaf and stalk come into contact with the surface of the compost. Cover with clear polythene and keep warm and semi-shaded. Small plants will form on the leaf, and can be detached and potted up separately.

Types to choose

Fibrous-rooted begonias include the angel-wing begonia (*B.coccinea*); the metallic-leaf begonia (*B.metallica*); and the elephant ear begonia (*B.scharffii* or *B.haageana*). The angel-wing begonia is erect growing, to a height of 1.8m (6ft). Its glossy green leaves have red edges, and its red flowers are carried in winter. The metallic-leaf begonia reaches a height of 1.2m (4ft). Its red-veined, green leaves are covered in tiny, silvery white hairs and have a metallic sheen. Its pale-pink flowers are carried in summer and autumn. The elephant ear begonia, to 1.2m (4ft) high, has an accurately descriptive common name: its leaves are large, hairy and shaped rather like elephant's ears. Its pale-pink flowers appear during the summer months.

Rhizomatous-rooted begonias include the eyelash begonia (*B.boweri*); the beefsteak begonia (*B.* × *feastii*); *Begonia manicata*; the iron cross begonia (*B.masoniana*); and the painted-leaf begonia (*B.rex*).

Begonia rex

The eyelash begonia is a small-scale plant, to 20cm (8in) in height, with velvety, heart-shaped bright-green leaves, with delicate brown markings on the slightly hairy edges. Its small, pale-pink flowers are carried in spring. The unfortunately named beefsteak begonia is a similar height, but with larger, thick, glossy, rounded leaves, crimson underneath, and small pink flowers in winter. A particularly popular form is *B.* × *f.* 'Bunchii', with frilly leaf edges.

Begonia manicata, up to 45cm (18in) high, is identifiable by the ring of red scales that surround the top of each leaf stalk. Its large green leaves are edged in red, and its clusters of small pink flowers are carried in winter.

The iron-cross begonia is so called because of its cross-like markings, in deep brown, on its dull-green, hairy, heavily corrugated leaves. It reaches a height of 25cm (10in), and rarely comes into flower.

Begonia rex is perhaps the most well known of all the 'foliage' begonias. There are innumerable named and unnamed hybrids, – up to 60cm (2ft) in height. The asymmetrical, roughly heart-shaped leaves may be splashed, edged, spotted or veined in any of several colours or colour combinations: – silvery white, pink, red, pale or dark-green, purple and bronze. There are dwarf forms available, with pretty, scaled-down leaves.

Caladium

Angel's Wings, Elephant's Ears

These are very enticing tuberous-rooted perennial plants, with their large, arrow-shaped leaves in a wild mix of

Caladium x *hortulanum* variety

colours and patterns. Unfortunately, caladiums are very demanding in their requirements, and even if you manage to cultivate them successfully, they have a completely dormant period of nearly half the year. You can treat them as short-term plants, to be enjoyed for a brief period then discarded, or take up the longer-term challenge that this tropical plant presents.

Cultivation

Pot the tubers in spring, 2.5cm (1in) deep, in a peat-based compost. Provide a minimum temperature of 20°C (70°F) and water sparingly until growth appears, then gradually increase watering. When in full leaf, water generously and feed fortnightly. (Plants can be bought at this stage, in full display.) Caladiums have very thin leaves that shrivel in dry conditions, so provide steady, high humidity. For the same reason, they cannot be exposed to direct sunlight, though bright light is needed for the leaf colours – white, yellow, pink, crimson, red or green, in various combinations – to develop intensity.

In autumn, when the leaves start to wither, stop feeding and gradually decrease the amount of water given. Once the leaves have completely died down, store the tubers at a minimum temperature of 16°C (60°F) until spring, then re-pot in fresh compost and proceed as above.

Types to choose

Caladiums available today are hybrids sometimes still sold as *Caladium bicolor*, the species from which the hybrids were largely derived. There are unnamed and named forms. One of the most popular named form is *C.* × *hortulanum* 'Candidum', with pure-white leaves, edged and veined green.

Calathea

Peacock Plant, Cathedral Windows, Zebra Plant

The main point about calatheas is that they are tropical plants, and need tropical growing conditions if they are to survive, let alone show off their exquisitely patterned and 'painted' leaves.

Cultivation

A minimum temperature of 16°C (60°F), higher temperatures in summer and high humidity to match, are necessary. Grow in John Innes potting compost No.3, with extra peat added or use a peat-based compost. Feed weekly and water generously in spring and summer; water sparingly in winter. Provide shade from direct sunlight at all times, especially in summer. If the plants are happy, they are quick growing, and can easily be propagated by division in spring.

Types to choose

All calatheas are evergreen perennials that form clumps of oval, lance-shaped or round leaves, carried on graceful stems. The most popular is *Calathea makoyana*, the peacock plant or cathedral windows. The oval leaves grow to a height of up to 90cm (3ft). They are silvery green above, with dark-green lines, edging and blotches, like paint strokes radiating from the central vein. The leaf undersides are similarly patterned, but in brown-purple.

Calathea lancifolia, sometimes still sold as *C.insignis* its former name, has narrower, wavy-edged leaves, up to a length of 60cm (2ft). They are lance-shaped, light-green with dark-green oval markings radiating from the central vein. Large and small markings alternate down each side of the vein, giving the plant a hand-painted look. The leaf undersides are dark purple.

The zebra plant, *C.zebrina*, has soft leaves, marked in a chevron pattern with pale and deep green, and purple leaf undersides. It grows to 60cm (24in) or more in height.

Calathea zebrina

Ceropegia

Hearts Entangled, Rosary Vine

Ceropegia woodii is a graceful and delicate looking trailing plant, ideal for hanging baskets or pots displayed at high level. The wiry, purple-tinged stems can reach 90cm (3ft) in length or more, and are produced from rounded woody tubers. The heart-shaped succulent leaves are carried in pairs along the stems. The leaves are small and the spaces between the pairs relatively large. The leaf undersides are rich purple, and the upper surfaces are marbled grey-green and white. In summer, curious-looking, small white flowers appear, which are of little visual merit.

Cultivation

Plant the tubers in a mixture of equal parts of John Innes potting compost No.2 and coarse sand. The top half of the tuber should sit above the surface of the compost. Provide maximum light and a minimum winter temperature of 10°C (50°F). Water moderately and feed occasionally in Spring and Summer. Keep nearly dry the rest of the year.

Ceropegia is easily propagated from the tiny tubers produced, here and there, along the stems. Detach the tubers, lay them on the surface of the compost mixture (see above), and water lightly. Leave in a semi-shaded spot and once new growth appears, provide more light.

Chlorophytum

Spider Plant

This is a real beginner's plant, tolerant of wide variations in growing conditions and extreme neglect. However, as a thriving specimen is infinitely more attractive than one that is barely surviving, a little extra care is worthwhile. Chlorophytums carry insignificant flowers along long pale arching stems, followed by small plantlets at the tips of the stems. In due course, further flowering stems may appear from the plantlets, until the combined stems reach a length of 1.5m (5ft) or more. This makes chlorophytum ideal for hanging baskets. Alternatively, train the stems vertically, tying them to canes, wire or trellis-work.

Cultivation

Grow in John Innes potting compost No.2 and, for best colour contrast, provide bright light, with a bit of shade from fierce summer sun. Water generously in spring and summer, moderately the rest of the year. Provide a minimum winter temperature of 7°C (45°F). Chlorophytum can be propagated by division in spring, or by detaching plantlets and potting them up as above.

Types to choose

There are several named forms, all with thin, arching, strap-shaped leaves that grow from thick, tuberous roots and form, in time, substantial clumps. Most often seen is *Chlorophytum comosum* 'Vittatum', with creamy white, green-edged leaves. Rarer, but equally pretty, is *C.c.*'Variegatum', with reverse colouring: green, white-edged leaves. The leaves of *C.c.*'Picturatum' are striped yellow, as are those of *C.c.*'Mandaianum'. The latter is a dwarf form, with leaves up to 15cm (6in) high, compared to the 30-38cm (12-15in) height of other cultivars.

Cissus

Grape Ivy, Kangaroo Vine, Begonia Rex Vine

These quick-growing climbers are, on the whole, tolerant of a wide range of environments and even a certain amount of benign neglect. Most climb by means of tendrils and need canes, wires or trellis-work for support. In the wild, cissus can easily reach 6m (20ft) in height; confined to a pot and with the growing tips pinched out regularly, it can be kept to far smaller proportions and makes a suitable subject for a hanging basket.

Cultivation

Grow in John Innes potting compost No.2 or a peat-based compost. Provide bright light but shade from strong summer sunlight, a minimum temperature of 7°C (45°F), higher for *C.discolor* (see below), and high humidity in high temperatures. Water moderately and feed fortnightly in spring and summer; water sparingly the rest of the year. Leggy specimens can be pruned back hard in spring; new growth should quickly sprout.

Cissus antarctica

Types to choose

The well known and much grown kangaroo vine, *C.antarctica*, has large, glossy, heart-shaped leaves. Grape ivy or Venezuelan treebine, *C.rhombifolia* is often confused with *Rhoicissus rhomboidea* (see page 105). Both are similar in appearance, with glossy leaves made of three leaflets, but *C.rhombifolia* has forked tendrils while *Rhoicissus rhomboidea* has unforked tendrils. The miniature grape ivy, *C.striata*, is a more delicate-looking climber, each small leaf composed of five coppery-green leaflets, purple on the undersides.

The most temperamental species, and the most exotic looking, is *C.discolor*, or rex begonia vine. (It has nothing to do with begonias at all; like other cissus, it is a member of the grape family, *Vitaceae*.) Its elongated heart-shaped leaves are variegated silvery white, purple and green, with the veins and mid-ribs picked out in dark green, and red-purple undersides. It needs higher temperatures – a minimum of 16°C (60°F) – and sparing supplies of water if it is not to drop its leaves. High humidity is also necessary, as is protection from all direct sunlight.

Codiaeum

Croton

Either you like crotons or you don't. They are certainly striking, with their leaves splashed, spotted, marbled or veined with combinations of white, yellow, orange, pink, red, crimson, green and deep browny black. Many people consider them the aristocrats of variegated pot plants. On the other hand, their slightly upright habit of growth and shiny, leathery leaves, combined with their hectic colouring, give them an unnatural – almost plastic – look and, indeed, it is genuinely hard to tell a real croton from its plastic counterpart.

Cultivation

If your taste does run to crotons, grow them in a peat-based mix, or John Innes potting compost No.3. Provide maximum light to intensify their contrasting colours, though some shade is necessary in summer. High humidity and a minimum temperature of 16°C (60°F) are needed; fluctuations in temperature are likely to result in a loss of lower leaves. Water generously and feed fortnightly in the growing season; water sparingly the rest of the year. If a croton becomes leggy or outgrows its allotted space, prune back hard in spring.

Types to choose

Crotons available commercially are named or unnamed forms of *Codiaeum variegatum pictum*. In ideal conditions, the woody shrubs may eventually reach a height of 3m (10ft) or more, though they usually remain much smaller. The evergreen leaves can be long and narrow, variously indented, rounded or pointed and oval, or even contorted and twisted, according to the form chosen.

Coleus

Flame Nettle, Painted Nettle

These cheerful, short-term plants have roughly nettle-shaped leaves in a vivid range of colours and colour combinations. Though technically perennials, coleus are usually treated as annuals, for spring and summer display, then discarded at the end of the season.

Cultivation

Grow in John Innes potting compost No.2. Provide maximum light and a minimum temperature of 10°C (50°F). In high temperatures, high humidity is beneficial, as the plants are prone to wilting and dropping lower leaves in dry conditions. Water generously in the growing season, and feed fortnightly. If you want to over-winter coleus, cut them back hard and keep almost dry until the following spring, then increase watering and proceed as above.

Coleus are easily propagated from cuttings, which will form roots in a jar of water. Once rooted, pot up and pinch out the growing tips at frequent intervals to make the plant bushy. Established plants also benefit from regular pinching out. Any flower buds that form should be removed.

Types to choose

Coleus range in height and spread from 15-60cm (6-24in), according to the strain chosen. 'Old Lace' is a particularly attractive tall form, with ruffled, deeply divided leaves. The 'Dragon' strain has serrated leaves, and the 'Carefree' strain has scalloped leaves. The usual colour range includes white, orange, red, purple, green, brown, pink and yellow.

A word of warning. Simply because of this wide range of intense colouring, a large-scale display of coleus can look overwhelming and confused, rather than attractive. A bit of self control, either in the scale of the display or the range of colours grown, is advisable.

Cordyline

Cabbage Palm, Blue Dracaena, Ti Tree

Cordylines are slow-growing, evergreen trees of considerable height in the wild. Young specimens make good conservatory plants. Most combine a tough constitution with an extremely lush and tropical appearance.

Above, Mixed *Coleus*

Cultivation

Grow in John Innes potting compost No.2 or a peat-based compost. *Cordyline australis* and *C.indivisa* are nearly hardy and need a lowish winter temperature, 5-10°C (40-50°F). Provide maximum sunlight and ventilation, and give them a spell outdoors in the summer, if possible. The 'odd man out' in this genus is *Cordyline terminalis*. It needs a minimum temperature of 13° (55°F), high humidity and shade from summer sun. All should be watered generously in spring and summer, sparingly the rest of the year. Mature plants produce clusters of small white flowers in summer, followed by berries. Conservatory-grown cordylines rarely reach flowering stage.

Types to choose

The New Zealand cabbage tree, *Cordyline australis*, reaches a height of 1.8m (6ft) as a pot plant. Its single stem produces a loose rosette of narrow, arching leaves, up to 90cm (3ft) in

Below, *Cyperus alternifolius*

length. The form *C.a.*'Atropurpurea' has a purple tinge to the leaves.

Similar in structure and size is *C.indivisa*. Its sword-shaped leaves are larger scale, ultimately reaching a length of 1.2m (4ft) or more, and wider than *C.australis*. The form *C.i.*'Rubra' has red-flushed leaves.

The tree of heaven, or ti tree, *Cordyline terminalis*, is quite different in appearance from the other species. Its broad, sword-shaped leaves are tinged with crimson, pink, purple and bronze; they lack the noticeable rosette formation of the other cordylines. In a conservatory, it is unlikely to exceed 90cm (3ft) in height. There are several named forms, all with particular variegations; one of the most popular is the red-leaved *C.t.*'Firebrand'.

Cyperus

Umbrella Plant, Papyrus

Among the very few plants that thrive in waterlogged conditions, cyperus are elegant, evergreen, and grass-like perennials.

Cultivation

Provide a minimum temperature of 13°C (55°F) and bright light. Grow in John Innes potting compost No.2, and keep thoroughly wet all year round. It is a good idea to stand the pots in a large waterproof container kept topped up with water. Feed fortnightly in spring and summer.

They are quick-growing plants, and can be propagated by division in spring.

If you are lucky enough to have a pool in your conservatory, these plants would be suitable subjects to grow with their pots submerged in the water.

Types to choose

Cyperus alternifolius, or umbrella plant, gets its common name from its appearance: tall stems with leaf-like bracts radiating, like the ribs of an umbrella, from the top. Reaching a height of 90cm (3ft) or more, it carries small brownish flowers in summer. The form *C.a.*'Variegatus' has white-striped leaves, and *C.a.*'Gracilis' is a dwarf form. Umbrella plants can be propagated from their leafy flower heads as well as by division. Detach a 'head', with 2.5cm (1in) of stalk attached. Trim the leaf bracts back, then invert the 'head' in a shallow dish of water. When roots develop, pot up as above; a new plantlet will soon appear.

For large conservatories there is *Cyperus papyrus*, or papyrus, which can reach a height of 3m (10ft). It is a more demanding plant, in terms of humidity and heat as well as space. The tall stems are topped with dense, floppy tufts of pale-green 'threads', each ending in a tiny flower.

Dieffenbachia

Dumb Cane

These handsome evergreen perennials have a poisonous sap which, if taken into the mouth, renders its victim speechless (and quite ill!) for several days, hence its common name. Dieffenbachias can reach a height of 1.8m (6ft) or more, but are slow growing and remain small for some years. The variegated oval, sometimes pointed, leaves grow from fleshy stems which elongate and thicken as they age. With age, too, the lower leaves are shed, giving the plant a tufted, almost tree-like appearance.

Cultivation

Grow in John Innes potting compost No.2 or a peat-based compost. Provide bright but indirect light, with quite definite shading in the summer months, a minimum temperature of 16°C (60°F) and high humidity. Water moderately all year round; feed fortnightly in spring and summer.

Dieffenbachia maculata 'Superba'

Types to choose

The giant dumb cane, *Dieffenbachia amoena*, has dark green leaves up to 45cm (18in) long, with white markings along the veins. *D.maculata* (formerly *D.picta*), the spotted dumb cane, is less vigorous, with leaves up to 25cm (10in) long. Its oval, dark-green leaves are randomly spotted and splashed with white. Among the many popular named forms are *D.m.*'Rudolph Roehrs', with pale, yellow-green leaves, veined in dark green, and *D.m.*'Exotica', with creamy-white leaves, margined and veined in green.

Dizygotheca

False Aralia

The specific name *elegantissima* – most elegant – correctly describes the delicate and graceful appearance of this tropical shrub when young. Its coppery green leaves are composed of up to ten long, thin leaflets, arranged rather like the ribs of an umbrella from the central leaf stalk. Each leaflet is heavily indented and droops slightly, thus adding to the feeling of delicacy.

Cultivation

Grow in John Innes potting compost No.2 or a peat-based compost. Provide bright but indirect light and a minimum temperature of 16°C (60°F), with accompanying high humidity. Water moderately and feed fortnightly in the growing season; water sparingly during the rest of the year.

Young plants are available from a height of 30cm (12in) or thereabouts. Dizygothecas are slow growing but may eventually make small trees. Unfortunately, as the age they lose much of their charm (like the ugly duckling in reverse): their lower leaves tend to drop off, revealing a poker-straight central stem, and those leaves that remain become coarse and a dull, dark green. Pinching out the growing points regularly does help, and drastically pruned specimens will send up new growth, but a young replacement is usually the best solution.

Eriobotrya

Loquat, Japanese Medlar

Hardier than many people realize, *Eriobotrya japonica* is a handsome shrub which can be grown outdoors in mild areas, but it is also an unusual and impressive plant for a cool conservatory. Its evergreen leaves are glossy, toothed and up to 30 cm (12in) long, rather like huge versions of sweet chestnut leaves. The young leaves have a silvery sheen and are felted pale brown on the undersides. Though the loquat is grown commercially in warmer countries for its edible yellow fruit, neither these, nor its fragrant white flowers, are likely to be produced in a conservatory.

Cultivation

Grow in John Innes potting compost No.2, with a bit of coarse sand added for improved drainage. Provide maximum light and ventilation. Water generously and feed fortnightly in spring and summer. Water moderately the rest of the year. Loquats benefit from being stood outdoors in the garden for part of the summer; in high temperatures in the conservatory, provide high humidity. A cool temperature in winter, maximum 10°C (50°F) is necessary. Although a loquat can reach 4.6m (15ft) in the wild, it can be kept to smaller proportions in a conservatory. Any pruning necessary can be done in spring.

Loquat fruit is sometimes sold in specialist stores, and the stones germinate readily.

Eucalyptus

Gum Tree

Eucalyptus make pleasing, if temporary, guests in a conservatory. In the wild, they are quick-growing, huge trees, and can soon outgrow their welcome under glass. Eucalyptus are unusual in having two types of leaves: juvenile and mature. The former, which are oval or rounded, carried in pairs, and stalkless, are generally considered more attractive than the mature leaves, which are longer and thinner.

Cultivation

Grow in John Innes potting compost No.3. Provide maximum light and ventilation; no artificial heat should be necessary, except in prolonged cold spells. Water moderately and feed fortnightly in spring and summer; water sparingly the rest of the year.

Eucalyptus have a natural growth habit of a single-stemmed tree. For smaller, bushier specimens which are more suitable for small conservatories, pinch out the growing tips regularly; pruning back hard in early spring is another way of restricting size. Eucalyptus dislike pot-bound conditions, and after two or three years (or when your largest pot or tub can no longer contain the roots), plants are best replaced with new ones, grown from seed.

Types to choose

Eucalyptus citriodora, the lemon-scented gum, can fill a conservatory with its lemony fragrance. The young leaves are oval and can reach a length of 12.5cm (5in). *E.globulus* 'Compacta' is a relatively small-growing form of the Tasmanian blue gum. Its young leaves are lance-shaped, bluey-grey with a white coating. *E.gunnii*, the cider gum, has similarly coloured and coated leaves, but they are rounded, almost heart shaped. Foliage at the tips of shoots is sometimes suffused with pink.

Fatshedera

Ivy Tree, Tree Ivy

This rather ordinary-looking evergreen shrub has an unusual ancestry. It is a bigeneric hybrid between *Hedera helix* 'Hibernica', the large-leaved, quick-growing Irish ivy, and *Fatsia japonica* 'Moseri'. Fatshedera has inherited qualities from both parents: the toughness of ivy and the large palmate leaves of fatsia. Like ivy, it needs some form of support if its floppy woody stems are to remain erect. The stems, which lack ivy's aerial roots, eventually reach a height of 1.8m (6ft).

Cultivation

Grow in John Innes potting compost No.2. Either a fully lit or lightly shaded spot in the conservatory is suitable. Water moderately and feed fortnightly in spring and summer; water sparingly the rest of the year. A period of winter rest is beneficial, at a temperature of 5-10°C (40-50°F), and high humidity in high summer temperatures.

Types to choose

xFatshedera lizei 'Variegata' has white edged leaves, and needs bright light for the variegation to develop fully. *xF.lizei* has glossy green leaves.

Fatshedera lizei 'Variegata'

Fatsia

False Castor Oil Plant, Japanese Aralia, False Aralia

Fatsias are often grown outdoors in sheltered gardens, a good indication of the plant's tough character and also its need for cool growing conditions. In a conservatory, this upright evergreen shrub may reach a height of 1.8m (6ft), and carries large, shiny, palmate (hand-shaped) leaves. It is a relative of the ivy and, like it, produces insignificant flowers followed by clusters of black berries, though fatsias in conservatories are shy of flowering.

Cultivation

Grow in John Innes potting compost No.3. Provide bright light, either direct or indirect, and maximum ventilation. A low winter temperature is essential, in the region of 5°C (40°F), and high humidity in high temperatures. A spell outdoors in the summer is beneficial, in a lightly shaded spot. Water moderately and feed fortnightly in spring and summer; water sparingly for the rest of the year.

Types to choose

Fatsia japonica is sometimes sold as *Aralia sieboldii* or *A.japonica*. As well as the species, there is a pretty variegated form, *F.j.*'Variegata', with white edges to the leaves.

Ficus

Fig, Rubber Plant

This genus includes hundreds of species of trees, shrubs and climbers. Those grown indoors are far fewer, but still quite varied in thier appearance and cultivation. It is difficult to make sweeping generalizations about ornamental figs, except to state that they are evergreen and either non-flowering or with insignificant flowers when grown in a conservatory.

Cultivation

The following is a general guideline to growing conditions. Exceptions are listed under the various species. Grow in John Innes potting compost No.2 or a peat-based compost. Pot-bound conditions are tolerated quite happily and plants can remain in the same pot for several years. Provide bright light, but shade from direct sunlight. Variegated forms need some exposure to sunlight to fully develop their leaf colour. All-green species tolerate a certain amount of shade.

Ornamental figs are frost tender; winter temperatures should not really fall much below 13°C (55°F). Provide good ventilation and high humidity in high temperatures. Water moderately and feed fortnightly in spring and summer; water sparingly the rest of the year. Wash the leaves of large-leaved forms from time to time.

Types to choose

The weeping fig, *Ficus benjamina*, is a slow-growing elegant tree – one of the few indoor plants that actually is tree-like in appearance. In a conservatory, its pale-grey trunk may reach a height of 3m (10ft) or more. The plant's drooping branches carry shiny, pale green, oval leaves that darken as they age. Some older leaves are shed naturally in the beginning of spring, but new leaves normally appear as replacements. Small plants are available from 30cm (12in) high; larger, more impressive ones tend to be very expensive. There is also a variegated form available.

The mistletoe fig, *F.deltoidea* (formerly *F.diversifolia*), is bushier and lower growing, to 90cm (3ft). Its small leathery leaves are round, slightly triangular in shape. Its inedible yellow 'figs' are produced generously, starting when the plant is quite young.

The enormously popular but visually boring rubber plant, *F.elastica*, is fast growing and single stemmed, with huge, oval, glossy, leathery leaves along its poker-straight length. Pinching out the growing tips helps to encourage the production of a side shoot or two, but even then the plant retains much of its ungainly, awkward appearance. Indoors, it may grow to 3m (10ft) or more. There are several named forms which have virtually replaced the species. *F.e.*'Decora' has dark-green leaves with red undersides. Variegated forms include *F.e.*'Variegata', with creamy yellow and green leaves, and *F.e.*'Doescheri', with pink, white and grey markings on its green leaves.

Ficus sagittata 'Variegata'

The fiddle-leaf fig, *F.lyrata*, is similar in form and habit to the rubber plant, but its huge – up to 60cm (2ft) long – leaves are wavy edged and shaped like a fiddle. Both plants are immensely tolerant of shade, in which they will survive, but not grow.

The creeping fig, *F.pumila*, is an unlikely member of the fig family. Its small, paper-thin juvenile leaves are heart shaped and carried on creeping stems. These produce aerial roots, like those of ivy, if given a surface up which to climb. The creeping fig can be grown up a moss pole or trained to wires or trellis-work; it can also be grown in a hanging basket. The stems can reach a length of 1.8m (6ft) or more, though pinching out the growing tips helps keep it compact. Mature plants carry larger, less attractive leaves, but these are unlikely to be produced in a conservatory. There is a naturally compact form, *F.p.*'Minima', with tiny leaves, 6mm (¼in) long. In spite of its delicate appearance, the creeping fig is nearly hardy and is grown outdoors in sheltered gardens. It needs a definite winter rest period, with lowish temperatures, around 5°C (40°F), protection from hot summer sunlight, and a continual supply of water, or its leaves will dry up.

The rooting fig, *F.sagittata* (formerly *F.radicans*), is another candidate for a hanging basket. It is most often grown in its variegated form, *F.s.*'Variegata': the lance-shaped leaves are grey-green and creamy-white. Both the rooting and creeping fig grow best in peat-based compost.

Fittonia

Painted Net Leaf, Silver Net Leaf

These evergreen perennial creeping plants are from the tropics, and need a tropical forest environment to thrive. For this reason, they are better suited to terrariums and bottle gardens than the airy conditions of a conservatory.

Fittonia argyroneura 'Nana'

Cultivation
If you are determined to 'have a go', grow in peat-based potting compost, to ensure perfect drainage. Provide a minimum temperature of 16°C (60°F), higher in the summer, and continually high humidity. Bright light is necessary, with shade from direct summer sunlight. Water moderately and feed monthly in spring and summer; water sparingly the rest of the year. Pinch out the growing tips regularly to prompt bushy growth, though the plants will inevitably become straggly. Replace with fresh stock, easily grown from cuttings.
Types to choose
Fittonia verschaffeltii, or painted net leaf, has oval green leaves, prettily veined in pink, and carried on stems 25-30cm (19-12in) long. The silver net leaf, *F.v.argyroneura* (sometimes sold as *F.argyroneura*) has silvery-white veins; *F.v.argyroneura* 'Nana' is a dwarf form.

Grevillea
Silk Oak
Silk oak makes a huge evergreen tree in warm climates, but seedlings are valuable in the conservatory for their lush, soft, fern-like foliage. Young plants, 30-60cm (12-24in) high, are often used in summer bedding-out schemes or in mixed displays of pot plants, where their natural grace is sometimes lost in the general muddle. In the conservatory, a silk oak can quickly reach a height of 1.8m (6ft). Unfortunately, older plants tend to drop their lower leaves and are best replaced with fresh stock, grown from seed.
Cultivation
Provide bright light, though a bit of shade in summer is tolerated. Water generously and feed fortnightly in spring and summer; water sparingly the rest of the year. Grevilleas benefit from a spell outdoors in summer; in the conservatory, provide high humidity in high temperatures. A minimum winter temperature of 7°C (45°F) is necessary, and lime-free potting compost, as grevilleas are lime haters.
Types to choose
The silk oak, *Grevillea robusta*, is usually seen as a single-stemmed plant, with leaves up to 45cm (18in) long. Flowers are not produced in a conservatory. Rarer is *G.rosmarinifolia*, a shrub up to 1.8m (6ft) high, with red flowers in summer and rosemary-like, dark-green leaves.

Gynura
Velvet Plant
These are tropical evergreen perennials, with a sprawling or climbing habit of growth. Their common name and main attraction come from the fine purple hairs that clothe the upper surfaces and undersides of the leaves and stems, giving the plants, especially young growth, an intensely purple colour. Gynura is an unlikely relative of the daisy – both belong to the *Compositae* family – and it produces deep-yellow flowers. These are unattractive, though, both visually and in terms of scent, and are best nipped off as soon as the flower buds are visible.
Cultivation
Grow in a peat-based compost or John Innes potting compost No.2. Provide a minimum winter temperature of 13°C (55°F) and maximum light. In summer, the plants need shade from strong sunlight and high humidity in high temperatures. Feed fortnightly with weak fertilizer in spring and summer and water moderately; water sparingly the rest of the year. Pinch out the growing tips from time to time to keep the plants bushy. Eventually mature plants will become leggy and tend to lose their purple colouring, and are best replaced by young plants, grown from cuttings.
Types to choose
Nomenclature in the case of gynuras is tricky. The plant most often seen is *Gynura sarmentosa*, a climbing plant suitable for growing in hanging baskets or training up canes or wires. It is usually considered to be a variety of *G.aurantiaca*, which is bushier and more upright initially, though otherwise similar to *G.sarmentosa*. The stems of both can grow to a length of 90cm (3ft) in a conservatory, more in the wild.

Hedera
Ivy
Ivy – self-clinging, evergreen, uncomplaining – is often undervalued, in the garden as well as the conservatory. Though the wild form, *Hedera helix*, is perhaps too omnipresent to warrant space in the conservatory, there are dozens of attractive named forms, as well as other unusual species and their cultivars.

Cultivation
Unheated or cool conservatories are ideal for ivy, as they need a winter rest period, with a maximum temperature of 10°C (50°F). Grow in John Innes potting compost No.2, and provide canes or wires up which the ivy can climb. (Slow-growing forms are suitable for hanging baskets.) Feed fortnightly and water moderately in spring and summer; water sparingly the rest of the year. In high temperatures, provide high humidity, and good ventilation is always beneficial.

Though ivies are shade tolerant, colouring of variegated forms is stronger in direct sunlight, though some protection from fierce summer sun is necessary. Non-variegated ivies are happy in indirect light, but deep shade will result in drawn out, weak plants. Ivies that outgrow their allotted space or those that produce spindly growth can be cut back hard as and when necessary. Propagation is easy from cuttings, which will root in water.

Types to choose
The following includes commonly available ivies; a specialist nursery will offer a much wider range.

Hedera canariensis, or Canary Island ivy, is a less hardy species, with leaves up to 20cm (8in) long. It is most often seen in the form *H.c.*'Variegata', sometimes called *H.*'Gloire de Marengo', with leaves edged in greeny grey and white. Persian ivy (*H.colchica*) has even larger leaves, up to 25cm (10in). The form *H.c.*'Dentata Variegata' has finely toothed leaves with creamy white margins, and *H.c.*'Paddy's Pride' has bold central markings of bright yellow on its dark-green leaves.

A few of the particularly good forms of *Hedera helix* are *H.h.*'Glacier', with small, grey-green leaves edged in cream; *H.h.*'Green Ripple', with small, jagged and frilled leaves; *H.h.*'Buttercup' with deep-yellow new leaves, which eventually turn green as they age; *H.h.*'Goldheart', with small, bright-yellow leaves edged in dark green; *H.h.*'Parsley Crested', with lacy, heavily frilled leaves; and *H.h.*'Atropurpurea', with purple-tinged leaves in winter.

Jacaranda

Jacarandas are forest trees in their native Brazil. In a conservatory, they make unusual shrubs, though they will eventually outgrow their welcome.

Cultivation
Grow in John Innes potting compost No.2, with a bit of coarse sand and peat added. Provide maximum light and a minimum winter temperature of 10°C (50°F). Water moderately and feed fortnightly in spring and summer; water sparingly the rest of the year. Jacarandas benefit from a spell outdoors in summer; if they remain in the conservatory, provide good ventilation in hot weather.

Any pruning necessary can be done in spring, but older plants tend to drop their lower leaves and lose their graceful appearance, and are best replaced.

Types to choose
Jacaranda acutifolia is sometimes sold as *J.mimosifolia* or *J.ovalifolia*; its single (later branching) stem carries lush, fern-like leaves up to 45cm (18in) long. The leaves are semi-evergreen and very delicate in appearance, each leaf being subdivided into hundreds of tiny leaflets. Though blue flowers are produced in the wild, small plants in cultivation are non-flowering.

Lippia

Lemon-scented Verbena
A modest-looking deciduous shrub, lemon-scented verbena, *Lippia citriodora* (*Aloysia triphylla*), is worth including in a cool conservatory for its aromatic, light-green leaves. It can grow to a height of 3m (10ft) outdoors, but can be confined to much smaller proportions by regular pruning and confining the roots in a pot or tub. In summer, sprays of tiny, pale-lilac flowers are produced, which are charming rather than showy.

Cultivation
Grow in John Innes potting compost No.2. Provide bright light and a minimum temperature of 7°C (45°F) during its dormant period in winter. Water moderately and ventilate freely in spring and summer; water sparingly the rest of the year. If practical, stand the plant outdoors in a sunny, sheltered spot for part of the summer to ripen the wood. In spring, once the allotted space is outgrown or if the shrub starts to get leggy, prune back the previous year's growth by up to half.

Maranta

Prayer Plant, Rabbit's Tracks, Red Herringbone Plant
This tropical evergreen perennial carries its oval leaves fully open during the day; at night, they close from the midrib upwards, like hands in prayer.

Cultivation
Grow in John Innes potting compost

Maranta leuconeura kerchoviana

No.2 with coarse sand or peat added, or a peat-based potting compost. Provide a minimum temperature of 13°C (55°F). Because the leaves are thin and can dry out quickly in high temperatures, high humidity is needed. Bright light helps intensify the leaf colouring, but direct sunlight is as harmful as dry air, and should be avoided, especially in the summer months. Water generously and feed fortnightly in spring and summer; water sparingly the rest of the year. Marantas are quick growing, and can easily be propagated by division in spring.

Types to choose

Marantas available commercially are named forms of *Maranta leuconeura*. All have basically oval leaves, 20-30cm (8-12in) high, produced by spreading rhizomes. The red herringbone plant, *M.l.erythroneura* is so called because the leaf veins and midribs are bright red. The dark, greeny brown leaves are further enhanced by yellow-green markings along the midribs, and purple undersides; the overall effect is exotic without being garish. *M.leuconeura massangeana*, sometimes sold as *M.*'Massangeana', is more subtle, with prominent silver veining to the green leaves, and purple undersides. Rabbit's tracks, or *M.l.kerchoviana*, has dark green or brown track-like blotches on both sides of the midrib.

Mimosa

Sensitive Plant, Humble Plant

This plant is a distant cousin of the popular, yellow-flowered florists' mimosa (*Acacia dealbata,* page 58). *Mimosa pudica* gets its common name from the curious ability of the fern-like leaves to close up if touched, or even if disturbed by wind. This is immediately followed by the leaf stalks drooping in a humble manner, though both the leaves and stalks soon return to normal.

In summer, the shrub-like plant, which can reach a height of 60cm (24in), carries small pink flowers, like tiny puff-balls, where the leaves join the slightly spiny stems. Though the humble plant is a perennial in its native Brazil, in conservatories it is best treated as an annual, grown from seed sown in late winter or early spring.

Cultivation

Use John Innes potting compost No.1, with coarse sand and peat added for extra drainage. Provide a minimum temperature of 18°C (65°F) and bright light, but protection from strong summer sun. In high temperatures, high humidity and good ventilation are necessary. Water moderately and feed fortnightly during the growing season; discard in autumn.

Monstera

Swiss Cheese Plant

Monstera offers large-scale, lush, tropical growth in return for modest care and cultivation, and for this reason has always been popular as a house plant. In a conservatory this evergreen climber can reach a height of 6m (20ft) or more, and its shiny, characteristically perforated and indented leaves can reach a length of 1.2m (4ft). Young plants have unperforated, heart-shaped leaves, which gradually change as they mature. Aerial roots are also produced; in nature, they cling to nearby trees and help the plant grow towards light, as well as absorbing food and water. In the artificial environment of a conservatory, the roots can be trained to a large moss pole.

Cultivation

Grow in John Innes potting compost No.3. Either strong light or semi-shade is suitable, but in deep shade, the leaf perforations and indentations are less likely to occur. Provide a minimum temperature of 10°C (50°F) and high humidity in high temperatures. Water generously and feed fortnightly in spring and summer; water sparingly the rest of the year. Keep the moss pole damp, as a source of water for the aerial roots. As with any large-leaved plant, an occasional dusting or washing of the leaves is important for the sake of its appearance and health.

Neoregelia

Blushing Bromeliad, Fingernail Plant

These tough, slow-growing bromeliads are valued for their rosettes of arching, strap-shaped leaves, and the ability of some forms to change leaf colour at flowering time. The flowers themselves are tiny and insignificant, carried deep within the rosette.

Cultivation

Provide bright light, ideally direct sunlight, high humidity and a minimum temperature of 10°C (50°F). Grow in small pots of peat-based compost or a mixture of equal parts John Innes potting compost No.2, coarse sand, and peat or leafmould. Water moderately and feed monthly all year round, filling the central cup of the rosette as well as the compost. Any offsets produced can be potted up separately.

Types to choose

The blushing bromeliad, *Neoregelia carolinae*, has dark-green, toothed leaves, to 30cm (12in) long; the centre of the plant changes from green to red at flowering time. *N.c.*'Marechalii' is a smaller form; *N.c.*'Tricolor' has creamy white central stripes to the leaves. An unusual species is *N.marmorata*, with browny-red patches on the leaves. The

Neoregelia carolinae variety

fingernail plant, *N.spectabilis*, is so called because its leaf tips are red.

Ophiopogon

Snake's Beard, Lily Turf, Mondo Grass

This moderately hardy evergreen perennial is sometimes grown under the staging of cold or cool greenhouses, where its graceful, arching, grass-like leaves form a dense carpet of greenery. In warm Mediterranean climates, ophiopogon is grown as a substitute for grass. The plant is a member of the lily family, and is doubly attractive in summer, when its sprays of small, tubular, pendant flowers are carried on nodding stems. The flowers are occasionally followed in autumn by blue berries.

Cultivation

Grow in John Innes potting compost No.2, with coarse sand added for improved drainage. Provide bright light but shade from strong summer sunlight. Though vulnerable to severe frost, ophiopogon dislikes hot, arid growing conditions and needs good ventilation at all times. Water moderately and feed fortnightly in spring and summer; water sparingly the rest of the year. The plant is easily propagated by division of the clumps in spring.

Types to choose

Ophiopogon jaburan, or lily turf, is most often grown in its variegated form, *O.j.*'Variegatus'. Its leaves can be 60cm (24in) or more in length, and are striped with white. Its flowers are white, occasionally pale mauve. Smaller scale is *O.japonicus*, dwarf lily turf, snake's beard or mondo grass. Its deep-green leaves may reach a height of 25cm (10in); its white flowers are carried on 10cm (4in) stems. Rare and quite striking is the black-leaved *O.planiscapus* 'Nigrescens'. It is relatively slow growing, compared to other ophiopogons, and carries pale-pink flowers.

Peperomia

Peperomias are small-scale, modest and polite plants, with a tidy growth habit and mouse-tail-like flower spikes. Peperomias are not 'show-stoppers', but have pleasing evergreen foliage and are often used as part of mixed planting displays. There are many species and named forms, with a wide range of leaf texture, colour, shape and size: the sprawling or trailing sorts are suitable for hanging baskets.

Cultivation

Grow in a peat-based compost or John Innes potting compost No.2, with extra peat or coarse sand added. Provide bright light but shade from direct summer sunlight. For good colour contrast in variegated forms, direct sunlight is advisable. Peperomias need moist, warm growing conditions, with a minimum temperature of 13°C (55°F), and high humidity in high temperatures. Particularly vulnerable to rotting, peperomias also need careful watering: sparingly all year round, slightly increased in the summer. Feed monthly in spring and summer. Bushy and trailing types benefit from having their growing points pinched out occasionally.

Types to choose

The watermelon peperomia, *Peperomia argyreia* (formerly *P.sandersii*), has distinctive leaves: pointed, oval, with dark-green and silver markings resembling the stripes on the skin of a watermelon. The leaves are carried on red stalks, with a height of 25cm (10in).

Peperomia caperata has heart-shaped, velvety, heavily corrugated leaves, again carried on red stems and reaching a height of 25cm (10in). There are several named forms, of which the most popular is *P.c.* 'Green Ripple'.

Peperomia magnoliifolia (formerly *P.tithymaloides*) is sometimes called the

Peperomia magnoliifolia 'Variegata'

desert privet, an accurately descriptive common name. It has glossy, oval, privet-like leaves and makes a bushy, floppy plant, 30-38cm (12-15in) high. It is most often seen as the form *P.m.*'Variegata', with creamy-yellow young leaves that gradually turn green as they mature.

The baby rubber plant, *P.obtusifolia*, has a similar height and growth habit, though slightly more erect. The dark purple stems carry dark green, thick, glossy, rounded or oval leaves. There are several named forms available, with variegated leaves and dwarf growth habits.

The only form of *Peperomia scandens* available is *P.s.*'Variegata', a trailing or climbing plant, to 1.8m (6ft) or more in length, with pretty, heart-shaped leaves which begin life almost entirely creamy-yellow, gradually becoming green-centred as they age.

Philodendron

Panda Plant, Spade Leaf, Parlour Ivy, Velour Plant, Heart Leaf, Elephant's Ear

One of the most popular genera of tender foliage plants, *Philodendron* includes species of widely varying appearance. Leaf size, shape and colour vary, and many philodendrons have quite different juvenile and adult leaves. Some philodendrons are climbers, producing aerial roots primarily for clinging but also for intake of food and water; these plants need moss poles or other forms of support up which to climb.

Other philodendrons are trailing plants, suitable for hanging baskets, and others still are non-climbing, producing open rosettes of leaves carried on elegant leaf stalks which grow from a short central stem. What these evergreen plants share in common is their South American provenance, their basic toughness and resilience, and the unlikelihood of flower production in a conservatory.

Cultivation

Grow in John Innes potting compost No.2 with added peat, or a peat-based compost. Provide bright light but protection from direct sunlight, especially in summer. A minimum winter temperature of 13°C (55°F) is necessary, and high humidity is advisable at all times. Water generously and feed fortnightly in spring and summer; water sparingly the rest of the year. Keep moss poles moist to encourage rooting; large-leaved specimens should be dusted or washed from time to time.

Philodendron laciniatum

Types to choose

The panda plant, *Philodendron bipennifolium*, is a climber to 1.8m (6ft) or more. Its juvenile, heart-shaped leaves are eventually replaced by long, pointed leaves, shaped rather like a fiddle; it is sometimes called the fiddle-leaf plant.

The tree philodendron, *P.bipinnatifidum*, is an impressively sculptural plant. The huge leaves, up to 90cm (3ft) across, form a loose rosette; as the plant ages, it takes on a tree-like appearance. Again, the young leaves are heart-shaped and entire; the mature leaves are deeply divided into a dozen or more lobes.

Philodendron domesticum (sometimes sold as *P.hastatum*) is commonly called spade-leaf or elephant's ear. It is a vigorous climber, to 1.8m (6ft), with long, arrow-shaped, undivided leaves.

Blushing philodendron, *P.erubescens*,

is a climber reaching a similar height, with arrow-shaped leaves that start life bright pinky-red and gradually turn green with age. Mature leaves retain the red colouring on their undersides and stalks. *P.e.*'Burgundy' (sometimes sold as *P.*'Burgundy') is a hybrid form with intensely bronze-red young leaves, and dark-red leaf undersides, stalks and main stem. It is relatively slow growing.

Most philodendrons have glossy leaves, but the velour plant, *P.melanochrysum* (sometimes sold as *P.andreanum*) is an exception. Its elongated, heart-shaped leaves are a velvety blackish green, with striking pale midribs and veins. It is a climber and may reach 1.8m (6ft) in time.

Philodendron pedatum, sometimes sold as *P.laciniatum*, is a very slow-growing climber, with pointed, lobed leaves, the lobes themselves being subdivided.

One of the most popular philodendrons is *P.scandens*, or heart leaf. Its climbing or trailing stems can reach 3m (10ft) in length, and may need occasional pinching out of the growing tips. The leaves are heart-shaped and relatively small, though they can, on mature plants, be 30cm (12in) long. Parlour ivy, *P.s.oxycardium* (sometimes sold as *P.cordatum*) is the widely available form.

Pilea

Aluminium Plant, Artillery Plant, Panamiga

Familiar residents of mixed planting bowls, these evergreen perennials make pretty, small-scale displays in their own right. Their one drawback is their short-lived beauty; being quick growing, they are also quick to become leggy, losing their lower leaves after a year or so.

Cultivation

Grow in pots or shallow pans of John Innes potting compost No.2 with added peat, or a peat-based compost. Provide bright but indirect light, and quite definite shading in the summer months. A minimum temperature of 10°C (50°F) is needed, and high humidity all year round. (Pileas are often grown in the controlled environments of bottle gardens and terrariums for this reason.) Water moderately and feed fortnightly in spring and summer; water sparingly the rest of the year. Pinching out the growing tips from time to time helps

Pittosporum tobira 'Variegatum'

prolong their bushy appearance. Older plants can easily be replaced by cuttings; creeping forms can be divided.

Types to choose

The aluminium plant, *Pilea cadierei*, is an erect, branching species, to 30cm (12in) in height. Its oval leaves grow in pairs and are dark green, with deeply incised veins and silver patches between the veins. There is a dwarf form available.

The artillary plant, *P.microphylla* (formerly *P.muscosa*), is a shrubby plant, to 30cm (12in) high, with tiny, almost fern-like, leaves. Its common name comes from the fact that the insignificant flowers discharge their ripe pollen over great distances; the plant is of little merit otherwise.

Pilea involucrata, or panamiga, is a creeping plant that roots along the surface of the compost as it grows. There are several named forms, with deeply quilted, oval leaves on red-purple stems, and variegated bronzy-green, silver, copper or bright green, according to the form chosen.

Pittosporum

Japanese Pittosporum

Dividing plants into 'flowering' and 'foliage' chapters is often an arbitrary process, and *Pittosporum tobira* is a prime example of a dual-purpose plant. Its creamy white summer flowers are small and sweetly scented, reminiscent of orange blossom, but its shiny, dark, evergreen foliage is a slightly stronger 'selling point'. The thick oval leaves are carried in rosettes and though the shrub can reach a height of 4.6m (15ft) in the wild, it can be kept to 90cm-1.2m (3-4ft) in a conservatory.

Cultivation

Grow in John Innes potting compost No.2. Provide maximum light and a minimum winter temperature of 7°C (45°F). Water generously, provide maximum ventilation and feed fortnightly in spring and summer; water sparingly the rest of the year. Any pruning necessary can be done in spring.

Types to choose

Pittosporum tobira 'Variegatum' is an unusual form with white leaf margins; it sometimes flowers in winter.

Rhoeo

Boat Lily, Moses in the Cradle, Purple-leaved Spiderwort

This evergreen perennial is grown for its open rosettes of stiff, lance-shaped leaves, up to 30cm (12in) long. The first two of its common names come from the curious purple boat-like bracts that appear at the base of the rosettes. The boats' (or cradles') 'occupants' are tiny white flowers. Rhoeo is related to *Tradescantia*, or spiderwort, hence its third common name; its former name was *Tradescantia discolor*, and it is still occasionally sold as *Rhoeo discolor*.

Cultivation

Grow in pots or hanging baskets, using John Innes potting compost No.2. Provide a minimum winter temperature of 10°C (50°F) and bright light, but shade from strong summer sunlight. Water generously and feed fortnightly in spring and summer; water sparingly the rest of the year. In high temperatures, provide high humidity. Rhoeo is easily propagated from offsets which can be removed and potted up separately in spring.

Types to choose

As well as the species, *Rhoeo spathacea*, which has glossy green upper leaf surfaces and purple undersides, there is a variegated form, *R.s.*'Vittata', which has yellow, green and white leaf stripes, occasionally tinged pink. Like the species, it suffers from confused nomenclature, and is sold as *Rhoeo discolor vittata* or, occasionally, *R.s.*'Variegata'.

Rhoicissus

Cape Grape, Grape Ivy

Both of these evergreen woody climbers are tough as nails, and can quickly reach a height of 6m (20ft) or more.

They climb by means of tendrils, and need wires, canes or trellis-work for support. Occasionally plants get caught in a botanical nomenclature trap, and *Rhoicissus rhomboidea*, the grape ivy, is one such victim. It is often confused with a very similar plant, *Cissus rhombifolia* (see page 95); some books treat them as a single plant, and either may be offered for sale as *Rhoicissus* or *Cissus*. In fact, *Rhoicissus rhomboidea* is a South African plant, with unforked tendrils; *Cissus rhombifolia* is a South American species with forked tendrils. As their cultivation and appearance are much the same, it is really of theoretical interest only.

Cultivation

Grow in John Innes potting compost No.2. Bright light is necessary, with some shade in summer, and a minimum winter temperature of 10°C (50°F). Feed fortnightly and water moderately in spring and summer; water sparingly the rest of the year. Provide plenty of ventilation in hot weather. Though rhoicissus have the capacity to grow to enormous proportions, they can be kept smaller by severe pruning. Regularly pinching out of the growing tips also helps.

Types to choose

Rhoicissus rhomboidea has glossy, dark-green leaves, each made up of three leaflets. Young leaves are covered in fine hairs and look almost white. There is a variety *R.r.*'Ellen Danica' with more deeply cut leaves.

Rhoicissus capensis, or Cape Ivy, has glossy but lighter green leaves, entire rather then composite. They are toothed and slightly hairy and brown on the undersurfaces. Their rounded heart shape is reminiscent of the foliage of the hardy ornamental grape vine, *Vitis coignetiae*, to which it is related.

Rhoicissus rhomboidea

Sansevieria

Mother-in-law's Tongue, Snake Plant, Bowstring Hemp

This old-fashioned evergreen plant is slow growing and long suffering. Its fleshy, pointed, sword-shaped leaves grow from rhizomes, and are decoratively marbled with pale and dark green or silvery white.

Cultivation

Grow in John Innes potting compost No.2 and use a clay pot to provide stability. Sansevieria prefers bright light, even direct sunlight, but tolerates shade. Provide a minimum temperature of 13°C (55°F). Water moderately and feed monthly in spring and summer; water sparingly the rest of the year. (Because the leaves are succulent, overwatering can quickly lead to rotting.)

Sanservieria does not mind pot-bound conditions, and can remain in the same container for many years. The plants are easily propagated by dividing established clumps in spring.

Types to choose

Sansevieria trifasciata is most commonly seen in the form 'Laurentii'. The leaves, up to 1.2m (4ft) tall, are edged in yellow. More unusual is *S.t.*'Hahnii', a dwarf, rosette-forming plant, to 15cm (6in) high; *S.t.*'Golden Hahnii' has leaves broadly edged in yellow.

Schefflera

Umbrella Plant, Seven Fingers

These slow-growing, tropical evergreen trees are valued for their graceful composite leaves. These are glossy and dark-green, and give the plant a contemporary – almost architectural – elegance.

Cultivation

Grow in John Innes potting compost No.2. Provide maximum light, with some shade in strong summer sunlight, a minimum temperature of 13°C (55°F) and a humid atmosphere. Water moderately all year round; feed fortnightly in spring and summer. Left to their own devices, schefflera tend to grow rather vertically; pinching out the growing tips encourages the production of side shoots and a shrubby form.

Types to choose

Schefflera actinophylla (sometimes sold as *Brassaia actinophylla*) can reach a height of 1.8m (6ft) or more. Its slightly drooping young leaves are composed of three leaflets, each up to 30cm (12in) long; mature plants produce leaves with five or more leaflets.

Schefflera arboricola (sometimes sold as *Heptapleurum arboricola*) grows to a similar height, but its leaves are composed of smaller leaflets and more of them, arranged like the spokes of a wheel around the central stalk. Seven fingers, or *S.digitata*, actually has seven or more finger-like leaflets on each stalk. It eventually makes a taller plant than the other species, and is distinguishable from the others by its wavy leaf edges.

Scindapsus

Devil's Ivy, Pothos

This easy-going evergreen climber has no rarity or horticultural 'snob value' at all, but is quite pretty and a good stand-by if you want lush growth with straightforward cultivation needs. The heart-shaped leaves are carried on stems that can reach a length of 10m (30ft) or more, though they are usually much shorter and can easily be kept to a reasonable size by pruning.

Scindapsus aureus

The stems produce aerial roots at each leaf node, rather like those of philodendrons, to which scindapsus is related. The plants can be grown in hanging baskets, trained up wires or trellis-work, or provided with bark or moss poles, to which the aerial roots can cling.

Cultivation

Grow in peat-based compost, of John Innes potting compost No.2. Provide bright light but shade from strong summer sunlight and a minimum temperature of 10°C (50°F). In high temperatures, high humidity is beneficial. Water moderately and feed fortnightly in spring and summer; water sparingly the rest of the year.

Types to choose

Scindapsus aureus (more correctly *Epipremnum aureum*) is the most familiar species, with shiny, heart-shaped, dark-green leaves splashed and marked with yellow. The form *S.a.*'Marble Queen' is basically white, with grey and green markings. *S.pictus* has smaller, less shiny leaves, 8cm (3in) long; the form usually grown is *S.p.*'Argyraeus', with grey-spotted leaves.

Selaginella

Spike Moss

More akin to ferns than mosses, these flowerless plants are not easy to grow in a 'normal' conservatory, as they need shade and constant high humidity to thrive. Many are very attractive, though, with their tiny, lacy leaves, and could be accommodated within the closed environment of a bottle garden, terrarium or old-fashioned bell jar in the conservatory.

Cultivation

Grow in shallow pots of peat-based mixture, with coarse sand added to improve the drainage. Alternatively, use a mixture of equal parts John Innes potting compost No.2, leafmould and peat. Provide a minimum temperature of 10°C (50°F); water generously in spring and summer, moderately the rest of the year. Feed monthly with half-strength fertilizer. If selaginella is unhappy, it will shrivel and die; if happy, it will grow at top speed. Prune hard as and when necessary, and propagate by division.

Types to choose

Selaginella apoda is a creeping form, with bright-green, moss-like foliage and stems to 8-10cm (3-4in) high. *S. kraussiana* is a trailing plant, to 30cm (12in), that also roots where the stems touch the compost. It was often used at the front of staging, to form a curtain of green, or gold in the form *S.k.*'Aurea', and is equally good in hanging baskets.

Another species for hanging baskets is *S.martensii*. Its fern-like, much divided fronds are arching in habit and can reach a length of 30cm (12in). The relatively large leaves are rich green, and there are variegated forms, with green and white leaves.

Senecio

German Ivy, Parlour Ivy, Wax Vine, Cape Ivy

Senecios belong to the daisy (*Compositae*) family, and the genus spans an incredible range: hardy and tender plants; those grown primarily for foliage and those grown primarily for flowers. The tender evergreen climbing plants listed here are pretty foliage subjects for growing in hanging baskets or training up wires, trellis-work or canes.

From a distance the plants look like ivy; close to, the soft, waxy texture of the leaves and stems and lack of aerial roots declares them to be quite different. In addition, they occasionally produce bright-yellow, daisy-like flowers.

Cultivation

Grow in pots or hanging baskets of John Innes potting compost No.2. Provide maximum light and a winter rest period, with a minimum temperature of 5°C (40°F). Water moderately and feed monthly in spring and summer; water sparingly the rest of the year. The thin stems can reach a length of 1.2m (4ft) or more, but old plants tend to get leggy, and are best replaced. New plants can easily be propagated from cuttings, which will root in water.

Types to choose

Senecio macroglossus 'Variegatus' (wax vine or Cape ivy) has attractively variegated leaves, dark green and creamy white, carried on dark red stems. *S.mikanioides* (German ivy or parlour ivy) is similar, but with larger, dark-green leaves, with decorative deep veining.

Setcreasea

This is a sprawling evergreen perennial, though 'everpurple' would be a more accurate description, as its lance-shaped leaves and stems are a rich, deep purple colour. The tiny flowers that are produced in summer are pinky purple as well, but it is the leaves, up to 15cm (6in) long, that are the main attraction.

Cultivation

Grow in pots or hanging baskets of John Innes potting compost No.2. Bright light is necessary for good colouring, but provide some shade from direct summer sunlight. Water moderately and feed fortnightly in spring and summer; water sparingly the rest of the year. Provide a minimum winter temperature of 7°C (45°F). In a suitable environment, setcreasea is a quick-growing plant, but it tends to get leggy with age, losing its lower leaves, and is best replaced with young plants grown from cuttings.

Types to choose

Setcreasea pallida 'Purple Heart' is

sometimes sold as *S.purpurea*; in any event the plants' stems grow to a length of 40cm (16in).

Sparmannia

House Lime, African Hemp

This large-scale evergreen shrub is a tender relative of the garden lime (*Tilia*). In the wild it produces clusters of yellow-centred white flowers in summer, but in a conservatory flowering is an unusual occurrence, and the plant is grown for the visual value of its foliage. The heart-shaped, light-green leaves are huge, up to 30cm (12in) across, and covered in fine hairs on both the upper and under surfaces.

Cultivation

Provide bright light but some protection from strong summer sunlight, and a minimum winter temperature of 7°C (45°F). Water generously and feed fortnightly in the growing season; water sparingly the rest of the year. Sparmannia benefits from being stood outdoors for part of the summer and in high temperatures high humidity is beneficial too. John Innes potting compost No.2 is a suitable growing medium. Sparmannias can get leggy, which is easily remedied by pruning back hard in spring. However, they are just as easily propagated by cuttings – which form roots even in water – and young plants tend to be more graceful.

Types to choose

Sparmannia africana 'Nana' is a dwarf form, reaching a height of 90cm (3ft), compared to the 3m (10ft) height of the species, though the latter can be kept to smaller dimensions by pruning and regular pinching out of the growing tips. Hillier's, the famous English nursery, says of sparmannia in its catalogue, 'This marvellous plant not only tolerates but appears to thrive on the cigarette and cigar ends and tea and coffee dregs of the second-class continental cafés.' While these conditions are unlikely to be met in a conservatory, it is an indication of the good-natured character of the plant.

Tolmeia

Piggy-back Plant, Mother-of-thousands

The common names of this evergreen perennial plant come from its curious way of producing small plantlets where the leaves join the leaf stalks. It is a modest plant in size and appearance, reaching a height of 15cm (6in), rather more across, with hairy, roughly heart-shaped leaves. Although it produces small spikes of tiny white flowers outdoors, it is unlikely to flower in a conservatory. In its favour, *Tolmeia menziesii* is an undemanding plant, frost tolerant, and amusing to propagate. It is also a prime candidate for a hanging basket.

Cultivation

Grow in John Innes potting compost No.2, in a well lit or lightly shaded spot. Provide plenty of ventilation at all times. Water generously and feed fortnightly during spring and summer; water sparingly the rest of the year. Plantlets growing from leaves in contact with the compost will send down roots naturally; for new specimens, simply detach the plantlets and pot them up separately.

Tradescantia

Wandering Jew, Inch Plant, White Velvet

These trailing perennials are a lot tougher than their appearance would lead you to believe, and make admirable subjects for hanging baskets. Tradescantias provide quick-growing greenery in return for a modicum of care and attention, and a single plant can provide an almost endless supply of cuttings, and thus new plants.

Tradescantia fluminensis 'Quicksilver'

Cultivation

Grow in pots or hanging baskets filled with John Innes potting compost No.2, or else a peat-based potting compost. Tradescantias need bright light, which intensifies the contrasting colours in variegated forms, but some shade from fierce summer sunlight. A minimum winter temperature of 7°C (45°F) is necessary, and high humidity in high temperatures. Water generously and feed fortnightly in spring and summer; water sparingly the rest of the year.

Their only possible drawback is their tendency to get leggy and lose their lower leaves. Pinching out the growing tips regularly helps combat this. Cuttings root easily in water, and old plants which can grow to 90cm (3ft) or more in length should be replaced with fresh material whenever necessary. Variegated forms occasionally produce all-green shoots; remove them as soon as they appear.

Types to choose

The Wandering Jew or inch plant, *Tradescantia albiflora*, rarely flowers, and is usually seen in one of its named forms: the white-striped *T.a.*'Albovittata' (or giant inch plant); the golden-leaved *T.a.*'Aurea'; or the purple, white and gold-striped *T.a.*'Tricolor'.

The flowering inch plant, *T.blossfeldiana*, is larger scale, with leaves to 10cm (4in) long. These are glossy green above, purple underneath and carried on purple, semi-erect stems. There is a white-striped form, *T.b.*'Variegata', with an occasional all-white leaf amongst the striped ones. Flowering inch plants carry purple and white flowers in summer and, like all tradescantias, they are three-petalled and appear on the tips of the stems.

Speedy Jenny (*T.fluminensis*) is also, and confusingly, called Wandering Jew. Its pointed green leaves have purple undersides and are usually carried on purple stems. There are two named forms with white-striped leaves: *T.f.*'Variegata', with thick stripes, and *T.f.*'Quicksilver', with thin stripes and a strong growth habit. Speedy Jennies have white flowers in summer.

Tradescantia sillamontana, or white velvet, is particularly pretty, but slightly tricky. Its pale-green leaves and stems are covered in white hairs, the effect of which its common name aptly de-

scribes. Its flowers are bright magenta. As with all woolly-leaved plants, it is vulnerable to rot; add coarse sand to the potting compost for improved drainage, and water sparingly, even in the growing season.

Yucca

Spanish Bayonet, Our Lord's Candle

In spite of their tropical appearance, most yuccas are surprisingly hardy, and are used to give an exotic touch to temperate climate gardens. Two species, though, benefit from the winter protection of a conservatory, where their tropical appearance is equally effective. They are evergreen plants, with rosettes of sword-like, extremely tough leaves. Some species are stemless, while others produce their rosettes on slow-growing, woody stems. Their tall spikes of white or red-flushed, bell-shaped flowers are not normally produced on plants grown under glass.

Cultivation

Grow in John Innes potting compost No.2, with coarse sand added for extra drainage. Provide maximum light and a minimum winter temperature of 5°C (40°F). If possible, stand the pots outdoors in a sunny sheltered spot in summer, returning them to the conservatory before the first autumn frost. Water generously and feed fortnightly in spring and summer; keep almost dry the rest of the year. Yuccas are slow growing, and don't seem to mind pot-bound conditions, so can stay for several years in the same pot. Stemless yuccas can be propagated from offsets detached in spring and then potted up separately.

Types to choose

Yucca aloifolia, or Spanish bayonet, is the most commonly available yucca for growing under glass. It is not a pretty plant, by any stretch of the imagination, with its stout single truncated stem topped with rosettes of sharply pointed, spine-tipped, grey-green leaves. The form *Y.a.*'Draconis' is slightly less awkward looking, with several stems and softer, drooping leaves.

The Spanish bayonet, Yucca aloifolia, is a dramatic specimen plant

There are variegated forms of *Y.aloifolia* available, with white, yellow or pink stripes, or combinations of these colours. All may eventually reach a height of 1.8m (6ft), with the leaves reaching a length of 60cm (24in) or more.

Yucca whipplei, or Our Lord's candle, is a stemless species, with sharply pointed, stiff, grey' narrow leaves, to 90cm (3ft) in length. Its common name comes from its extraordinary, 3-m (10-ft) high flower spike, covered with fragrant, red-tinged white flowers.

Zebrina

Wandering Jew, Inch Plant

Not a rare plant, but a useful one for hanging baskets or training up trelliswork, zebrina is grown for its colourful leaves. These are oval and pointed, and carried on soft stems up to 45cm (18in) long; the leaf undersides are purple, the upper surfaces various colours, according to the form chosen.

Cultivation

Grow in John Innes potting compost No.2 or a peat-based compost. Provide maximum light for intense leaf colour, though some protection from strong summer sunlight is necessary. Water generously and feed fortnightly in spring and summer, sparingly the rest of the year. A minimum winter temperature of 7°C (45°F) is necessary, and good ventilation all year round. Pinch out the growing points from time to time to encourage compact, bushy growth. New plants are easily propagated from cuttings, which will root in water, and once old plants become leggy and sparse, they are best replaced.

Occasionally zebrinas produce stems with all-green leaves; these should be removed as soon as they appear.

Types to choose

Zebrina pendula is the most familiar form, and the species from which various cultivars have been developed. Its leaves have upper surfaces striped with green and silvery white. *Z.p.*'Purpusii' is sometimes sold as *Z.purpusii*; its upper leaf surfaces are a solid greeny purple, with brighter undersides. *Z.p.*'Quadricolor' is variegated rose-pink, white, cream and green. It requires higher winter temperatures.

Special Collections

Very few people have the option today of owning several specialized collections of plants, each collection housed in a separate conservatory or greenhouse. Most contemporary conservatories are, of necessity, a 'mixed bag', containing plants of quite different provenance and qualities that, for one reason or another, appeal to the owner's taste.

Huge collections of a single family, or even genus, are usually confined to botanical gardens and to the homes of the very wealthy. Still, certain types of plant – ferns, orchids, alpine plants or cacti, for example – hold a strong fascination for some people, and there is no reason why a conservatory can not be given over entirely to the cultivation of one or other of these groups. Even a small conservatory can then become a paradise and haven for the committed orchid lover, or the 'alpine-ophile'.

The most popular groups of plants which often comprise specialized collections are described here.

One thing that all the entries in this section have in common is their relative ease of cultivation. 'Plants for the beginner' sounds more condescending than helpful, but realistically, nothing encourages like success, and the best way to become involved in growing the more difficult, specialist plants, is to succeed with those you do try. Once past the initial stages, there are many, detailed and more comprehensive books for the enthusiast, and specialist nurseries which will supply the plants.

Palms are a universal symbol of the warmth and sunshine so often lacking in cold climates: remembrances of summer holidays past, glimmers of summer holidays to come. Palms are also reminders of the elegant living of bygone days, when huge palms invariably graced Victorian and Edwardian parlours, hotel lobbies and ballrooms. On a more mundane level, palms are toughies in the tender plant world, enduring a wide range of temperatures and light conditions, silently suffering in dimly lit rooms, draughty halls and dusty public places. And although palms will survive an amazing amount of neglect and ill suited surroundings, they look nicer and actually grow if reasonably well cared for.

Cultivation

Temperature requirements vary from palm to palm, and are detailed below, but none tolerates exposure to hard frost, and all like high humidity in hot weather. Ironically, many palms, particularly young ones, dislike exposure to intense summer sunlight, and light shade should be provided. The rest of the year, bright indirect light is best.

Grow in John Innes potting compost No.2, with peat or coarse sand added for extra drainage. Many palms are potentially very tall trees, but in the confines of a pot in the conservatory, they are usually slow growing. You can buy very large palms, but they are expensive. Smaller young palms are much cheaper, but you will have to face the fact that they are likely to remain small for many years.

Palms prefer relatively pot-bound conditions, and can remain in the same container for several years. Repot only when the roots are visibly cramped. Water generously and feed fortnightly in spring and summer; water sparingly the rest of the year. Palms are evergreen, but naturally shed older, lower leaves as they grow. Cut these off in spring, when any suckers can be removed and potted up separately, if you wish. Many palms, such as the date palm, can be germinated easily from seed, but are ungainly looking and un-palm-like to start with, and not really suited for instant display.

Another drawback to the display of palms is that they are a dust trap; wash or dust the leaf fronds from time to time, for the health of the plant as well as its appearance. (If you notice brown tips to the fronds while cleaning them, chances are increased humidity is needed.)

Chamaedorea elegans

This popular, easy-going, pinnate palm is burdened with names. It is sometimes sold as *Collinia elegans* or *Neanthe bella*, and popularly called the parlour palm, good-luck palm or dwarf mountain palm. Its delicate, pinnate fronds and short trunk are usually less than 1.2m (4ft) high. Provide a minimum winter temperature of 16°C (60°F). It is more tolerant of dry air and dim light than many palms, and produces its very small, yellow flowers when only two or three years old.

Chamaedorea elegans

Chamaerops humilis

The European fan palm grows wild on the hills overlooking the Mediterranean. It is nearly, but not quite, hardy, requiring a minimum winter temperature of 5°C (40°F), or even slightly lower. Its leathery, greeny-grey, fan-shaped fronds can eventually be 90cm (3ft) across; in mature plants, the fronds grow from a short trunk, although this is unlikely to develop in a conservatory. Even so, a well grown conservatory

Phoenix canariensis

specimen can produce leaf stalks 1.2m (4ft) or more in length. The form *C.h.elegans* is compact, more suitable for small spaces. Provide bright, direct light for European fan palms, and a spell outdoors in summer, if possible.

Howea

Kentia, or sentry, palms are rented 'guests' at innumerable social occasions: delivered and unwrapped at the start of the event, wrapped up again and carted away at the end. There are two species: *H.forsteriana (Kentia forsteriana)*, the thatch-leaf palm; and *H.belmoreana* (*Kentia belmoreana*), the curly palm. Both are quite similar, with feathery, pinnate arching fronds, to 3.6m (12ft) high, but usually less. The leaflets of *H.belmoreana* are held more upright than those of *H.forsteriana*, which droop. Provide a minimum temperature of 7°C (45°F).

Livistonia

These palms are relatively unusual. Except for young specimens, they are too large-scale for most conservatories; their fan-shaped fronds can be 1.8m (6ft) across, on stalks of equal length. The dark-green Australian fountain palm, or Australian fan palm, (*L.australis*), and the lighter-green Chinese fan palm, (*L.chinensis*), both have pleated, fan-shaped fronds, drooping at the tips. Provide a minimum temperature of 7°C (45°F).

Microcoelum weddellianum

The weddell, or cocos palm, is sometimes sold as *Cocos weddelliana*, sometimes *Syagrus weddellianus*. Its rather erect, pinnate, shiny fronds may reach a height of 90cm (3ft) in a conservatory, but are usually smaller. Provide a minimum temperature of 16°C (60°F); humidity in high temperatures is essential.

Phoenix

There are three species of the well known date palm available, all with pinnate fronds, slightly folded along the midribs. The true, commercial date palm, *P.dactylifera*, is the least suitable as a long-term conservatory plant. Its stiff, grey-green fronds grow from a thick trunk that can eventually reach a height of 30cm (100ft) or more. Its young foliage is relatively sparse looking, compared to that of the other two species.

The Canary Island date palm, *P.canariensis*, is ultimately smaller – to 12m (40ft) in height – with darker green, denser, arching fronds. It is the least tender of the three, and tolerates winter temperatures as low as 5°C (40°F). Smallest of all is the pygmy date palm, *P.roebelinii*, with a maximum height, even in the wild, of 1.8m (6ft). Its fronds are softer, with a more graceful, pendant habit of growth. This secies and *P.dactylifera*, need a minimum temperature of 13°C (55°F).

Rhapis

The lady palm looks like a cross between a palm and a bamboo, retaining the elegant qualities of both. It is a clump forming plant, usually less than 1.5m (5ft) high, with bright-green, cane-like stems. These are produced in dense clusters and carry fan-shaped fronds, divided into finger-like, leathery, flat leaflets. These, too, are a fresh, shiny green, and slightly toothed along the edges. The two species in cultivation are *R.excelsa* and *R.humilis*. The former is smaller, with thicker stems; the latter is taller-growing and more delicate in appearance, with more finely divided fronds. Provide a mininum temperature of 7°C (45°F).

Trachycarpus fortunei

The Chusan, or windmill palm, is similar in appearance to chamaerops and is sometimes sold as *C.excelsa*. Like chamaerops, it is an almost hardy plant, needing protection from frost but not much else. Its large, fan-shaped leaves can eventually be 1.5m (5ft) or more across, and are composed of long, slender leaflets. Provide plenty of direct sunlight, and a spell outdoors in summer, if possible. It is unlikely to exceed a height of 2.7m (9ft) in a conservatory, but is usually much smaller. Both the Chusan palm and chamaerops are more attractive as containerized, small plants than as fully grown trees, which are largely clothed in un-shed, dead fronds, giving them a bedraggled appearance.

Unlike flowering plants that rarely flower or have insignificant blooms, ferns make no pretence of flowering. Indeed, these primitive plants do not flower, but instead reproduce sexually by means of dust-like spores. These are usually found on the undersides of the plant's leaves. Spores, though botanically interesting (they grow into tiny green 'prothalli' which in turn produce the male and female cells that combine to form a new fern) are hardly beautiful.

The beauty of a fern is in its foliage alone. Their fronds, made up of blades and stalks, grow from rhizomes, or underground stems. The fronds can be thick and leathery, delicate and semi-transparent, shiny or even woolly, according to species, and range in length from tiny to 1.2m (4ft) or more. And although the adjective 'ferny' connotes laciness and delicate intricacy, some ferns have undivided, or entire, fronds. There are deciduous and evergreen ferns, but those grown under glass are usually evergreen.

Cultivation

Some ferns – maidenhair, for example – are notoriously difficult to grow outside the controlled environment of a terrarium but most others have easy-going natures, if you meet their basic requirements. Shade is perhaps the primary one: not total darkness, but good protection from exposure to direct sunlight. In a conservatory, this means you can grow ferns in the shade of staging or tables, and reserve the sunny spots for more light-demanding subjects.

A lush, natural environment created with a dense display of palms and ferns at the Fernery, Southport Botanical Gardens

Adiantum capillus-veneris

Humidity is another major factor. The warmer the temperature, the higher the atmospheric moisture required. Ferns need a steady supply of moisture to their roots, but they do not like waterlogged conditions.

For this reason, an especially free-draining compost is necessary: a mixture of equal parts John Innes potting compost No.2, peat and coarse sand. Ferns tolerate, perhaps even prefer pot-bound conditions and need relatively small pots.

Temperature requirements vary, and are covered individually below. And although watering should be generous, and combined with occasional weak feeds in spring and summer, as the temperatures and light levels drop in autumn and winter, watering should decrease accordingly, and feeding stop. The compost, though, should never be allowed to become bone dry.

Adiantum

Maidenhair ferns are the most popular, but also one of the most temperamental, entries in the following list. Their delicate, lacy fronds demand high humidity and subdued light, and usually will not settle for anything less. The ideal minimum temperature is 16°C (60°F), although a few degrees lower will be tolerated. They really are easier in bottle gardens or terrariums, where high humidity and draught-free conditions can be maintained. Large specimens can be propagated by division of the rhizomes – the underground stems – during the spring months

Adiantum capillus-veneris, is the most popular species, with black, wiry stalks and delicate fronds made up of small, triangular pinnae. Well established specimens can have fronds to 60cm (24in) or more in length, but they are usually less than half this size. The Australian maidenhair, *A.hispidulum*, has the same size and delicacy, but its stalks are much branched and the pinnae are pointed and narrow, and tinged red when young. The delta maidenhair, *A.raddianum*, formerly *A.cuneatum*, is a similar size, but its fronds have a more arching habit of growth. The named form 'Fragrantissima' is scented; *A.r.*'Fritz-Luthii' has longer fronds. Larger still is the brittle maidenhair, *A.tenerum*, with fronds to 90cm (3ft). The form *A.t.*'Farleyense' has intricately ruffled pinnae. In an unheated conservatory, try growing the deciduous *Adiantum venustum*, a smaller look-alike of *A.capillus-veneris*.

Asplenium

There are two commonly grown species of spleenwort, quite different in appearance. The hen-and-chicken fern, *Asplenium bulbiferum*, has much-divided, typically 'ferny' fronds to 60cm (24in). Its botanical and common names come from the tiny bulbils which appear along the fronds of mature plants and which produce, in time, baby ferns. (These can be detached and planted up in another container.)

Asplenium nidus

Asplenium nidus, the bird's nest fern, grows in the wild as an epiphyte on tree branches. Its fronds are undivided and rather broad, and form a loose rosette. The leaves are usually no more than 30cm (12in) long, though in ideal conditions they can be several times this length. It can only be propagated from spores, as division of the rosette is not possible and offsets are not formed. *Asplenium bulbiferum* needs little in the way of artificial heating; *A.nidus* will need a minimum temperature of 13°C (55°F).

Blechnum

The following are unusual tropical or sub-tropical ferns, needing a minimum temperature of 10°C (50°F). The rib fern, *Blechnum brasiliense*, is a large-scale plant, which eventually forms a tree-like trunk, topped by a loose rosette of

Blechnum gibbum

fronds. These are 90cm (3ft) or more in length, leathery, and much divided. *B.gibbum* (formerly *Lomaria gibba*) is more often grown, and has a similar size and growth habit. Smaller, with fronds to 30cm (12in), is *B.moorei*. It is sometimes sold as *Lomaria ciliata*. Blechnums occasionally produce offsets and these can be potted up separately.

Cyrtomium falcatum

The aptly-named holly-leaf fern has fronds composed of tough, glossy, leathery, holly-like leaflets. The fronds can be 90cm (3ft) long; the form *Cyrtomium falcatum* 'Rochfordiana' is more compact. Cyrtomiums are almost hardy, and are grown outdoors in mild areas. In the conservatory, keep them frost-free. Propagate by division in spring.

Davallia

The rabbit's foot fern is so called because of the creeping, furry rhizomes that extend from the base of the plant and root as they grow. In the wild, davallias are epiphytes, and are suitable for growing in hanging baskets, from which the rhizomes can trail. Davallias need somewhat less humidity than other ferns, another bonus. Against this, they are deciduous, and disappear for a short spell in winter. The hare's foot fern, *Davallia canariensis*, has lacy, pale-green fronds to 45cm (18in) in length. It needs a minimum temperature of 10°C (50°F). The ball fern, or squirrel's foot fern, *D.mariesii*, is nearly hardy; it is smaller but otherwise similar to *D.canariensis*. Its rhizomes can be trained in the shape of a ball. Rooted rhizomes of davallias can be detached and potted up separately.

Nephrolepis

The ladder fern, or sword fern, is beautiful and relatively easy. They were traditionally displayed on pedestals, where their elegant fronds, up to 90cm (3ft) long, could gracefully arch and droop. Hanging baskets are equally suitable, or, failing these, pots. *Nephrolepis exaltata* has given rise to many named forms, each with slightly different qualities. The Boston fern, *N.e.*'Bostoniensis', sometimes sold as *N.bostoniensis,* is particularly beautiful with drooping fronds made up of much sub-divided pinnae, resembling lace or moss. *N.e.*'Elegantissima' has compact, light-green fronds, and -*N.e.*'Rooseveltii' has darker-green, heavily subdivided fronds.

As with many plants having minor variations from one named form to another, nomenclature can be nightmarish. At the height of their popularity, there were over 100 named forms, though most of these have, sadly, disappeared. Provide a minimum temperature of 10°C (50°F). Nephrolepis produce surface runners which root and eventually send up tiny ferns; these can be detached and potted up separately.

Pellaea

The species most often grown under glass is *Pellaea rotundifolia*, the button fern. Its rounded pinnae are carried alternately on arching fronds up to 30cm (12in) long. The fronds themselves are densely packed and rather haphazardly arranged, compared to the rosettes of *Asplenium nidus*, or the orderly grace of *Nephrolepis exaltata*. Still, they are very attractive, and suitable for growing in hanging baskets.

Less well known is the green cliff brake, *P.viridis*, and less easily identified. Its fronds, more archetypical 'ferny' can be 90cm (3ft) in length. The roughly

Cyrtomium falcatum

triangular blades are carried on short, bare stalks, and are made up of pairs of pinnae, themselves subdivided. There are named forms available. Provide a minimum winter temperature of 7°C (45°F), and propagate by division of the rhizomes in spring. For an unheated conservatory, try the purple cliff brake, *P.atropurpurea*, a small-growing and purple-stalked species.

Phyllitis scolopendrium

The hart's tongue fern is perfectly hardy, and is found growing wild in woodlands and shady hedgerows. In the conservatory, it likes an equally cool and shady environment. Its glossy-green, strap-shaped fronds are carried, rosette-fashion, on dark stalks; the plant rarely exceeds a height of 30cm (12in).

As with *Nephrolepis*, there are fewer named forms available now than in the heyday of ferns, when avid collectors had dozens of crested, frilled, ruffled or otherwise embellished sports of the common hart's tongue. Among those that still can be found in specialist nurseries are *P.s.*'Crispum', with wavy-edged margins; *P.s.*'Capitatum', with striking, crested tips to the fronds; *P.s.laceratum* 'Kaye's Variety', with crested and deeply cut fronds; and *P.s.*'Undulatum', a compact form with wavy-edged fronds. Phyllitis is sometimes sold as *Scolopendrium vulgare*, sometimes (and actually more correctly) as *Asplenium scolopendrium*. All can be propagated by division of the rhizomes in spring, and the named forms can only be propagated by division, as they do not come true from spores.

Platycerium

The stag's horn fern is in a class of its own, both visually and in its cultivation requirements. It is epiphytic in its native Australia, growing on the branches of forest trees. In a conservatory, it is best grown in hanging baskets or with its relatively small root system padded with a mixture of leafmould and damp sphagnum moss, and wired to a substantial piece of bark. The stag's horn fern has two types of fronds; a rounded, sterile frond at the base, and the fertile, antler-shaped fronds which emerge from the centre. The rounded front clasps or surrounds its support and also helps to collect nutrients, in the form of rotted leaves and other forest debris, for the plant's sustenance. When young, the round frond is green and fleshy; as it ages, it becomes brown and dried out, and is eventually replaced by a new young frond. The species most often grown is *Platycerium bifurcatum*, sometimes sold as *P.alcicorne*. Its much forked, fertile fronds, which can be 90cm (3ft) long, appear silvery grey due to the overlay of white felting.

On a far larger scale is the regal elk's horn fern, *P.grande*, with 1.8m (6ft) long fronds – definitely not for the small conservatory! The enormous fertile fronds are roughly triangular in shape and erect, creating a rather basket-like structure, before arching at the branched and subdivided tips.

Provide a minimum temperature of 7°C (45°F), slightly higher for *P.grande*; high humidity is essential in high temperatures. Watering is often more successful when carried out from below – soaking the basket or root-ball in water – than from above, where the

Platycerium bifurcatum

sterile fronds act as a waterproof shield. Feed by adding liquid fertilizer to the water from time to time in spring and summer. Small plantlets are sometimes produced at the base, and these can be detached and potted up separately.

Polypodium

The polypody is a far less exotic fern than the stag's horn fern, and less peculiar in its requirements. There are many hardy North American polypodys, tough enough to be used as evergreen ground cover in shady gardens; the species most often grown under glass is *Polypodium aureum*, the hare's foot fern, from tropical America. Its deeply divided, leathery fronds can grow up to 1.2m (4ft) tall, and are carried on tough, wiry stems. The form *P.a.*'Glaucum' has blue-grey fronds; *P.a.*'Mandaianum' is similar, but with crimped and ruffled fronds. The creeping rhizomes are furry and do resemble hare's feet as they grow along the surface of the compost; propagate by detaching a rooted 'foot' and potting it up separately. Provide a minimum temperature of 10°C (50°F).

If you are an avid fern collector, but have an unheated conservatory, try growing some of the hardy species and their named forms: *P.vulgare* (more correctly *P.virginianum*), to 30cm (12in) high; *P.v.*'Cornubiense', with lacy, much-divided fronds; *P.v.*'Cristatum', with drooping crests; and *P.v.*'Cambricum', with finely toothed fronds. New fronds, of a lovely fresh green, are produced in late spring, when the old fronds should be cut off – incidentally, a good idea with Phyllitis as well.

Polystichum

The shield fern resembles the polypody, in that they are both hardy and tender species. For a conservatory with a minimum temperature of 10°C (50°F), *Polystichum tsu-simense* is the best choice. It is a small fern, up to 30cm (12in) high, with clumps of shiny, leathery fronds growing from much-branched, dark brown rhizomes. Because the pinnae of shield ferns are sharply pointed, they are sometimes called the holly fern and, indeed *Cyrtomium falcatum*, the holly leaf fern, (see page 116) is sometimes classified as *Polystichum falcatum*.

For an unheated conservatory, try the exquisite and larger scale, up to 1.2m (4ft) high, soft shield fern, *P.setiferum*. For the specialist collector, there are many choice named forms: *P.s.*'Acutilobum', half the size of the species, with delicately divided fronds growing spiral fashion from the crown; *P.s.*'Densum' with fronds so finely divided and subdivided the effect is that of parsley foliage; and *P.s.*'Proliferum', which carries many bulbils and plantlets along its fronds. All shield ferns can be propagated by division; those which produce bulbils can have these detached and potted up.

Pteris

The brake fern combines availability, easy cultivation and a wide range of species and named forms from which to choose. Provide a minimum temperature of 7°C (45°F). Most well known is the Cretan brake, *Pteris cretica*; though often included in bowls of mixed plants (which tend to look congested and haphazard), it is worthy of being displayed on its own. Its strap-shaped, finger-like fronds are carried on stalks up to 60cm (24in) tall. The form *P.t.*'Albolineata' has central markings of pale green. The sword brake, *P.ensiformis*, is similar, but with narrower fronds; the form *P.e.*'Victoriae', the Victoria brake or silver table fern, has silver-white markings on the fronds. The Australian brake, *P.tremula*, is larger growing, to 1.5m (5ft), with bright-green, heavily divided fronds.

Alpine Plants and Dwarf Bulbs

Alpines

Although an unheated conservatory in winter and spring may not seem a hospitable place, it makes an ideal home for alpines in flower then. Like much else in the plant world, alpines suffer from identity crises, and alpine sections in garden centres are likely to contain a jolly mixture of true alpines, rock plants (the two aren't necessarily the same thing) and dwarf forms of plants which are neither.

Technically, alpine plants are those which grow in the wild above the tree line but below the line of perpetual snow. This is often, but not always, in high altitudes; alpine plants can also be found near sea level in polar regions. There are alpine meadows as well as rocky mountains and cliff faces, and 'rock' plants need not come from alpine regions, although many do. What most true alpines and alpine look-alikes share in common is their diminutive size, hardy constitution, willingness to be containerized, and winter or spring flowering. This means that even a relatively small unheated conservatory can house several flowering alpines at an otherwise grim time of year.

Alpine plants are available – common ones from garden centres, less common ones from specialist nurseries – all year round. Buy them in the autumn if you have a cold frame to keep them in until they are ready to flower; buy them just as they are coming into flower if you don't have a cold frame.

In traditional alpine houses, the plants are displayed on waist-high benches, in shallow pans or half pots sunk up to their rims in pea shingle. For the odd plant or two, a table is fine, minus the pea shingle, although half pots or pans are still a good idea. Pots range in diameter from 15-30cm (6-12in); several plants can be housed in one large pot, as long as they are not crowded.

Cultivation of Alpine Plants

Alpines are tough and used to harsh conditions. The low, tight rosettes and waxy or hairy leaves often associated with alpines cut down transpiration in the drying winds, summer heat and droughts of their native environments. Humidity and/or soggy compost combined with cold or excessive warmth are the plants' worst enemies, and will lead to rotting. Free-draining compost is, therefore, vital. John Innes potting compost No.1, with a third extra of coarse sand or grit, is a sensible basic mixture. Place a generous layer of drainage material at the bottom of the container first. Plant firmly, then cover the surface of the compost with a layer of grit or chippings. This keeps the above-ground growth from coming into contact with moist soil, keeps the compost from drying out too rapidly in hot weather, and looks nicer, like a scaled-down replica of the original environment.

Minimal artificial heat, bright light and maximum ventilation are also essential, so alpines won't be able to share lodgings with tropical conservatory plants. Provide just enough heat to keep the temperature frost free, as exposure to long, hard frosts can crack the pots, if they're clay, as well as damage the plants. (Remember, the layer of snow that normally covers alpines in winter acts as a form of insulation.)

Water *very* sparingly in cold weather, moderately in the growing season, when weak feeds should be given from time to time, and light shade from the strongest spring and summer sun.

Mixed display of alpines and bulbs

Cultivation of Dwarf Bulbs

Dwarf winter- and spring-flowering bulbs complement alpines, and require much the same growing conditions. Pot them up in shallow pans or half pots in early autumn (mid-autumn for tulips), in John Innes potting compost No.1 or 2. Crock as before, add a firm layer of compost, then the bulbs, almost – but not quite – touching one another. Cover with their own depth in compost. Keep outdoors, but frost free, until green shoots appear, towards the end of autumn. Bring the pots into the conservatory and treat as for alpines. After flowering, return the pots to the garden, keep frost free and watered until leaves start to die down, then cease watering. Re-pot in fresh compost in the autumn as above. Because the bulbs (and alpine plants) have not been forced in unnaturally high heat, they can be brought into the conservatory to provide a display of flowers from one year to the next.

Care after Flowering

This may present a problem. If you have a cold frame or sunny sheltered bit of garden to which alpines and dwarf bulbs can be returned for rest and recuperation, from the time they finish flowering until the following early winter, all is well and good. This frees the space in the conservatory for late spring and summer-flowering or foliage displays, and allows alpines and bulbs as near a natural environment as possible. Cold frame lights, or even a pane of glass positioned above the plants and held in place with strong wire, can protect them from frost and excessive wet, while the sides of the frame, and a layer of ash or peat built up to the rim of the pot, offer additional protection.

Choosing Alpines and Dwarf Bulbs

For the fanatic alpine enthusiast, there are thousands of plants from which to choose, including temperamental ones requiring special compost, care and nursing on the part of the grower. For the non-fanatic, who just wants something nice to look at without emotional commitment on a vast scale, the following list should be helpful. The alpine plants are listed first in alphabetical order, followed by a selection of winter and spring-flowering bulbs.

ALPINE PLANTS

The plants listed all make attractive pot-grown specimens to brighten the conservatory in spring or early summer.

Androsace

Rock jasmines form cushions or mats of foliage and carry tiny, primrose-shaped flowers in late spring. Some, particularly the mat-forming types, are very difficult, but two relatively easy species are *Androsace helvetica* and *A.sarmentosa* (more correctly, *A.primuloides*). The former has white, almost stalkless flowers just above its cushion of tightly packed, grey-green foliage; the latter has pink flowers and mats of grey-green leaves, growing in rosettes. The form *A.s.*'Chumbyi' is a more compact form, with noticeable silky hairs on the leaves. Late spring. 5-10cm (2-4in) high.

Arabis caucasica

This rock cress, sometimes sold as *Arabis alpina*, can be quite invasive in the open ground, but makes a well-behaved plant when containerized. It has greeny-grey leaves and white, typically *Cruciferae* flowers. More compact named forms include the pink 'Rosabella', the deep-red 'Coccinea', and the pink-flowered 'Variegata', with yellow and white leaves. Late spring. 20cm (8in) high.

Campanula

The alpine species of this huge genus have typically blue or white, bell- or star-shaped flowers. The sweetly named fairy's thimble, *Campanula cochlearifolia* (sometimes sold as *C.pusilla*) has light-blue, nodding flowers. Good named forms include the double-flowered 'Elizabeth Oliver' and, with deep-blue flowers, 'Oakington'. Or try *C.portenschlagiana* (sometimes sold as *C.muralis*), with spreading mats of foliage and sprays of light-blue, starry flowers. Late spring. 10-15cm (4-6in) high.

Dianthus

Another multi-faceted genus, the easiest species for an alpine house or conservatory is *Dianthus alpinus*, the alpine pink. The white-centred, light or dark-pink flowers are carried above mats of dark-green foliage. The form *D.a.*'Red Velvet' is dark crimson, with an almost black 'eye'. Spring flowering. Or try the glacier pink, *D.neglectus* (more correctly *D.pavonius*), though it normally flowers in summer, when you may have other plans for the conservatory. 10-20cm (4-8in) high.

Draba aizoides

Whitlow grass is not a grass at all, but a member of the *Cruciferae* family. Its minute leaves form densely packed rosettes, above which tiny yellow flowers are carried on wiry stems. Curious rather than beautiful. Spring. 10cm (4in) high.

Edraianthus serpyllifolius

Grassy bells is another non-grass, this time a member of the *Campanulaceae* family. It is an easy, mat-forming plant with blue-violet, campanula-like flowers, dark purple in *Edraianthus serpyllifolius* 'Major', and 5cm (2in) in diameter. Late spring. 2.5cm (1in) high.

Gentiana verna

F. Kingdon-Ward, in his book *Common Sense Rock Gardening*, calls this gentian 'The glory of the Alps'. It is among the most easy-going gentians – not an easy genus – and carries small, star-shaped blue flowers. The form usually available is *Gentiana verna angulosa*. Spring. 8cm (3in) high.

Geranium cinereum subcaulescens

Sometimes sold as *Geranium subcaulescens*, this tiny cranesbill has saucer-shaped, black-centred, magenta flowers. Salmon-pink flowers are carried by the form *G.c.s.*'Splendens'. Alpine geraniums, incidentally, have nothing to do with the regal, zonal or ivy-leaved 'geraniums'. The latter are more correctly referred to as pelargoniums, but their old-fashioned, incorrect name lingers on. Summer. 10-15cm (4-6in) high.

Phlox subulata

The moss phlox, or moss pink, comes in many named forms, all carrying five-petalled flowers above narrow, shiny leaves. The species has flowers ranging from pink to purple; *Phlox subulata* 'Emerald Cushion Blue' has bright-blue flowers, *P.s.*'Amazing Grace' has pretty, red-eyed, white flowers. For dark-centred, crimson flowers try *P.s.*'Red Wing'. 5-10cm (2-4in) high.

Phlox subulata

Primula

Primulas sold as short-lived pot plants have been covered elsewhere (see page ref), but there are also lovely, unusual alpine primulas worth growing. *Primula x pubescens* are hybrids of complex parentage, but simple in their requirements. Good varieties include 'Mrs. J.H.Wilson', with white-centred, violet flowers, 'Alba', with white flowers, and the carmine-flowered 'Carmen'. Especially vulnerable to winter wet is *P.allionii*, and particularly happy in an unheated conservatory. It has small, slightly sticky leaves and large, pink, white or purple flowers, several to a stem. Work some lime into the compost. Spring. 5-10cm (2-4in) high.

Saxifraga
There are dozens of pretty saxifrages, but the 'Cushion' types (sometimes called Kabschia and Engleria saxifrages), with their rosettes of grey, lime-encrusted leaves, benefit particularly from winter protection. Try *Saxifraga burseriana*, with white flowers, or *S.b.*'Major Lutea', with large, light-yellow ones. *S.* × 'Cranbourne' has small pink flowers, and *S.* × *elizabethae* (sometimes sold as *S.* × *godseffiana*), has small yellow flowers. Early spring. 2.5-8cm (1-3in) high.

Sedum
Stonecrops, with their succulent, fleshy leaves, are well-known residents of rock gardens, where they often become invasive. Containerized, they are better behaved. Varieties of *Sedum spathulifolium*, with rosettes of spoon-shaped leaves, are easy plants: 'Aureum' has yellow, grey and pink leaves; 'Capa Blanca' has pale-grey, almost white leaves, and 'Purpureum' has puple leaves. All have yellow flowers. *S.oreganum* is similar, but with leaves tinted red in summer. Late spring. 5-10cm (2-4in) high.

Sempervivum
Houseleeks produce clusters of succulent rosettes which have a beautiful, sculptural quality; the flowers are really a secondary attraction. The cobweb, or spider, houseleek, *Sempervivum arachnoideum*, has fine hairs covering the leaves and bright-pink, starry flowers. The common, or roof, houseleek is *S.tectorum*; sempervivums were grown on roofs, traditionally, which gives an indication of their toughness. This species comes in many named forms, variously coloured mahogany, grey, green or pink, often with contrasting edging. The colours of the plants vary according to the seasons, giving added interest. They rarely flower. 5-15cm (2-6in) high.

EARLY FLOWERING BULBS
Pots of dwarf bulbs are a cheering sight in late winter and spring. The following are especially recommended.

Anemone blanda
The daisy-like blossoms of windflower are blue in the species, rose-pink in *Anemone blanda* 'Charmer', and white in *A.b.*'White Splendour'. Early spring. 15cm (6in) high.

Chionodoxa
Glory-of-the-snow has spikes of starry flowers, bright blue in *Chionodoxa luciliae*, pink in *C.l.*'Rosea', and dark blue in *C.sardensis*. Early spring. 8-15cm (3-6in) high.

Crocus
Most spring-flowering crocuses can be potted up in autumn, but the ones you are likely to come across are the varieties and hybrids of *Crocus chrysanthus*. They are available in white, cream, yellow, blue, wine-red, bronzy purple and various combinations, according to the form chosen. Late winter onwards. 5cm (2in) high.

Cyclamen
The alpine cousins of the well known and much bought pot plant are exquisite and charming. Try *Cyclamen coum* (sometimes sold as *C.orbiculatum*, *C.vernum* or *C.atkinsii*), with purple-blotched white, pink or red flowers, or *C.persicum*, the parent of the large, florists' cyclamen, in the same colours. Winter to early spring. 8-20cm (3-8in) high.

Iris reticulata 'Joyce'

Tulipa kaumanniana 'Aneilla'

Eranthis hyemalis
The winter aconite carries cheerful yellow, buttercup-like flowers, backed by a ruff of green leaves, from late winter onwards. 5-8cm (2-3in) high.

Galanthus
The common snowdrop, *Galanthus nivalis*, with its green-tipped white nodding bells, is as good a choice as any. For the more adventurous, there is a double-flowered form, *G.n.*'Flore Pleno'. Mid-winter. Later, in mid-spring, and with larger flowers and fresh green leaves, is *G.ikariae latifolius*. 15-20cm (6-8in) high.

Iris
The winter-flowering bulbous, or netted, irises include the blue-flowered *Iris reticulata*, and its various named forms;

I.danfordiae, in bright yellow; and the deep-blue *I.histrioides* 'Major', probably the easiest for container growing. Mid-winter. 10-15cm (4-6in) high.

Leucojum vernum
The spring snowflake has snowdrop-like flowers, flushed with yellow in the form *Leucojum vernum carpathicum.* Late winter, early spring. 20cm (8in) high.

Muscari
The grape hyacinths have tiny, bell-shaped flowers, packed together on short stems, like bunches of grapes. An easy species is *Muscari armeniacum*, with white edged, deep-blue flowers; *M.a.*'Cantab' has pale-blue flowers. For pure-white flowers, try *M.botryoides* 'Album', a sky-blue variety of the wild European grape hyacinth. Mid-spring. 20cm (8in) high.

Narcissus
Large-flowered daffodils are often forced, in heat, for winter flowering, but the tiny species narcissi are equally – perhaps even more – attractive. There are many from which to choose, but for the beginner, *Narcissus asturiensis (N.minimus),* the tiniest daffodil, only 8cm (3in) high, would be fun. Others to try are *N.bulbocodium*, the hoop-petticoat daffodil, with huge, conical trumpets; *N.cyclamineus,* the cyclamen-flowered narcissus, with swept-back petals; and *N.juncifolius,* the rush-leaved jonquil, with clusters of flowers. Late winter onwards. 8-15cm (3-6in) high.

Puschkinia scilloides
The striped squill has pale-blue, star-shaped flowers, striped with darker blue, or white flowers in the form *Puschkinia scilloides* 'Alba'. Spring. 10-20cm (4-8in) high.

Scilla
The true squills are similar in appearance to the striped squills, minus the stripes. The twinleaf squill, *Scilla bifolia*, has gentian-blue flowers, pale pink in the form *S.b.*'Rosea'; the Siberian squill, *S.siberica*, has blue-violet, intensely brilliant flowers; and *S.tubergeniana* has light-blue flowers. From late winter onwards. 8-20cm (3-8in) high.

Tulipa
The species tulips are less showy than their cousins, the large-flowered garden cultivars, but earlier and more graceful. The water-lily tulip, *Tulipa kaufmanniana*, is white, with a yellow and red centre; it opens out fully, like a water lily. *Tulipa pulchella*, carries up to three, dark-red or purple flowers to each stem, and *T.tarda* (sometimes sold as *T.dasystemon*), also carries several flowers to a stem, yellow with white edges to the petals. 8-25cm (3-10in) high. *T.sylvestris* is a taller species, with scented yellow flowers and grey green leaves.

Scilla siberica

Cacti and Succulents

Few cacti could be called graceful, yet they have many other endearing (and practical) charms. Like alpines, their generally small scale, slow growth habit, often intriguing structure and pretty flowers, combined with relative ease of cultivation, make them immensely popular. Like palms, they conjure up a picture of hot, dry, far-away places.

Compared with most other plants, cacti have an oddly modern appearance, like abstract sculptures in miniature. As always, it is an example of nature's pragmatism: their round or cylindrical shapes help cut down water loss, or transpiration, as do their grey colouring, waxy or farinose (floury) coating, hairs and spines. Even the rigidly formal, vetical ridging is purposeful, helping the plant expand to store water, and to shrink as the water is expended.

Another similarity between cacti and alpines is the confusion surrounding their definition. All cacti (members of the *Cactaceae* family) are succulents and have areoles. These are small, often felted or hairy, cushions from which the spines and flowers grow. The typical, plump above-ground growth of a cactus is, in fact, a modified stem. The vast majority of cacti are leafless, the job of photosynthesis being taken over by the stem. Most cacti have spines.

Not all succulents are cacti; other succulents come from families as wide ranging as *Compositae*, which contains daisies, and *Euphorbiaceae*, which contains garden spurges and poinsettias. 'Non-cactus' succulents lack areoles, are usually spineless, their storage organs may be leaves.

Furthermore, there are two types of cacti: desert and forest. The latter usually grow as epiphytes on the branches and trunks of trees. Their jointed, flattened 'leaves' are actually stems, with a drooping or arching habit of growth. Christmas and Easter cacti are popular examples. Unlike desert cacti and succulents, which come from a brightly lit, dry environment, forest cacti come from lightly shaded, humid tropical conditions.

Cultivation

It is a common misconception that cacti and succulents need blistering heat, day and night, winter and summer. In the wild, temperatures can drop rapidly from 38°C (100°F) during the day, to freezing at night. In fact, when light levels dip in autumn and winter, cacti and succulents should have lowered temperatures, to induce a rest period. Provide a minimum temperature of 5°C (40°F) for desert cacti and succulents, and 10°C (50°F) for forest cacti.

Like alpines, cacti and succulents cannot tolerate cold combined with excess wet, either in the compost or in the air. Water for desert cacti and succulents should be almost nonexistent in autumn and winter, just enough to keep them from shrivelling up. Water moderately in spring and summer, allowing the compost to dry out a bit between waterings. Keep the air bone dry all year round. Forest cacti need a moderate supply of water all year round, again with semi-drying out periods between waterings, and high humidity in high temperatures. All cacti and succulents need good ventilation, especially in late spring and summer. Maximum light is essential, all-year-round, for desert cacti and succulents; provide light shade for forest cacti in spring and summer. All benefit from a spell outdoors in summer.

Cacti and succulents grow best in relatively small, well-crocked containers. Forest cacti can also be displayed in hanging baskets or wired to large pieces of bark or tree trunk. Always provide free-draining compost. There is a special compost available for cacti and succulents, or use a mixture of two-thirds John Innes potting compost No.2 and one-third coarse sand and grit. Add a touch of lime – old mortar rubble, if you can get it – and bonemeal, to encourage spine formation. Use the same basic mixture, minus the lime and with the addition of leafmould, for forest cacti, which prefer a slightly acid compost.

Epiphyllum Hybrid

Feed desert cacti and succulents monthly in spring and summer, forest cacti fortnightly then. Use a high-potassium fertilizer, as one high in nitrogen encourages soft, lush, un-cactus-like growth.

Potting on

Potting on and re-potting are only necessary when the plant overspills its pot, and is best done in spring. Protect your hands from spines, if necessary, by using a piece of thickly folded newspaper wrapped round the plant. Offsets can be removed and potted up separately then. If you have to cut them off, rather than gently prising them away leave the raw surfaces exposed to the air for a day or two to dry out, then plant shallowly in the above mixture. Forest cacti, tall-growing desert cacti and succulents can be propagated from stem cuttings, treated as above.

Flowering

Finally, there is a mystique surrounding the flowering of cacti. Cacti and succulents flower when they reach maturity, and are given a suitable environment. Naturally small-growing cacti flower sooner – in some cases, on one- or two-year old plants – than naturally large cacti, which may grow to a height of several metres. Once a cacti or succulent starts flowering, it should flower every year thereafter. Desert cacti usually flower in spring and summer, producing trumpet-shaped blooms. Forest cacti and succulents can bloom at any time of the year; the flowers of forest cacti are also basically trumpet-shaped, while those of succulents reflect their very wide and mixed origins.

FOREST CACTI

These epiphytes, with their spectacular flowers, are among the most popular of cactus species.

Aporocactus flagelliformis

The unfortunately named rat-tail cactus has trailing, cylindrical spiny stems to 90cm (3ft) in length, and pink flowers in spring. Unlike other forest cacti, it is tolerant of dry air and lime. The flowers close at night.

Epiphyllum

The orchid cacti, or epicacti, are usually available as complex hybrids, the parentage of which involves other genera besides *Epiphyllum*. Their flattened, jointed stems are up to 90cm (3ft) long, and their huge flowers, up to 20cm (8in) or more across, are available in all colours but blue, according to the form chosen; some are scented. One of the most popular hybrids is *E.*'Ackermanii', which may produce a hundred, bright-red flowers a year. Its main flowering period is spring and summer, though flowers can be produced at other times.

Rhipsalidopsis

The Easter cactus is *Rhipsalidopsis gaertneri*, though it is sometimes sold as *Rhipsalis gaertneri* or *Schlumbergera gaertneri*. Its short, flat, leaf-like stem sections are 2.5-5cm (1-2in) long, jointed together and arching rather than hanging in growth habit, up to 30cm (12in) long. Its bright scarlet flowers are produced in spring. *R.rosea* is a similar size, but with pink, slightly scented flowers, and with stem sections that can be angled or flat. There are numerous hybrids that have been developed from these two species.

Schlumbergera

Once again, confusion reigns over nomenclature. The Christmas cactus, with pendulous stems composed of leaf-like stem sections and deep-pink flowers at Christmas, is *Schlumbergera* × *buckleyi*, but it is often sold as *S.bridgesii* or *Zygocactus truncatus*. There are named forms with white, pink or orange flowers. The lobster or crab cactus, *S.truncata*, sometimes sold as *Zygocactus truncatus*, is similar but flowers earlier and has toothed edges to the leaf sections.

SUCCULENTS

Strictly speaking all cacti are succulents, but the word is used here to describe a range of popular fleshy leaf forms without spines.

Aeonium

There are many aeoniums, all with succulent leaf rosettes carried on bare stems. The flowers are usually yellow, but can be white, pink or red, according to the species chosen. Older specimens can get leggy and bare. Cut them back, using the clippings as cuttings if you wish; the mother plant should quickly produce fresh growth. *Aeonium arboreum* is the most common species, up to 90cm (3ft) high; *A.a.*'Atropurpureum' has leaves which turn a deep purple in full sunlight. Both can reach a height of 90cm (3ft).

Rhipsalidopsis gaertneri

Kalanchoe fedtschenkoi

Agave
(see page 90)

Aloe
(see page 60)

Ceropegia
(see page 94)

Crassula
The family *Crassulaceae* is a large one, and includes *Sedum* (see page 120, 125) and *Sempervivum* (see page 120). The genus *Crassula* includes shrubby plants of varying habits, from trailing to erect shrubs. The jade tree, *C.argentea*, sometimes sold as *C.portulaca*, is a popular, old-fashioned plant, looking rather like a stumpy tree. Its juicy leaves are oval, bright green and shiny, and are carried on an often single-stemmed, much-branched and gnarled-looking shrub. Its clusters of small white or pale-pink flowers are carried in spring. Similar to the Chinese jade tree, is *C.arborescens*, with greeny-grey, red-margined leaves. It rarely flowers in cultivation. Both can reach a height of 1.8m (6ft), but are very slow growing.

Echeveria
The greeny-grey or blue-grey rosettes of echeverias can often be seen in carpet-bedding schemes, where their dense, tidy habit of growth is much appreciated. Their yellow, orange or red, bell-shaped flowers are carried on graceful stems in summer. *Echeveria agavoides* resembles an 8cm (3in) high miniature agave. Taller growing, to 60cm (24in) or more, is *E.gibbiflora*, with thick, bare stems topped with rosettes of large, grey-green leaves. *E.g.*'Metallica' has a bronzy sheen to the leaves. At 5cm (2in) high, *E.derenbergii* is sometimes called the baby echeveria, for obvious reasons. Each leaf is tipped in red, and offsets are readily produced, quickly transforming a single rosette into a clump.

Gasteria
These mainly stemless plants belong to the lily family, *Liliaceae*. Their long, thick, fleshy leaves are usually in two rows, though they can sometimes grow in a spiral fashion; from the leaves come the common names: lawyer's tongue and ox tongue. *Gasteria brevifolia* has attractive white banding across its rounded leaves, up to 15cm (6in) long. The smallest species is *G.liliputiana*, with 5cm (2in) long, white-flecked leaves, and *G.verrucosa*, 15cm (6in) high, has long, tapering leaves arranged vertically in pairs. The leaves are covered with raised, pale-grey spots. All have red or pink flowers, carried on one side of arching stems, in spring and summer.

Haworthia
Sometimes called the wart plant because of the raised, wart-like patches on its waxy leaves, haworthia is a typical, rosette-forming succulent. The greeny-white flowers are insignificant, minute lilies, declaring the plant as a member of *Liliaceae*. In the wild, haworthia is found in slightly shaded spots, either in the shade of other plants or partially buried in sand, so provide light shade in the conservatory. Good species to start with include *Haworthia truncata*, with 2.5cm (1in) high rosettes of truncated leaves, translucent at the tips to absorb light; *H.fasciata*, or zebra haworthia, with raised, white banding on the leaves; and *H.reinwardtii*, with elongated rosettes up to 15cm (6in) high.

Kalanchoe
Kalanchoes take various forms, but all have succulent leaves. Grown for the flowers are *Kalanchoe blossfeldiana* hybrids, with shiny green leaves and red, yellow or orange blossoms, on bushy plants up to 30cm (12in) high. They are best discarded after flowering. *K.daigremontiana*, sometimes sold as *Bryophyllum daigremontianum*, produces tiny plantlets along the edges of its spotted, grey-green leaves. In time, the plantlets drop off and root quickly if they land on suitable compost. Devil's backbone, as the plant is sometimes called, can reach a height of 90cm (3ft). *K.tubiflora*, sometimes sold as *Bryophyllum tubiflorum*, is commonly called the chandelier plant, and eventually reaches a similar height. Its cylindrical, grey-green leaves are carried in whorls of three up the stem, and each leaf produces plantlets on its tip. In winter, the plant produces a cluster of orange, bell-shaped flowers.

The panda plant – or pussy ears – *K.tomentosa*, is so called because of the silvery white hairs that thickly cover the leaves. They are edged in rusty brown, and form loose rosettes which are produced on stems up to 45cm (18in) high.

Kleinia articulata

The candle plant is more correctly *Senecio articulatus*, but is usually sold under its old-fashioned name. It is a curious, rather than pretty, shrubby plant, to 60cm (24in) high. Its much branched stems are grey-green, cylindrical, fleshy and jointed. In late autumn and winter, small, triangular leaves are produced, which die in spring. Unusual for succulents, the growth period is autumn and winter, when watering and feeding are necessary; keep almost dry in spring and summer. It may occasionally carry yellow, daisy-like flowers in autumn.

Lithops

Living stones mimic perfectly the stones they grow amongst in South Africa. Two almost completely fused leaves make up the plant; the fissure where the two swollen leaves meet is the point from which the yellow or white, daisy-like flowers appear in autumn. The plant expands sideways, forming clumps of smaller, new 'stones', the oldest, central stones eventually dying. Add a generous amount of sharp sand to the compost; keep bone dry from mid-autumn to mid-spring, and provide maximum sunlight all year round. Easy species to start with are *Lithops fulleri, L.bella* and *L.leslei*, all with attractive markings on the flattened upper leaf surfaces. In the wild, these markings serve to admit light, as the plants are usually partially buried in the sand.

Sedum

As well as hardy plants (see page 120) this genus includes tender succulents for the conservatory; the latter are mostly Mexican in origin. The plants range from trailers to quite tall shrubs, usually with fleshy, stalkless leaves. Burro's tail, *Sedum morganianum*, is a trailer, to 60cm (24in) in length, ideal for a hanging basket. Its stems are covered with closely packed, overlapping grey leaves. Jelly beans, or Christmas cheer, *S.rubrotinctum*, is a much branched shrub, to 25cm (10in), with fleshy, cylindrical leaves. These are green, but become tinged red in hot, dry, sunny conditions. *S.sieboldii* is a moderately hardy trailing plant, sometimes grown in rock gardens. In cold conditions it is deciduous, but new shoots are formed in spring. The round, blue-grey leaves are carried in pairs along the stems; *S.s.*'Medio-variegatum' produces yellow centred leaves. Grow in hanging baskets, as the stems can be up to 45cm (18in) long.

DESERT CACTI

The cacti listed in this section include some of the most familiar and easily grown types.

Cephalocereus senilis

An enchanting plant, the old man cactus is columnar in habit, up to 9m (30ft) or more in the wild, but rarely exceeding 30cm (12in) in cultivation. It is entirely covered with long, silver hairs, concealing thin yellow spines. It does not flower as a small plant.

Chamaecereus sylvestrii

The peanut cactus is a freely branching plant with cylindrical, spiny stems. As the stems lengthen with age, to 15cm (6in), they tend to lie horizontally on the compost or even hang over the edge of the pot. Short-lived scarlet flowers are produced over several weeks in summer. Branches come away if the plant is handled at all roughly, or if it is lacking sufficient water, but these root easily if potted up.

Echinocactus

The barrel cacti are slow growing, but can eventually reach a height of 90cm (3ft) in cultivation. The golden barrel, or ball cactus, *Echinocactus grusonii*, is globe shaped, with well-defined ribs carrying yellow spines. Mature specimens produce a ring of yellow flowers in the summer. Smaller, and freer-flowering, is *E.horizonthalonius*. Its grey-green stem is globe-shaped, up to 25cm (10in) high, with grey spines and pink flowers.

Echinocereus

The hedgehog cactus can be round or cylindrical, upright or sprawling, and spiny or spineless, according to the species chosen. Most form branches, others are clump forming, but all are ribbed and all flower when quite young. The flowers are relatively large and usually close at night; they are sometimes followed by edible fruit. They are relatively low growing, and unlikely to exceed 40cm (16in) in height, even after many years. The lace cactus, *E.reichenbachii*, has bright-pink flowers on upright stems. The rainbow cactus, *E.pectinatus rigidissimus*, has comb-like spines in bands of white, yellow, pink, and brown around the upright stem, and deep-pink flowers. The sprawling stems of *E.pentalophus* have five ribs, arranged spirally and covered with warts. The lilac-pink flowers are bell-shaped.

Mixed displays of cacti show off best these plants' sculptural qualities.

Lobivia jajoiana

Lobivia

The red or yellow flowers of the cob cactus are produced on young plants. The flowers are short lived and open only in full light, but new flowers are produced over many weeks, in summer. Its botanical name is an anagram of Bolivia, where most of the species are found. *Lobivia hertrichiana* is an eleven-ribbed, dark-green, globe-shaped species, 10cm (4in) high, with yellow spines and bright-red flowers. Offsets are freely produced, even by young plants. *L.jajoiana* has pink spines and deep-purple flowers on cylindrical stems, 15cm (6in) high. *L.Allegraiana* flowers pink or red.

Mammillaria

The pincushion cacti are generally unribbed, cylindrical or rounded, and clump forming. They are slow growing but flower when young. The individual flowers are small, and are carried in a ring at the top of the cactus; flower colour varies according to species. The flowers are sometimes followed by red or black fruit. The snowball cactus, *Mammillaria bocasana*, is rounded, covered with silky, long white hair and tough, bristly spines. Its eventual height is 15cm (6in). The flowers are yellow and red. As its name suggests, *M.elongata* is an elongated, cylindrical shape, to 15cm (6in) high, with spines that can be white, yellow, red or brown. Its flowers are white. The silver cluster cactus, *M.prolifera*, produces offsets freely and quickly, forming an impressive clump. The dark-green, slightly cylindrical stems, 5cm (2in) high, are woolly looking, and carry pale-yellow flowers, followed by red fruit.

Notocactus

The flowers of notocactus are generally yellow, less often red, with red stigmas, and are freely produced, even on young plants. The stems of notocactus tend to be rounded, hence the common name, ball cactus, but they elongate with age. The scarlet ball cactus, *Notocactus haselbergii*, sometimes sold as *Brazilocactus haselbergii*, has white spines and intensely scarlet flowers, and an eventual height of 15cm (6in). *N.apricus*, 8cm (3in) high, has glossy yellow flowers and curved yellow spines, and the golden ball cactus, *N.leninghausii*, sometimes sold as *Eriocactus leninghausii*, has flat-topped, cylindrical stems up to 90cm (3ft) high, hairy yellow spines and, eventually, large yellow flowers. It is not fully dependable as a flowering cactus, though.

Opuntia

The most popular prickly pears look like a child's drawing of a cactus: a precarious build-up of oval flattened shapes. Opuntias don't often flower in cultivation. Be careful when handling them; all have tiny bristles, or glochids, growing from the areoles, which lodge under the skin and prove very painful. The beaver-tail cactus, *Opuntia basilaris*, is relatively spineless, with purple-tinged, flattened pads. It does produce flowers – pinky-purple and cup-shaped – after four or five years, when about 20cm (8in) high. Bunny ears, *O.microdasys*, is similar in appearance, spineless but with bright yellow glochids; there are named forms with white and red glochids. Like *O.basilaris*, its eventual height is 90cm (3ft).

Different from both of these species is *O.cylindrica*, a non-branching, columnar species which can grow to 1.8m (6ft) or more high. Diamond-shaped tubercles make a pleasing pattern over the bright-green surface. It can be induced to form branches, if its top is cut off; the result is a more interesting plant.

Rebutia

The crown cacti are rounded, clump-forming and flower prolifically when quite small; the flower colour varies with the species, but they all close at night. Spiny, wart-like tubercles are arranged spirally round the stems. Unlike most other cacti, they appreciate light shade in summer. *Rebutia calliantha, R.minuscula* and *R.deminuta* are similar in appearance, with orange-red or red flowers carried from late spring onwards around the base of the stems. Yellow flowers are carried on the spherical stems of the wallflower crown, *R.pseudodeminuta*. Maximum height is normally 15cm (6in).

Orchids

Orchids – most mysterious and intriguing of flowers – are steeped in symbolism and surrounded by myths. They embody the exotic, unobtainable and tropical; wealth and its conspicuous display; and love, with underlying sexuality – throughout history orchids have had lascivious connotations, and were thought to have great aphrodisiac powers. To many people, they represent all that is difficult in nurturing, in temperate climates, plants from hot, steamy ones.

The reality is quite different. Orchids make up an enormous family of over twenty thousand species and many thousands of hybrids. Though some are tropical or sub-tropical, many grow in temperate climates – consider the lovely and modest native orchids: the early purple orchid (*Ophrys mascula*), the bee orchid (*O.apifera*) and the very rare lady's slipper (*Cypripedium calceolus*), for example. In the conservatory, there are orchids for alpine conditions; others that are happy with a minimum winter temperature of 7°C (45°F), and those that really do need high temperatures all year round; the latter are not included in the selection of orchids that follows.

The entanglement of orchids with wealth and exclusivity is no longer as strong as it once was. Orchids as cut flowers are available from chain stores at modest prices, pre-wrapped in plastic and stripped of their snobbery. Orchid plants can be costlier than many others, but most are long lived if properly tended. Orchid plants that have just finished flowering can sometimes be bought at reduced prices; shopkeepers know that the plants have lost their 'instant appeal' until they come into flower again, and are only too happy to clear the space for more saleable items.

Cultivation

As already stated, the temperature requirements of orchids vary (and are given in detail below), but there are many requirements they have in common. One is for free-draining compost. Most orchids in cultivation are epiphytic, living in the wild on tree branches or rocks, clinging by means of aerial roots; they need little in the way of sustenance and less in the way of rich compost. There are many formulae for orchid composts, but a good general one is a mixture of equal parts of pine-bark chippings, sometimes sold as orchid bark, and sphagnum moss peat. The addition of a small amount of charcoal will keep the mixture from turning 'sour'. Old-fashioned books recommend osmunda fibre (the dried, chopped root of osmunda fern); though excellent as a growing medium, it is expensive and not readily available. If you can get it, mix it, as above, with sphagnum moss peat. Terrestrial orchids also need free-draining compost: a mixture of equal parts leafmould, loam, coarse sand and chopped sphagnum moss.

Grow orchids in relatively small, very well crocked pots, hanging baskets or special orchid baskets, made of slatted wood. Epiphytic ones can also have their roots wrapped in live sphagnum moss and then be wired to bark or epiphytic 'trees'.

Orchids need humidity, more in hot weather, less in cool, and plenty of ventilation, but protection from daughts. Orchids need light, but protection from strong summer sunlight; remember that, in nature, they usually grow in the dappled shade of trees.

Actively growing orchids need evenly moist compost: one which is neither waterlogged nor bone dry. Less water is needed in low temperatures. Very high summer temperatures – above 21°C (70°F) for orchids tolerating cool winter temperatures, and above 27°C (80°F) for those needing warm winter temperatures – can be as lethal as freezing ones.

It is much easier to harm orchids by over-feeding them than by under-feeding. Give weak feeds, monthly, in the growing season.

There are two types of orchids: sympodial, or those with thickened, and above-ground stems, called pseudobulbs; and monopodial, or those with a single, erect stem, with new growth and flowers carried at the top. The pseudobulbs act as storage organs; older, leafless ones can be detached and potted up

Despite their exotic appearance many orchids like these, are easy to grow.

separately. Those with a single stem are propagated by the removal of side shoots or from tip cuttings.

Cattleya

These are epiphytic, tropical orchids which grow from huge pseudobulbs. The flowers are archetypal 'corsage' orchids; tubular lipped, large and waxy. They are carried in groups or singly, and come in various colours, according to the form chosen. The evergreen leaves are thick and strap-shaped. The autumn cattleya, *Cattleya labiata*, carries several yellow-throated, lilac-rose, fragrant flowers in late autumn or winter. The Christmas orchid, *C.trianae*, flowers later; the blooms vary in colour from white to deep lilac. The tulip cattleya, *C.citrina*, carries single, yellow, bell-shaped flowers in late spring and summer.

Provide a minimum temperature of 13°C (55°F) for the first two species, and 7°C (45°F), for the third. For two months after flowering, the natural rest period, give only enough water to keep the pseudobulbs from shrivelling. Provide maximum light in autumn to encourage the formation of flower buds. The plants rarely exceed 60cm (24in) in height.

Coelogyne

Again, these are epiphytic evergreen orchids with pseudobulbs. The fragrant flowers are usually white or creamy yellow. One of the easiest species is *Coelogyne cristata,* with hanging clusters of heavily scented white flowers in late winter or early spring, and arching, pointed, strap-shaped leaves. *C.ochracea* carries spikes of white flowers, marked with bright ochre on the lip, in spring. Provide a minimum temperature of 7°C (45°F) and a dryish rest period after flowering. Approximately 30cm (12in) high.

Cymbidium hybrids

If you are thinking about growing orchids, or have room for only one, choose a cymbidium. These are terrestrial and epiphytic species, all producing pseudobulbs, but epiphytic types are more suitable for a conservatory. Very popular, and free flowering, are the dwarf hybrids, often less than 30cm (12in) high. The flowers, carried several to a stem, can be white, pink, yellow, acid-yellow, green, or rich brown, often with contrasting markings. The leathery evergreen, thin leaves can be upright or arching. Cymbidiums can be had in flower all through the year, according to the form chosen. If you can bear to cut them, the cut flowers last for several weeks in water; they are popular florists' flowers. Provide a minimum temperature of 7°C (45°F), and place them in a lightly shaded spot outdoors, for the summer months. Exposure to maximum light in the autumn encourages flowering.

Above, Cymbidium 'Tinsel'

Below, Cymbidium 'Flame Hawk'

Dendrobium

There are over 1000 species in this genus, with great variation among the plants, their flowers and their cultivation needs. For the 'one dendrobium conservatory', the evergreen *D.nobile* or one of its hybrids is a good choice. In winter or spring they carry sprays of fragrant flowers, variable in colour but usually ranging from white to pink, rose and lavender, blotched with maroon in the centre and edged with purple. Unfortunately, the pseudobulbs of this epiphyte are elongated and cane-like, and not terribly attractive. Cymbidiums make far more attractive plants. Provide a minimum temperature of 10°C (50°F), and water very sparingly during its winter rest.

Epidendrum

There are hundreds of species of buttonhole orchid, with all the variation that that entails. They tend to be deciduous, with small, but often brightly coloured, flowers, epiphytic, and grow from pseudobulbs. The cockle-shell orchid, *Epidendrum cochleatum*, has twisted flower stalks, so the curious flowers hang upside-down. The deep-purple and yellow lip is uppermost, and the yellow-green petals and sepals hang downwards. Flowering can occur at any time of the year. Spidery flowers, with thin, pale-green petals and a heavily fringed white lip, are carried by *E.ciliare* in winter. Heights are usually 45cm (18in) or less. Provide a minimum winter temperature of 13°C (55°F).

Lycaste

These relatively easy orchids are usually epiphytic, with pseudobulbs and handsome, pleated leaves. The waxy, heavily scented flowers are carried singly and in a wide range of colours; they have relatively small lips, and smaller petals than sepals. Flowering time varies, and some species are deciduous, losing their leaves when dormant. Fragrant, red-spotted, yellow flowers are carried in spring and summer by *Lycaste aromatica*. The Auburn hybrids have flowers ranging from pink to browny-red, and *L.virginalis*'s flowers range from pure white to crimson. Provide a minimum temperature of 10°C (50°F); water very sparingly during the winter rest period, even though the plant may be in flower. Height is usually 45cm (18in) or less.

Miltonia

The pansy orchid has large, flat-faced flowers and attractive, arching, strap-shaped leaves, growing from pseudobulbs. Both species and hybrids are grown, with various flowering times and colours, including white, cream, yellow, pink, rose, red, crimson and violet, usually blotched with a contrasting colour on the two-lobed lip. *Miltonia spectabilis* carries pink-flushed, white flowers, with a dark-purple lip, in autumn, one to each stem. In place of the species, *M.s.*'Moreliana' is usually offered for sale; its petals and sepals are dark rose, its lip bright rose. Heights range from 20-60cm (8-24in) according to the form chosen.

The main flowering period is in spring and summer, although a second, smaller 'crop' may appear in autumn. Pansy orchids do not have a well defined rest period, and need reasonable supplies of water right through the year.

Odontoglossum

In the days of cheap heat, land and labour, entire greenhouses were given over to the cultivation of this huge, immensely popular genus. They are worth growing on any scale, and vie with cymbidiums in general appeal. The plants are epiphytic, evergreen, and grow from pseudobulbs. The flowers come in a wide colour range, often with contrasting markings, and can appear all through the year, according to the form chosen. The lace orchid, *Odontoglossum crispum*, has arching stems up to 75cm (30in) long, each stem carrying several blooms of heavily frilled, pink-tinged, white flowers. The form *O.c.*'Lyoth Arctic' has pure white flowers. Spring is the main flowering season. The tiger orchid, *O.grande*, is comparatively easy. Its flowers, in autumn, are a striking combination of yellow, orange and chestnut brown. There are many varieties available, with red, pink, white, cream or yellow flowers, or various combinations; 30cm (12in) is the usual height of the flower spike.

Odontoglossums have been crossed with other genera as well. One such striking result is x*Odontonia*, the other parent being *Miltonia*. The variety x*O.atherior* 'Lyoth Majesty' has pink-flushed white flowers, marked and speckled in red. Provide a minimum temperature of 10°C (50°F). A spell in the garden during the summer months is much appreciated, provided there is high humidity.

Paphiopedilum

The lady's slipper orchid, Venus slipper, or slipper orchid, gets its common name from the large, pouch or slipper-shaped lower lip. It is the 'odd-orchid-out' in this list, in that most paphiopedilums are terrestrial, not epiphytic, and none have pseudobulbs. Over 3000 hybrids have been raised, many from the species and others from crossing existing hybrids. The period of flowering, the shape, size and colour of the flowers, and size of the plant, vary enormously, according to the form chosen. Temperature requirements can vary, too, so take care when making a selection.

Paphiopedilum callosum has mar-

Lycaste 'Auburn'

bled, strap-shaped leaves and waxy, long-lasting flowers on 30-45cm (12-18in) stems, in spring. The flowers have a dark-rose pouch, and drooping side petals and a large, upright petal of pale pink, striped handsomely with green and maroon. Flowers can appear in winter, spring and summer. The winter-flowering *P.insigne* has subtle, exquisitely marked flowers. They are yellow-green, with a rusty brown pouch, and dark brown spots on the wavy-edged upper petal. The 25cm (10in) flower stems carry the blossoms singly, or two to each stem. For the connoisseur, *P.venustum* has upper and side petals of white, with fine green striping, and a green-veined yellow-green lip. It flowers in winter, on 25cm (10in) stems. Provide an absolute minimum temperature of 13°C (55°F), though 16°C (60°F) is better. There is no well-defined rest period, so give a steady supply of water.

Pleione

Pleiones are 'odd-orchids-out' as well. Besides being terrestrial, they thrive in the alpine conditions of a just frost-free conservatory. Pleiones have pseudobulbs which live for a single season and are then replaced by (usually) two young pseudobulbs. They are deciduous plants, and the flowers appear in winter or early spring, before the ribbed, lance-shaped leaves. The flowers are relatively large, with attractively marked and fringed, trumpet-shaped lips.

The most popular and easily available species is *Pleione bulbocodioides*, sometimes sold as *P.formosana*. Its petals and petal-like sepals range in colour from pale pink to lilac and rose, with the pale, tubular lip marked in red and yellow. Named forms include the white *P.b.*'Alba', and the light pink and white *P.b.*'Blush of Dawn'. The dark-pink 'Oriental Jewel' and purple 'Oriental Splendour' are technically forms of the subspecies *P.b.limprichtii* but, in spite of their complicated names, are easy pleiones to grow.

All need a winter rest, and the old shrivelled pseudobulbs carefully removed each spring, when the plants should be re-potted. Leave the upper two-thirds of the pseudobulbs sitting above the compost. For out-of-season care, see Alpines, page 118.

Vanda

These monopodial, evergreen orchids are also epiphytic, and comprise a huge genus, with wide variation in flowering, habit and temperature requirements. Those listed below are good species to start with. Their single stems carry light-green leaves and masses of aerial roots; the fragrant flowers are carried at the top of the stems. *Vanda caeulea* has pale-blue flowers, darker-blue on the lip, carried in summer and autumn on stems up to 90cm (3ft) high. *V.teres* can reach 1.8m (6ft) or more in height. Its pale-pink, deep-pink and magenta flowers are carried, up to five to each stem, in late spring and summer. Equally tall is *V.tricolor,* with a reputation as a particularly easy vanda. The flowers, in autumn and winter, are very variable, but generally have creamy-pink to yellow petals, spotted brown, and a dark-pink or purple lip.

Provide a minimum temperature of 13°C (55°F); water less in winter than the rest of the year, but never let the compost dry out completely. They can be grown in pots, but hanging baskets more easily accommodate the aerial roots.

Paphiopedilum 'Rowan'

Some Manufacturers and Distributors of Conservatories

Edenlite Products,
Wern Works, Briton Ferry, Neath, West Glamorgan SA11 2JS.

F Pratten & Co., Ltd.,
Charlton Road, Midsomer Norton, Bath, Avon BA3 4AG.

Sun Aluminium Greenhouses, E M Sears & Co., Ltd.,
Sears House, Bailey Industrial Park, Mariner, Tamworth, Staffordshire B79 7UL.

Marley Buildings Ltd.,
Shurdington, Cheltenham, Gloucestershire GL5 5UE.

Florada Garden Products,
Chesterton Lane, Cirencester, Gloucestershire GL7 1YL.

Alexander Bartholomew Conservatories Ltd.,
277 Putney Bridge Road, London SW15 2PT.

Banbury Homes and Gardens Ltd.,
PO Box 17, Banbury, Oxfordshire OX17 3NS.

Solardome,
Rosedale Engineers Ltd., Hunmanby, Filey, North Yorks.

Aluminium Greenhouses Ltd.,
Birmingham Road, West Bromwich, West Midlands B17 4JY.

S Wernick & Sons Ltd.,
Lindon Road, Brownhills, Walsall, Staffordshire WS8 7BW.

M D Kidby Buildings Ltd.,
28 Kennylands Road, Sonning Common, Berkshire RG4 9JT.

Halls Homes and Gardens Ltd.,
Church Road, Paddock Wood, Kent TN12 6EU.

New England Conservatories Ltd.,
Whitney Road, Daneshill East, Basingstoke, Hampshire RG24 0NS.

Crittall Warmlife Ltd.,
Crittall Road, Witham, Essex CM8 3AW.

Room Outside Ltd.,
Goodwood Gardens, Waterbeach, Chichester, West Sussex PO18 0QB.

Amdega Ltd.,
Faverdale Industrial Estate, Darlington, Co. Durham DL3 0PW.

Baco Leisure Products,
Windover Road, Huntingdon, Cambs PE18 7EH.

Machin Designs,
4 Avenue Studies, Sydney Close, London SW3 6HW.

Leofric Conservatories,
Leofric Works, Ryton, Coventry, West Midlands CV8 3ED.

Waytogro,
Unit 5A, Bruce Grove, Heron Industrial Estate, Wickford, Essex.

Robinsons Ltd.,
Winnall Industrial Estate, Winchester, Hampshire SO23 8LH.

Wessex Conservatories,
Unit 8, Wyndham Road, Hawksworth Industrial Estate, Swindon, Wiltshire SN2 1EJ.

Index

Page numbers in **bold** refer to illustrations.

Picture credits

P. Ayers: 70 Baco Products: 11(t) Steve Bicknell: 66(r), 84(t), 85(b), 90, 91, 95, 100, 112, 125 Michael Boys: 22, 25, 40 Pat Brindley: 67, 69, 86, 88/9, 92, 97, 98, 114, 120, 124 Bruce Coleman Ltd.: 16 Crittall Warmlife Ltd: 10(b) Alan Duns: 62(b), 80, 104(t) Mary Evans Picture Library: endpapers Paul Forrester: 109 John Glover: 2, 7, 48/9, 54, 61, 64 Derek Gould: 62(t), 75, 76(t) Jerry Harpur: 37 David Kelly: 42 S & O Mathews: 1 John Melville: 93(t), 101, 107, 115(1), 116(b), 117 A. Robinson: 59 Robinson's of Winchester: 6 Ianthe Ruthven: 4/5, 19 Harry Smith Horticultural Photographic Collection: 20, 56/7, 58(b), 66(l), 68, 72, 73(tl,b), 81, 82/3, 84(b), 85(t), 93(b), 94, 96, 96/7, 99, 104(b), 106, 108, 113, 115(r), 116(t), 119, 121, 122, 128(t) Michael Warren: 18, 26, 44/5, 47, 58(t), 63, 65, 71, 74, 76(b), 77, 78/9, 87, 102/3, 105, 110/1, 118, 120/1, 123, 126, 127, 128(b), 129, 130 Colin Watmough: 60, 73(tr), Elizabeth Whiting: 14, 28

Artwork

Richard Phipps: 46, 50/1, 52, 53 Simon Roulston: 8/9, 10(t), 12/13, 15, 21, 23, 24, 27, 29, 30, 31, 32, 33, 34, 35, 36, 38, 39

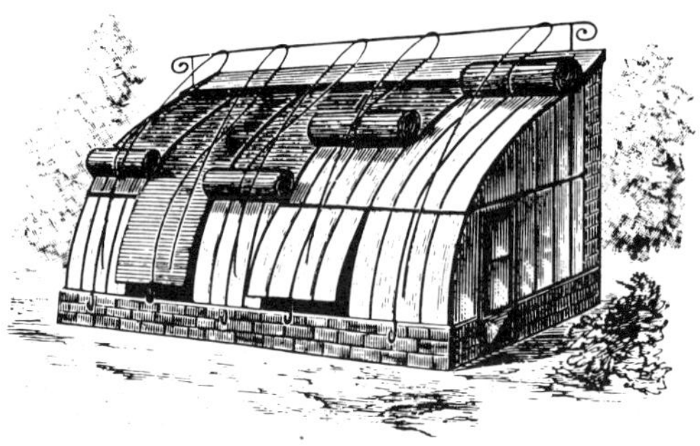